Gender Equality and Men

LEARNING FROM PRACTICE

Oxfam GB

Oxfam GB, founded in 1942, is a development, humanitarian, and campaigning agency dedicated to finding lasting solutions to poverty and suffering around the world. Oxfam believes that every human being is entitled to a life of dignity and opportunity, and it works with others worldwide to make this become a reality.

From its base in Oxford, UK, Oxfam GB publishes and distributes a wide range of books and other resource materials for development and relief workers, researchers, campaigners, schools and colleges, and the general public, as part of its programme of advocacy, education, and communications.

Oxfam GB is a member of Oxfam International, a confederation of 12 agencies of diverse cultures and languages, which share a commitment to working for an end to injustice and poverty – both in long-term development work and at times of crisis.

For further information about Oxfam's publishing, and online ordering, visit www.oxfam.org.uk/publications

For further information about Oxfam's development, advocacy, and humanitarian relief work around the world, visit www.oxfam.org.uk

Gender Equality and Men

LEARNING FROM PRACTICE

EDITED BY SANDY RUXTON

Oxfam

First published by Oxfam GB in 2004

ISBN 0 85598 514 3

A catalogue record for this publication is available from the British Library.

Available from:
Bournemouth English Book Centre, PO Box 1496, Parkstone, Dorset, BH12 3YD, UK
tel: +44 (0)1202 712933; fax: +44 (0)1202 712930; email: oxfam@bebc.co.uk

USA: Stylus Publishing LLC, PO Box 605, Herndon, VA 20172-0605, USA
tel: +1 (0)703 661 1581; fax: +1 (0)703 661 1547; email: styluspub@aol.com

For details of local agents and representatives in other countries, consult our website:
www.oxfam.org.uk/publications
or contact Oxfam Publishing, 274 Banbury Road, Oxford OX2 7DZ, UK
tel: +44 (0)1865 311 311; fax: +44 (0)1865 312 600; email: publish@oxfam.org.uk

Our website contains a fully searchable database of all our titles, and facilities for secure online ordering.

Published by Oxfam GB, 274 Banbury Road, Oxford OX2 7DZ, UK.

Printed by Biddles Ltd., King's Lynn

Oxfam GB is a registered charity, no. 202 918, and is a member of Oxfam International.

Contents

Foreword

Barbara Stocking

At the forty-eighth session of the UN Commission on the Status of Women in March 2004, participating governments agreed an important set of conclusions on 'the role of men and boys in achieving gender equality'. The text reflects a new emphasis in international debates, not just on men as holders of privileges or perpetrators of violence, but as potential and actual contributors to gender equality.

Of course there are risks to such an approach. For instance, involving men and boys in achieving gender equality must not be at the expense of the empowerment of women and girls, and resources for supporting the latter must not be undermined, as the conclusions of the Commission also recognise.

We must also acknowledge that the identities, experiences, and practices of different groups of men and boys vary widely, depending on factors such as age, race, culture, class, and sexual orientation – and that their interests may differ as a result.

Male leaders in dominant social groups will continue to resist attempts to challenge the power they hold. Other men who feel their masculinity threatened, particularly those at the sharp end of economic and social change, are likely to react with hostility towards other social groups (including women, ethnic minorities, and children), who they wrongly blame for their predicament.

But in all parts of the world, there are also men who are aware of the straightjacket imposed upon them by traditional notions of masculinity, and who are more open to reassessing their roles and responsibilities.

If we are to make progress towards gender equality, we must encourage more men to move out of the confines of rigid gender divisions at home, at work, and in the community. To reach a 'tipping point' where gender issues become visible, and therefore important, to the majority of men, it is essential that the benefits of gender equality for men as individuals and as members of families and communities should be more widely publicised. Seeing the effects of gender discrimination on people they are close to, be they wives, partners, girlfriends, or children; understanding that opportunities to build sustainable livelihoods are enhanced by more flexible gender roles; becoming aware of the stress of existing lifestyles and work patterns on personal health, and its impact on others; feeling the emotional pull of parenting – these are just some of the many triggers that can cause men to re-evaluate their circumstances and redirect their energy towards support for gender equality.

I came across a powerful example of this when talking to a small group in a village in the Rajasthan desert, in India. One man admitted that he now collected the wood for fires because his wife had become a weaver; it was brave of him to do it and even more brave of him to confess to it in front of his male peers.

Encouraging greater numbers of men to work actively for gender equality represents a considerable challenge for states, corporations, communities, and families. Development organisations also have their part to play in promoting positive policy and practice. In particular, they must ensure that all staff, especially men, are committed to gender equality and feel confident and able to make their own contribution to achieving it.

Within Oxfam GB, the experience gained by our Gender Equality and Men project in recent years has provided invaluable lessons about how the organisation should engage with men, whether as workers or as beneficiaries. This publication documents much of this learning, bringing together experience from practitioners around the world who are exploring in diverse ways how to work effectively with men for gender equality.

We recognise that much still needs to be done in order to improve our thinking and programming in this area, and we hope that this book will help to stimulate further debate and action both within and beyond Oxfam GB.

Barbara Stocking

Director, Oxfam GB

Acknowledgements

Gender Equality and Men: Learning from Practice includes contributions from those with substantial writing experience and those have not had their work published before. The majority of contributors are development practitioners from both the global North and South. Most are employed by Oxfam GB or partner organisations; in some cases they have links to another of the 12 member organisations of Oxfam International. A smaller number are external consultants or researchers, several of whom have played a significant role in advancing thinking in this area over the past decade or more. The voices and views all the authors express here are their own.

This book reflects the tenacity and flexibility of the contributors, many of whom had to overcome significant constraints in order to take part. These included juggling considerable work and travel pressures with personal and family commitments – one of the authors even gave birth during the period in which her article was written! For some who wanted to participate, the pressures of external events, such as seeking to research material in societies where conflict and curfews are a fact of life, unfortunately proved insuperable; their efforts must also be acknowledged.

Thanks are also due to people and groups without whom the development and publication of the book would have been impossible. At institutional level, Oxfam GB especially wishes to record its gratitude to the UK government's Department for International Development, which part-funded the Gender Equality and Men project.

Oxfam GB international programme staff who provided advice and information, or read and commented on specific drafts include: Aimee Ansari, Harold Brown, Juan Cheaz, Rose Gawaya, Keti Getiashvili, Maxime Houinato, Adam Leach, Walid Qawasmi, Jo Rowlands, Claude St Pierre, Tamar Sabedashvili, Eddie Thomas, Franz Wong, Mandy Woodhouse, and Tahera Yasmin. Staff from other member organisations of Oxfam International who provided ideas, contacts, and support were Inga Mepham and Keryn Clark (Oxfam CAA, Australia), Hazel Wong (Oxfam Hong Kong), and Denise Parmentier and Marleen Nolten (Novib, Oxfam Netherlands).

A particularly crucial role was played by the readers who commented on the full draft text: Michael Flood (The Australia Institute), Fiona Gell (Oxfam GB), Chris Roche and Reihana Mohideen (Oxfam CAA, Australia), and Rajni Khanna (Oxfam GB, Yemen). The editorial group provided an essential sounding board: James Lang (formerly development officer for the Gender Equality and Men project), Caroline Sweetman, Maree Keating, Jon Horsley, and Sue Smith (all of Oxfam GB). Jon Horsley and Sue Smith deserve particular thanks for co-managing the GEM project, and for providing advice, encouragement, and comments throughout. Thanks also to Anna Coryndon of Oxfam GB's publishing team, who edited this book.

On a personal basis, thanks are due to all my colleagues in Oxfam GB, especially: Michelle Matheron and Sarah Griffiths, who provided practical assistance; Ann Marsden, who diligently followed up my regular requests for information; Xin Moreton and Ruth Emsley, who looked after the budget; and Audrey Bronstein, who supported my secondment to the project.

Sandy Ruxton

Contributors

Mario de Araujo is a founding member of the Men's Group Against Violence in Timor Leste, and a long-term social activist. For the past two years he has worked for Oxfam CAA Australia as advocacy officer and programme co-ordinator. He is committed personally and professionally to promoting greater gender and social equity, particularly at the community level.

Gary Barker is executive director of Instituto Promundo, a non-government organisation (NGO) based in Rio de Janeiro, Brazil, that works to promote gender equality, the health of young people, and equitable community development. His doctorate is in child and adolescent development, and he has worked throughout Latin America on gender socialisation, violence prevention, HIV/AIDS prevention, and the promotion of sexual and reproductive health. g.barker@promundo.org.br

Cinnamon Bennett is a local government officer in the UK, holding the post of gender manager for the 'Objective 1' programme in South Yorkshire. Formerly a lecturer in sociology at Sheffield Hallam University, she has worked on several research projects on gender equality issues in local and regional development. Most recently, she prepared guidelines for the Scottish Parliament on mainstreaming equal opportunities in parliamentary committees. Her Ph.D. explored the changing strategies for delivering equal opportunities for women in British local government.
CinnamonBennett.goyh@go-regions.gov.uk

Lissette Bernal is the 'Knowledge to Practice' co-ordinator for the ACQUIRE reproductive health project at EngenderHealth. She has 12 years of progressive experience as a technical adviser and programme manager for USAID-funded reproductive-health and family-planning programmes, with special expertise in men's reproductive health and male-involvement strategies. In her role as senior programme associate for the Men As Partners programme, she organised and conducted training workshops to stimulate increased attention and innovative programming for male involvement in reproductive health.

Janet Brown, MSW (Columbia), has since 1981 been social worker, then director, of the Caribbean Child Development Centre (CCDC), School of

Continuing Studies, at the University of the West Indies (UWI), based in Kingston, Jamaica. CCDC serves the wider Caribbean region in curriculum development, research, training, and advocacy in the areas of early childhood development and parenting support. Since the late 1980s, she has worked collaboratively with UWI's faculty of social sciences in the under-researched area of Caribbean fathers and in the gender-socialisation of children. With colleagues, she has helped to translate the research into user-friendly outputs for broad applications in public and parenting education, teacher training, and policy development.

Magda Mohammed Elsanousi is a graduate of Ahfad University for Women in Sudan. She holds MAs in Gender and Development and in Rural Development, both from the University of Sussex. She has mainly worked on development, poverty reduction, and humanitarian assistance in general, and on gender issues in particular. She has worked on gender and peace activities with a number of INGOs and with the UN in Sudan. She joined Oxfam GB in Yemen in 2001, and in the course of this work, developed interests in approaches to gender equality and men. She was invited by the UN Division for the Advancement of Women to participate in the meeting held in Brazil in 2003 on the 'Role of Men and Boys in Promoting Gender Equality'. Her published work includes 'Political engagement of Sudanese women: displaced and rural women as tools for economic development: the case of Sudan', in Barbara J. Nelson and Najma Chowdhury (eds.), *Women and Politics Worldwide*, Yale University Press, 1994.

Gaetane le Grange has been a part of Targeted AIDS Interventions (TAI) since 2001, and during that time she has tremendously enjoyed participating in the pioneering projects that have been implemented by TAI. She has been involved in administration, project management, the analysis of research results, and the monitoring and evaluation of the various projects. Gaetane is currently completing her degree in Development Studies with a special focus on poverty and issues relating to human rights.

Michael Kaufman is a founder of the White Ribbon Campaign and the author or editor of books on gender issues, on democracy and development, and an award-winning novel. Dr. Kaufman has worked in over thirty countries as a writer, public speaker, consultant, and workshop leader on gender relations for governments, corporations, professional firms, trade unions, universities, NGOs, and bodies of the United Nations. A former university professor, he lives in Toronto, Canada. A number of his articles are available at: www.michaelkaufman.com

Maree Keating is based in Melbourne, Australia, and since 1998 has managed country-level development programmes in Indonesia, Cambodia, and East Timor. She previously worked as a teacher, trainer, and adult educator, as well as a project manager, musician, and performer. She completed a thesis on 'The Women's Movement in Indonesia in the Post-Suharto Era', and has been one of Oxfam GB's advisers on gender equality since 2002. Maree has recently guest-edited an issue on trade of the journal *Gender and Development.*

Benno de Keijzer is based in Mexico, and is an MD with a Master's degree in Social Antropology and is currently completing a Doctorate in Community Mental Health. He is founder and current co-ordinator of Salud y Género (Mexico) and the Program H initiative. A teacher and international consultant in themes related to gender, masculinities, health, and community work in several local and national educational institutions, he is currently Fellow in Reproductive Health and Rights with the Open Society Institute and Columbia University.

Nana Khoshtaria is a psychologist and graduate of Tbilisi State University, Faculty of Psychology and Philosophy. She was a scientific worker in the 1980s at the D. Uznadze Institute of Psychology, working on the role of psychological factors in the development of cancer. Since 2000, she has worked for the 'Sakhli' Advice Centre for Women, Georgia, as a project assistant, where her primary responsibilities are psychological consultations and research design and implementation.

Thalia Kidder has worked since 1997 as a policy adviser on livelihoods for Oxfam GB. During five years working in Central America, she focused on local economic projects, microfinance, and gender, and has carried out training in West Africa, the Caribbean, and Asia, as well as publishing articles on the issues of microfinance and gender. Based on her previous experience in workers' organising in North America, she has recently helped to develop and co-ordinate research for Oxfam into labour rights in 12 countries in South and East Asia, Africa, Latin America, the UK, and the USA. She is committed to finding new and practical ways to communicate and inspire people about gender-equality issues in economics. She has an MA in Community and Economic Development from the University of Minnesota.

James L. Lang is an independent consultant working on issues of gender-based violence and on men as partners for gender equality and social justice. James is currently working with the United Nations system and the Family Violence Prevention Fund (San Francisco, USA). He has worked with Oxfam GB on the Gender Equality and Men project, served as the research co-ordinator for the United Nations International Research and Training Institute for the Advancement of Women (INSTRAW), and as a programme officer and researcher for the United Nations Development Programme (UNDP). James has published numerous articles and edited books on the topics of poverty, men and gender, gender-based violence, and other development issues.

Manisha Mehta is currently the senior technical adviser for client–provider interaction for the ACQUIRE reproductive health project at EngenderHealth. Ms. Mehta has 12 years of progressive experience as a technical adviser and manager in the field of international family planning and reproductive health, with special expertise in working with under-served populations, most notably men and youth. During her tenure as programme manager for the Men As Partners programme at EngenderHealth, she led the development, implementation, and evaluation of innovative male-involvement strategies and tools to constructively increase male involvement in reproductive health.

Marcos Nascimento is a clinical psychologist who holds an M.Phil. in Gender, Sexuality, and Health from the University of Rio de Janeiro. He has conducted research on young men and gender-based violence in Brazil, and has also carried out training activities on working with young men in Brazil, Latin America, and the USA. He is currently co-ordinator of the Gender, Youth and Health Initiative at Instituto Promundo, an NGO based in Rio de Janeiro.

Dean Peacock is the South Africa programme manager of EngenderHealth, and technical adviser for the South and East Africa Men as Partners programme. In South Africa, he provides training and technical assistance to a wide range of organisations on the development and implementation of the Men as Partners programme. For the past 11 years, he has worked in South Africa, the USA, and Latin America to end men's violence and to promote egalitarian, non-abusive models of masculinity that improve the lives of men, women, and children and contribute to a more just society. He has worked as a consultant to many national and international organisations, including the United Nations Division for the Advancement of Women, the Commonwealth Secretariat's Gender, HIV/AIDS and Human Rights programme, the San Francisco-based Family Violence Prevention Fund, and the Vera Institute of Justice in New York.

Rusudan Pkhakadze is a psychologist and graduate of Tbilisi State University, Faculty of Psychology and Philosophy, and carried out scientific work in the D. Uznadze Institute of Psychology in the 1980s. She worked for Oxfam GB in Georgia as a social worker in 1997–98. From 2000, she has been a director of the 'Sakhli' Advice Centre for Women, and is also a chairperson of the Tbilisi Coalition Against Domestic Violence. Ms. Pkhakadze is the author of a number of publications and articles on domestic violence.

Julie Pulerwitz is a behavioural scientist with the Horizons Program at Population Council/PATH, a global HIV/AIDS research project. Dr. Pulerwitz received her masters and doctoral degrees from the Harvard School of Public Health. Her main research areas include HIV/STI prevention, gender and male involvement, and stigma and discrimination. She is co-principal investigator with Gary Barker on an evaluation study in Brazil, and is also implementing studies in Nicaragua, South Africa, and India. She has published articles on HIV/AIDS and gender in the *American Journal of Public Health,* among others.

Sharon E. Rogers joined Oxfam in 2002 as South Asia regional campaign adviser for the Campaign to End Violence Against Women, and works as part of a team to develop five national campaigns to change the attitudes and beliefs that perpetuate gender violence. Prior to joining Oxfam, she worked in Kyrgyzstan on a democracy and civil society strengthening programme and in Nicaragua on women's human-rights education. In the USA, she was a lobbyist and organiser for NGOs working for gender and racial and ethnic equality, civil rights, and reproductive health. A passionate activist against gender-based violence, Sharon has also been a volunteer for a rape crisis hotline, a legal advocate for survivors, a shelter worker and chair of a shelter board of directors, and the co-curator of a multi-site exhibition of art by survivors of violence. She holds a BA in Women's Studies and an MA in Public Policy and Women's Studies, and has focused on alliance building and organisational development.

Sandy Ruxton, who edited this publication, works as an Oxfam GB policy adviser on UK and EU poverty issues. He is the author of *Men, Masculinities, and Poverty in the UK* (Oxfam GB, 2002) and co-author of *Beyond Civil Rights: Developing Economic, Social, and Cultural Rights in the United Kingdom* (Oxfam GB, 2001). Other published work is in the areas of children's rights, asylum and migration, poverty and social exclusion, and European policy. He has worked in policy and research for fifteen years, having previously trained as a teacher, and has worked in a range of community settings (mainly with young male offenders). He is a graduate of the Universities of Oxford, York, and North London.
sruxton@oxfam.org.uk

Márcio Segundo holds a Master's degree in Political Science from the University of Brasilia, Brazil. His expertise is in political and social development, and his work has focused on the design, implementation, and management of social-impact evaluation programmes. He has also provided training on research methodology and strategic planning, specifically for education and health-related interventions. He currently co-ordinates the research and evaluation arm of Instituto Promundo, an NGO based in Rio de Janeiro. In this position, he oversees the evaluation of an intervention to promote health and gender equity among young men from local low-income communities.

Sue Smith is currently gender adviser to Oxfam GB's UK Poverty Programme. Based on its international work, Oxfam has a gender perspective on poverty in the UK, exploring through gender analysis how poverty affects women and men differently, and how gender relations impact on poverty. Sue has worked for Oxfam for the last ten years, as resource officer in the Gender and Development Unit, and information manager in the Oxfam GB's Policy department. She edited *Links,* Oxfam's newsletter on gender and development, for five years. She has taught in the Middle East, and lectured in further education.

Introduction

Sandy Ruxton

The main aim of *Gender Equality and Men: Learning from Practice* is to share knowledge and experience of work with men on gender equality in programmes run by Oxfam GB and other organisations. It also seeks to explore how work with men can be developed to promote broader gender equality and poverty reduction strategies, and to encourage a more active engagement with men through gender programming.

The book provides a critical account of practical experience in this field, and therefore complements other recent edited collections that adopt a more academic or theoretical perspective.[1] A range of key issues is addressed, including the value of including men in gender equality and anti-poverty work; the difficulties that are likely to arise – both for men and women – and how they can be overcome; practical evidence from different spheres (for example, in relation to sustainable livelihoods, gender-based violence, sexual and reproductive health); lessons about the impact of including men in gender analysis and action; and future strategies and directions for development organisations and practitioners.

Developing work with men for gender equality is still 'work in progress' for Oxfam GB and other organisations. Contributors to this book were therefore asked in particular to reflect on their experience, and to describe, analyse, and highlight learning for others. While we believe that *Gender Equality and Men* will provide an important contribution to the debate – and will be relevant to development practitioners, researchers, academics, students, and policy makers – we accept that it is by no means the last word in this complex field.

This book is the latest of many publications from Oxfam GB on gender and development, and draws together contributions from authors working in many parts of the world who are seeking to involve men in gender-equality strategies. Exploring work with men is not a new departure for Oxfam, as we have published a range of papers[2] and co-hosted a series of seminars[3] on this topic in recent years. Nevertheless, the focus of this book on the practice of working with men and masculinities confirms the increasing emergence of this strand in the organisation's thinking.

This introduction sets out Oxfam GB's approach to gender equality, and explains the organisation's gender policy and how the specific position of men is integrated into it. It goes on to describe the development of Oxfam GB's 'Gender Equality and Men' project between 2002 and 2004; this publication represents a key outcome of the second phase of the project. The introduction then examines arguments for and against the inclusion of men in gender-equality work. Drawing on recent research, it outlines a framework for understanding men and masculinities, and concludes with an overview of the contributions to the book.

Tackling gender inequality: Oxfam's approach

Oxfam GB is a member of Oxfam International, an international grouping of development agencies whose mission is to work with local partners to alleviate poverty and injustice, working in more than 100 countries worldwide. Oxfam GB works in more than 75 countries, and its activities include advocacy, education, campaigning, and development and humanitarian programmes. It focuses on five key aims: to uphold people's rights to sustainable livelihoods; quality education and healthcare; protection from disasters and violence; communities' participation in the decisions that affect their lives; and the right to equity (including gender equality and diversity issues).[4]

Oxfam GB's commitment to gender equality is rooted in 20 years of analysis and practical action in line with feminist goals. Oxfam[5] understands gender as one of a number of 'social relations': the various structural relationships within society which create and maintain differences in the positioning of various groups according to age, race, ethnicity, class, disability, and sexual orientation.[6] Gender relations are thus about power relations between the sexes, and between different groups of women and men. Gender analysis explores inequalities in gender roles and responsibilities in society, and identifies the practical needs and strategic interests of men and women. It asks key questions such as 'who does what?', 'who has what?', 'who decides?', 'who gains?', and 'who loses?'.

Oxfam's approach to working for gender equality has tended to focus on developing programmes aimed directly at improving the lives of women, based on continuing evidence that women are the majority in the poorest groups in all societies, and that their experience of poverty consists not only of economic want, but also of social and political exclusion. For example, in many developing countries women earn on average only 60 to 70 per cent of what men are paid for similar work (and in Africa and Asia only 50 per cent). Women also work longer hours than men, with women's working hours estimated to exceed men's by about 30 per cent.[7]

This reality remains at the core of Oxfam's approach, and its updated 'Policy on Gender Equality' (2003) reasserts that women often have less recourse than men to legal recognition and protection, less access to public knowledge and information, and less decision-making power both within and outside the home.[8] The policy also confirms that in many parts of the world, women frequently have little control over fertility, sexuality, and marital choices. It concludes that such discrimination increases their vulnerability to poverty, violence, and ill-health, and results in women representing a disproportionate percentage of the poor population of the world.

In order to mainstream work for gender equality throughout Oxfam's programme, the gender policy also states that Oxfam 'will address the policies, practices, ideas and beliefs that perpetuate gender inequality and prevent women and girls (and sometimes men and boys) from enjoying a decent livelihood, participation in public life, protection, and basic services'. Oxfam's strategy is to work with both men and women, together and separately, to have a more lasting impact on beliefs and behaviour. And in an implicit endorsement of the need to undertake work with men – the first time this has been recognised in Oxfam's gender policy – it highlights that 'We will ensure that any work we do with men and men's groups supports the promotion of gender equality'.

The emerging focus on men in this book does not signal a retreat from Oxfam's long-standing concern to tackle poverty among women. Nor does it argue that men have been 'left out' of gender programming because of an inappropriate focus on women, and that the former need now to be 'included'. Rather, it reflects increasing recognition that examining men's power and privilege and responding to masculinity issues are vital elements of the efforts to build gender equality.

Why work with men to find solutions to gender inequality and poverty?

The emphasis on work with men in Oxfam's gender policy reflects a growing international acknowledgement of the importance of the issue. Over the past 10 to 15 years, interest in men's involvement in gender equality has increased significantly. This is demonstrated by the growing body of research, the emergence of websites[9] and academic journals,[10] and the establishment of campaigns (e.g. the White Ribbon Campaign, see chapter by Kaufman in this volume) and educational programmes focusing on men and masculinities.

At the 1995 UN Fourth World Conference on Women, the *Beijing Declaration* committed participating governments to 'encourage men to participate fully in all actions towards equality'.[11] Five years later, at its twenty-third special session

3

('Beijing + 5'), the UN General Assembly went on to emphasise that 'men must involve themselves and take joint responsibility with women for the promotion of gender equality'.[12] Consolidating these commitments, one of the two major themes addressed at the UN Commission on the Status of Women in its 48th session in March 2004 was 'The role of men and boys in achieving gender equality' (see Appendix).

These statements and events reflect long-standing debates within development policy and practice, where a conceptual shift from focusing on 'Women in Development' (WID) to 'Gender and Development' (GAD) has been underway over the past decade. Although these terms have often been used synonymously, they are intended to describe different approaches. The former tends to focus on women as an analytical category, and envisages the setting up of separate organisational structures for the development of women-specific policies and projects. The latter suggests that 'gender relations' should be the key analytical framework, and that a gender perspective should be integrated (or 'mainstreamed') into all development activities and planning structures in order to transform the power balance between men and women within society. The emphasis of GAD on 'gender relations' inevitably encourages a more active approach to men and masculinity issues than in the past.[13] It is important to note, however, that addressing men through GAD does not necessarily involve abandoning projects and strategies that focus on women, which may still be justified by gender analysis.

The extent to which this conceptual shift has been reproduced at grassroots level is unclear, however, and in practice many projects and programmes continue to target women without considering the need to transform men's attitudes and behaviour. In part, this reflects uncertainties about working with men. Work with men could be seen as a distraction from the fundamental work of empowering women, or as an attempt by men to co-opt existing gender work for their own purposes. It could divert (or be seen to be diverting) resources away from the empowerment of women, raising concerns in the current context of shrinking development assistance.

Moreover, many men are resistant to changing ideas, beliefs, and behaviours. Progress towards gender equality can be undermined by boy's and men's expectations of receiving services from women; by difficulties in accepting new roles (e.g. as carers) and sharing power with women; by cultural or political support for existing unequal power structures; and by male hostility to gender-equality programmes. In practical terms, programming in this area is still relatively new, and strong impact assessments have not yet been undertaken to evaluate the effectiveness of such work.

Yet these concerns, although sometimes borne out in practice, ignore the risks of *not* engaging with men. Unless men's practices, attitudes, and relations change, efforts to promote gender inequality will face an uphill struggle. Involving women in development programmes can lead to overload and exhaustion for them, and may entrench stereotypes of women (as 'carers', for example) and men (as 'breadwinners').[14] The majority of male decision makers will continue to ignore the relevance of gender, and as a result, it will remain a peripheral issue and will not be integrated effectively into development policy and programmes at all levels.

The concerns regarding the risks also fail to acknowledge sufficiently the potential for positive outcomes of involving men in gender-equality strategies. Echoing the conclusions of a Gender Equality and Men workshop in Oxford in June 2002,[15] and of a UN-backed Expert Group meeting in 2003,[16] a report of the UN Secretary General on the role of men and boys in achieving gender equality recently suggested that:

> *Where men are key decision-makers and holders of economic and organisational power and public resources, they can facilitate gender-responsive policy reform and support laws designed to protect the rights of women and children. Men and boys can play a crucial role in combating HIV/AIDS and violence against women; in achieving gender equality in the workplace and the labour market; and in promoting the sharing of family responsibilities, including domestic work and care of children, and older, disabled and sick family members.[17]*

In this volume, Kaufman describes the broader benefits for society as a whole, drawing on his 'AIM' framework.[18] He believes that the beneficial impact of involving men and boys is likely to be felt in the longer-term, and that such an approach will contribute to raising the next generation of boys and girls in a framework of gender equity and equality, and respect for human rights. Shifting the attitudes and behaviour of men and boys should also improve the lives of women and girls in the home, the workplace, and the community.

Kaufman goes on to suggest that involving men may help to create wider consensus and support on issues which have previously been marginalised as of interest to women only (in relation to family, violence, sexual and reproductive health, for example). Targeting men, especially those who have a powerful role within institutions, may also unlock additional financial resources and improve the overall funding levels available to meet the needs of women and girls. And engaging with men may encourage the development of effective partnerships between men's and women's organisations. Such efforts may also help to undermine the position of those men who are working to preserve men's power and privilege and deny rights to women and children.

Exploring work with men: Oxfam GB's Gender Equality and Men project

Oxfam GB's Gender Equality and Men (GEM) project began in 2002 as a joint initiative between two Oxfam programmes: the UK Poverty Programme, and the Middle East, Eastern Europe, and CIS region – with funding from Oxfam and the UK government Department for International Development. That the project was led by staff located in these geographical areas reflects the growing debate over the position of men and boys in these countries in recent years.

The notion that men as a group are 'in crisis' is common in populist discussions of changing gender relations, but clearly is overstated. It is more useful to focus on evidence of significant shifts in gender relations as a result of economic, social, and political change. For example, a World Bank report in 2002[19] on 27 transition countries in Europe and Central Asia (ECA) suggested that there has been a sharp increase in unemployment, mental illness, suicide, and risk-taking behaviour among men in some countries in this region.[20] But at the same time, the reduction of state support for women in ECA over the past decade has led to them increasingly carrying the double burden of working and caring.

A 'gender perspective' implies looking at the connections between the issues facing men and women. For instance, the negative changes for men outlined above (unemployment, mental illness, suicide) are also likely to have a negative impact on women, creating a growing number of women-headed (or maintained) households, increasing the social and economic burdens on women, reducing their protection, and so on.

The need to develop responses to trends such as these, and to generate a closer understanding of the potential and reality of work with men, provided the impetus for the GEM project. The project has been assisting Oxfam to explore ways to advance gender equality and poverty reduction by incorporating men and boys more fully into its gender work.

The first phase of the GEM project ended in a workshop held in June 2002, bringing together representatives from six Oxfam regions with other organisations with expertise in working with men.[21] As a result, staff in each region drafted an action plan to generate new thinking and approaches to including men in work promoting gender equality, and to increase the impact of poverty-reduction programmes.

Since then, the GEM project has stimulated and contributed to a range of activities. These include the development of improved tools and frameworks for gender analysis, the initiation of pilot projects and exploratory seminars, the production of good-practice case studies, and improvements to programme design. For example, the revision of Oxfam's gender policy recognises the need to work with men as well as with women to achieve gender equality. Regional workshops on men and masculinities have taken place in East Asia and South Africa, and an internal course has trained a number of key male advocates for gender equality within the organisation. Progress has been made in developing pilot approaches in Azerbaijan, Georgia (see the chapter by Pkhakadze and Khoshtaria), Albania, and the Negev Desert (Israel). The development of Oxfam GB's campaign to end violence against women in South Asia has involved consideration of how men can be encouraged to support gender equality (see the chapter by Rogers). In Yemen (see the chapter by Elsanousi) and the UK,[22] changes in policy and practice have been achieved at different levels of government.

We make reference to some of the learning from these initiatives in the concluding chapter of this book. While this book brings to a close the second phase of the GEM project, we are currently exploring ways to consolidate the lessons learned within Oxfam's future policy and practice.

A framework for understanding masculinity

A key part of the GEM project's approach is the recognition that improving policy and practice in work with men depends on developing a framework for understanding contemporary masculinities. The available research and analysis reflects increasing interest among academics over the past 15 years in studying who men are and what they do. This growing body of literature draws on a range of intellectual traditions, and in particular diverse feminist and pro-feminist approaches (for example, Kimmel 1987, Connell 1987 and 1995, Segal 1997).[23] These approaches have, in turn, influenced the development of specific studies of men, for example, in criminology, education, and health.

Much of this theoretical work has originated in developed-country contexts, especially in the USA, Australia, and parts of Europe (such as Scandinavia, Germany, and the UK). There is evidence to suggest that the range is expanding, however, and studies are emerging to fill existing gaps. They include the exploration of masculinity issues in Southern Africa by Morrell (2001),[24] in the Caribbean by Reddock (2004),[25] in Japan by Roberson and Suzuki (2003),[26] in Latin America by Vigoya (2001),[27] and in the Middle East by Ghoussoub and Sinclair-Webb (2000).[28]

The most significant attempt to outline a comprehensive framework for understanding masculinity is widely accepted as being the work of Australian sociologist Robert Connell.[29] Connell's framework amounts to a significant critique of the often negative expressions of men's power around the world, and it remains essential to criticise oppressive or destructive aspects of men's behaviours and attitudes.

However, it is also important to emphasise that men are as capable as women of being caring human beings and of living in ways that are not damaging to other men, women, or children. As Connell's framework shows, there is no fundamental or biological reason preventing men from living in this way. Indeed, it is increasingly accepted that men have a positive role to play in efforts towards gender equality. As Connell himself emphasised recently, 'Our task is to consider men and boys not just as beneficiaries of women's work or holders of privilege or perpetrators of violence against women, but also explicitly as agents of change, participants in reform, and potential allies in search of gender justice'. Below, we draw upon and extend Connell's summary of the findings of current research into masculinities.

Multiple 'masculinities'

There is no universal form of masculinity (hence the term 'masculinities'), and differences among men exist according to class, race, age, religious belief, disability, and sexual orientation (as they do for women).[30] This is confirmed by various studies: the collection edited by Morrell on Southern Africa, for instance, explores *inter alia* the masculinities of Afrikaner reactionaries, gay men, migrant labourers, unemployed youth, and white surfers.[31] In this volume, de Keijzer highlights the crucial role played by gay men in Mexico (as elsewhere) in destabilising heterosexual expressions of masculinity.

The invisibility of men's gender identity

Men as a group occupy a relatively privileged position in relation to women in the economic, social, and sexual spheres, as Lang and Smith identify in their contribution. Given their relatively powerful position, men are often unaware of the fact that many of their privileges (such as higher incomes, care and domestic services from women) are derived *purely from being male;* therefore their 'gender', and gender issues, remain invisible, and therefore unimportant, to them.[32] In other words, men, both as individuals and as a group, benefit from what Connell calls the 'patriarchal dividend' – 'the advantage men in general gain from the overall subordination of women' – which they can call upon when they want to.[33] One effect of the patriarchal dividend is that most statistics, institutions, and interventions, although they appear to be gender-neutral, are shaped around men representing the 'norm', thus giving them a structural advantage.

Dominant ('hegemonic') expressions of masculinity and other forms

There is usually a dominant form of masculinity that subordinates, co-opts, or marginalises other forms (as well as women); this has been described as 'hegemonic' masculinity.[34] Men as a group, in particular those in higher income groups, hold a relatively powerful structural position in relation to women and to young men, to men from ethnic or religious minorities, gay men, disabled men, and men on lower incomes (or some combination of these factors). Meanwhile, men in the subordinate groups feel entitled to the patriarchal dividend, but in practice do not see how they benefit from it. This situation is often a cause of male hostility and aggression, particularly towards other groups that lack power, such as women and children. However, a number of contributions in this collection – notably those of Kaufman and de Keijzer – show that such tensions can also provide an opportunity to shift gender relations towards equality.

Globalised masculinities

Hegemonic masculinity is often based on economic success, racial superiority, and overt heterosexuality – and reinforced, especially in developed countries, by the growth of transnational business and the wider circulation of the symbols and imagery of individualism and competition (through sport, for example). However, some commentators are cautious about the extent to which such features of globalisation can be said to be having an impact on masculinity generally.[35] They argue that although the forces of globalisation are having an increasing influence on the development of gender relations, local diversity remains hugely significant. Moreover, the global and the local are inextricably linked to each other, interacting in diverse ways.

Collective masculinities

Masculinities are also collectively constructed and enacted within cultures, groups, and institutions beyond the individual, such as the classroom, factory, the military, the sports club, and the mass media. Using the example of violent masculinities, Connell highlights how such violence is not just a matter of individual pathology, but is collectively defined or institutionally supported, whether in informal peer groups, formal armies, or militias somewhere between the two.[36] In this volume, Pkhakadze and Khoshtaria explore the dismissive attitudes and behaviour of male police officers towards violence against women and children, and how this relates to the culture within the police force. Similar work has been undertaken by the non-government organisation (NGO) ROZAN in Pakistan.[37] The importance of Connell's insight overall is that if change is to be achieved, it is essential to focus not only on individual, but also on institutional transformation.

Masculinities are actively constructed

Although cultural differences may exist in the ways in which masculinities are constructed, in general it appears that they are 'produced' through social inter-action, rather than being programmed by genes or fixed by social structures. A good example of this process is the way in which individual boys (and girls) in schools constantly negotiate and re-negotiate gender relations within peer groups, formal classes, and adult–child relationships, as research in British schools has shown.[38] As Barker observes in his chapter, young men in Latin America are not just 'sponges' of cultural norms; learning about gender involves a more active process than the passive and linear 'socialisation' model implies.

Masculinities are dynamic

Masculinities change according to specific historical circumstances. For example, in an essay on Soviet masculinities, Novikova describes how, from the 1917 Revolution onwards, the State was formally committed to equal rights for women (through the education of girls and women, childcare provision, and health services, for example), although in practice the reality for many women was far from the principle of gender equality.[39] Following the collapse of the Soviet system at the end of the 1980s, strong pressure to reject its heritage fuelled the idea that men had become 'emasculated' during the Soviet period. There followed a celebration of competitive masculinity in the adjustment to the new structures of capitalism, resulting in the reassertion of male power and privilege among some men, and in unemployment and poverty for others. This insightful analysis mirrors the development of gender relations in Georgia described by Pkhakadze and Khoshtaria in this volume. Similarly, de Araujo charts how, following independence in East Timor, a small number of men are beginning to challenge the widely accepted norms of male power and violence established under Indonesian occupation.

Negative impacts of masculinities

Conformity to restrictive definitions of masculinity ('be tough, compete, don't cry') can lead to disengaged fatherhood, poor health, aggression, overwork, and lack of emotional responsiveness. It is important to understand and respond to effects such as these – especially among men at the sharp end of social and economic change. The contribution of Mehta, Peacock, and Bernal, and that of le Grange, highlight how narrow notions of masculinity can lead to risk-taking behaviour among such men.

However, acknowledging effects such as these can slip too easily into making misleading claims that men are 'losing out' to women, or even 'oppressed' by them. The difficulties some men undoubtedly face in particular societies are often misinterpreted by small but vocal 'men's rights' groups, who argue that it is essential to reinforce traditional masculinities, usually by seeking to undermine the important advances that have been achieved in the status and rights of women and children. In her chapter, Brown argues that it is important to listen to the voices of fathers, particularly those on the margins, but she highlights the risks of men and women developing opposing perspectives. De Araujo goes further, drawing attention to the importance of collaboration between men's and women's organisations, and the long-standing role of the women's movement in generating analysis and action in relation to men and masculinities.

Challenges in achieving change: the contributions to this book

The contributions to this book suggest that there is a nascent shift in the attitudes and behaviour of small numbers of men around the world, who are increasingly involved as fathers to their children, are keen to develop more egalitarian partnerships with their wives and partners, who support opportunities for women to earn an income outside the home, and who reject domestic and other forms of violence.[40] Positive change is by no means universal, however, nor can it be expected to become so. It remains a crucial task for men and women to nurture, promote, and sustain such change. The contributions in this volume, outlined below, are intended to help them achieve this.

The book is divided into four sections, responding to some of the key challenges facing practitioners and organisations developing work with men.

Why is it important to include men in gender equality and anti-poverty work?

In the first section, Michael Kaufman puts the case for involving men and boys in working for gender equality. He argues that development interventions have usually failed to focus on men and boys, and that as a result male power remains dominant in gender relations, and women and women's struggles are marginalised. He suggests that in societies where male power is threatened, there is a risk that addressing the challenges to men and boys can encourage erroneous analyses of men as the new 'victims'. Kaufman believes, however, that it is also possible in such circumstances to open up space for a more progressive gender discourse. He outlines a range of potentially positive outcomes of involving men and boys, and concludes with a set of principles for guiding the development of programmes and interventions in the future.

Benno de Keijzer identifies economic and social changes affecting masculinities in Mexico, and highlights important shifts in family relations, such as the erosion of men's breadwinner role. While these changes provide opportunities for altering unequal power relations, the risks (of domestic violence, unemployment, and alcohol abuse, for example) tend to dominate. Nevertheless, de Keijzer argues that positive change is possible, influenced by a range of factors including: significant life events (relationships, the birth of a child); the influence of schools, peer groups, and older men; the experience of migration; and the support of women and women's groups. Drawing on the activities of the NGO Salud y Género over the past decade, de Keijzer analyses how change occurs, and the tensions and contradictions that surround it. Finally, he explores key entry-points to work with men, including reproductive and sexual health, fatherhood, gender-based violence, and youth work.

What works with men in practice?

In section two, Maree Keating reflects on her own experience of facilitating gender workshops with men and women in a range of countries (including Afghanistan, Cambodia, Democratic Republic of Congo, Ghana, and Nigeria), and explores why many facilitators shy away from sensitive discussions related to gender. She argues that it is critical in gender workshops to bring into the open power and equality issues (for example, changing social and family norms, or male violence), even with predominantly male groups. Failure to engage with such issues means that opportunities are missed that could help participants develop the tools to discuss gender equality beyond the workshop. Furthermore, women in the group may be left frustrated at the lack of progress, and men may remain secure in their view that changing gender relations is either unnecessary or unachievable.

Thalia Kidder's chapter first identifies the common limitations of gender analyses of livelihoods programmes, which tend to focus on social factors and fail to address gendered economics. Drawing on examples from workshops in Albania, El Salvador, Haiti, Indonesia, Malawi, Nicaragua, and Senegal, she describes attempts to encourage male participants to value women's unpaid contributions to households, and to allow women space to market their products and use financial services. She also acknowledges that some men may be disadvantaged by gender stereotypes and roles in relation to livelihoods. Rather than raise gender issues explicitly in workshops (as Maree Keating does), Kidder sets out methods that rely more heavily on indirect economic efficiency arguments; in her view, men may be more receptive if they appreciate that gender stereotypes are making projects less effective. She ends by observing, among other things, that it is vital in each setting to find key questions that jolt men (and women) into thinking and acting differently.

Magda Elsanousi outlines the socialisation process for men and women, and the key factors that maintain gender inequality in the conservative society of Yemen. She then describes attempts by three women's groups to work with influential men as allies in combating violence against women. Given the lack of power and voice that Yemeni women have, she believes that this is the most effective way of getting women's concerns on the agenda. Identifying the key principles of such partnerships, she argues that, although change is slow and hard to sustain, these initiatives demonstrate the enormous potential of alliance building of this kind.

EngenderHealth's 'Men As Partners' programme (MAP), has been implemented in a number of countries worldwide (including Bolivia, India, Nepal, Pakistan, and South Africa), and its experience is described by Manisha Mehta, Dean Peacock, and Lissette Bernal. The authors show how MAP encourages men to prevent gender-based violence and to take greater responsibility for improving their sexual and reproductive health and that of their partners. To be effective, they suggest it is essential that programmes enable men to play a positive role, build organisational cultures that are committed to working with men, involve key stakeholders from the outset, and develop strategic alliances.

Two specific initiatives established by the Targeted AIDS Intervention Project to educate young men in KwaZulu-Natal about sexual and reproductive health are examined by Gaetane le Grange. The initiatives are attempts to respond to the HIV/AIDS crisis in South Africa, which has been fuelled by increasing risk-taking behaviour by men – particularly those affected by poverty, unemployment, and alcoholism. The author describes how the project contacted groups of young men through soccer clubs and schools, and how networks of peer educators were trained to disseminate accurate information to their friends and partners about issues such as puberty, sexually transmitted diseases, HIV/AIDS, and condom use. Le Grange describes the surprisingly enthusiastic response of young men, and suggests that this was due to the participatory approach of the educators, the space the project provided for young men to discuss sensitive topics, and the fact that project activities came to be seen by young men as 'cool'.

Janet Brown reviews fatherhood initiatives in the Caribbean region, arguing that narrow perceptions of fathers as providers and protectors are deeply embedded in society, and undermine positive efforts to support men as fathers. She identifies a range of programmes, including work with vulnerable men; men-only public forums; parenting and public education activities; and reproductive health interventions. Although little impact analysis has been carried out on these programmes as yet, Brown believes that developmental approaches based on men's own expressed needs and views are more likely to engage men. She also suggests that there is a need to create spaces for men alone, but warns that there is a danger of polarising men's and women's positions on family issues.

Rusudan Pkhakadze and Nana Khoshtaria describe in their article how gender relations have changed in the post-Soviet period in Georgia. They highlight in particular the links between economic hardship, unemployment, and men's violence within families, and argue that women's roles increasingly involve not only caring, but also breadwinning. Drawing on their practical experience with the unique Sakhli Women's Advice Centre, they show how counselling services can help men to respond positively to their changing circumstances. They also describe wider action to prevent domestic violence, including public-awareness campaigning and a programme to raise awareness of the issue among police officers.

Another perspective on tackling domestic violence is provided by Mario de Araujo. He has been a prime mover in the work of the Men's Association Against Violence (AMKV) in East Timor, a country which only gained independence from Indonesia in 2002. As in other states which have recently emerged from domination or occupation by a larger neighbour, the level of violence against women and children is high. Learning from an international exchange with men's groups in Nicaragua and Brazil and working in collaboration with women's groups in East Timor, AMKV have used popular education techniques to initiate discussion in communities and schools. Their approach is rooted in practical everyday experience and avoids the dissemination of gender theory, because they believe that the former has a more immediate impact on attitudes and behaviour.

What is the impact of including men in gender analysis and action?

In the third section, Gary Barker explores the impact of programme intervention with young men, drawing on a case study of the joint work of a number of NGOs with low-income men in Brazil. He describes the activities undertaken by Program H, which seeks to help young men to question traditional norms related to manhood using educational manuals, videos, and marketing campaigns. Recognising the importance of measuring changes in attitudes and behaviour – a crucial aspect of interventions with men which is rarely considered – he outlines how researchers developed an appropriate tool (the 'Gender-equitable Attitudes in Men Scale') to undertake such evaluation. Although the efforts need to be sustained, the early findings demonstrate the value of the programme and of the evaluation method.

How should organisations develop work with men?

The final section begins with the only contribution to analyse in depth the development of a funding programme to support initiatives targeting men. Cinnamon Bennett describes the design and development of the 'Objective 1' programme in South Yorkshire in the UK. She explores how men who have lost their jobs – and their self-esteem as 'breadwinners' – can be drawn back into educational and employment contexts. Bennett is aware of the risk of recruiting men to traditional training projects that fail to challenge outdated notions of masculinity, and she highlights the view of practitioners that this can only be achieved indirectly. She concludes with recommendations for integrating a gender perspective into every stage of policy making and project delivery.

Sharon Rogers explores the thinking about gender equality of male staff in Oxfam GB in Bangladesh and India. The interviews and group discussions she initiated show that the men acknowledged that male dominance and gender inequality was central to their societies. However, they tended to believe that women as well as men had a role in maintaining such domination, and that simplistic stereotypes were unhelpful. Citing the influence of families, education, and NGO work on the development of their own gender awareness, they identified several obstacles to progress, including the fear of condemnation and conservative interpretations of Islam. Interviewees concurred that they often felt uncomfortable and defensive when discussing gender issues with women, and recommended that more space should be made available for informal, open dialogue. This would allow them to explore more fully the personal perspectives (on relationships, children, and the media, for example) that influenced their understanding and commitment to gender equality.

James Lang and Sue Smith address the responsibilities and challenges facing development organisations in engaging men, using the examples of the UN Working Group on Men and Gender Equality and the gender mainstreaming efforts in Oxfam GB. In particular, they highlight the constraints – conceptual, structural, policy, and personal – to greater male involvement. If these are to be overcome, they suggest it is essential to explore the linkages between personal and organisational change, to undertake internal advocacy, to establish male role models, and to implement gender-sensitive policies for all staff.

In the concluding chapter, we draw together lessons from the rest of the book. A range of issues is explored, such as effective practice in engaging men, and learning from work on specific issues. We end with some reflections on how development organisations and practitioners should work with both men and women in the future, if their programmes are to enhance and support gender equality.

Notes

1. For example, B. Pease and K. Pringle (2001) *A Man's World? Changing Men's Practices in a Globalized World*, London and New York: Zed Books; F. Cleaver (2002) *Masculinities Matter! Men, Gender and Development*, London and New York: Zed Books.

2 C. Sweetman (1997) *Men and Masculinity*, Oxford: Oxfam GB; S. Chant and M. Gutmann (2000) *Mainstreaming Men into Gender and Development*, Oxford: Oxfam GB.

3 C. Sweetman (ed.) (2001) *Men's Involvement in Gender and Development Policy and Practice: Beyond Rhetoric*, Oxford: Oxfam GB.

4 See www.oxfam.org.uk for further details. Oxfam's recent research on women workers in global supply chains is reported in *Trading Away our Rights*, Oxfam International (2004), available online at www.maketradefair.com

5 'Oxfam' for the purposes of this introduction refers to Oxfam GB and its programmes.

6 N. Kabeer (1994) *Reversed Realities: Gender Hierarchies in Development Thought*, London: Verso.

7 UNPFA (2000) 'Women's Empowerment and Reproductive Health: Links Through the Life Cycle', available at www.unfpa.org/modules/intercenter/cycle/index.htm (last accessed February 2004).

8 Oxfam GB (2003) 'Policy on Gender Equality', available at www.oxfam.org.uk/what_we_do/issues/gender/policy.htm

9 See *The Men's Bibliography* for a comprehensive list of international academic publications on men and masculinities: www.xyonline.net/mensbiblio/

10 For example, *Men and Masculinities*, published by Sage.

11 Paragraph 25: United Nations (1995) *Beijing Declaration and Platform for Action, Report of the Fourth World Conference on Women*, Beijing 4–15 September, UN Document A/CONF 177/20, New York, NY: United Nations. The accompanying Plan of Action reaffirmed the principle of shared power and responsibility between men and women, suggesting that women's concerns could only be addressed 'in partnership with men' towards gender equality.

12 Paragraph 6 of the Political Declaration, 5–9 June 2000, available at www.un.org/womenwatch/daw/followup/reports.htm

13 S. Chant and M. Gutmann (2000) *op. cit.*

14 C. Sweetman (1997) *op. cit.*

15 J. Lang (2002) 'Gender is Everyone's Business: Programming with Men to Achieve Gender Equality', workshop report 10–12 June 2002, Oxfam GB. Available on www.oxfam.org.uk/what_we_do/issues/gender/gem/

16 'The Role of Men and Boys in Achieving Gender Equality', report of the Expert Group Meeting, Brasilia, Brazil, 21–24 October 2003, UN Division for the Advancement of Women, EGM/MEN-BOYS-GE/2003/REPORT, 12 January 2004.

17 See UN Economic and Social Council, 'The Role of Men and Boys in Achieving Gender Equality', report of the Secretary General, E/CN.6/2004/9, 22 December 2003.

18 M. Kaufman (2003) 'The Aim Framework: Addressing and Involving Men and Boys to Promote Gender Equality and End Gender Discrimination and Violence', UNICEF. Available on www.michaelkaufman.com/articles

19 P. Paci (2002) 'Gender in Transition', Washington DC: World Bank. Available in pdf format on: http://lnweb18.worldbank.org/ECA/eca.nsf/General/F55E7337BA69423985256BFA0053F091? OpenDocument

20 The World Bank's Europe and Central Asia (ECA) region consists of the following countries of the former Soviet Union: Russia, Ukraine, Belarus, Moldova, Latvia, Lithuania, Estonia, Armenia, Azerbaijan, Georgia, Kazakhstan, Kyrgyz Republic, Tajikistan, Turkmenistan, and Uzbekistan, and the following countries of Central and Eastern Europe: Poland, Czech Republic, Slovakia, Hungary, Albania, Bulgaria, Romania, Slovenia, Croatia, FYR Macedonia, Bosnia and Herzegovina, Serbia and Montenegro, and Kosovo.

21 For further details, see www.oxfam.org.uk/what_we_do/issues/gender/gem/

22 S. Ruxton (2002) *Men, Masculinities, and Poverty in the UK*, Oxford: Oxfam GB.

23 M.Kimmel (1987) *Changing Men: New Directions in Research on Men and Masculinities*, Newbury Park, CA: Sage; R.W. Connell (1987) *Gender and Power: Society, the Person and Sexual Politics*, Palo Alto, CA: University of California Press, and (1995) *Masculinities*, Cambridge: Polity Press; and L. Segal (1997) *Slow Motion*, London: Virago.

24 R. Morrell (ed.) (2001) *Changing Men in Southern Africa*, London and Durban: University of Natal Press and Zed Books.

25 R. Reddock (2004) *Interrogating Caribbean Masculinity*, Kingston, Jamaica: University of the West Indies Press.

26 J. Roberson and N. Suzuki (eds.) (2002) *Men and Masculinities in Contemporary Japan: Dislocating the Salaryman Doxa*, London and New York: Routledge

27 M.V. Vigoya (2001) 'Contemporary Latin American Perspectives on Masculinity', *Men and Masculinities*, 3 (3).

28 M. Ghoussoub and E. Sinclair-Webb (2001) *Imagined Masculinities: Male Identity and Culture in the Modern Middle East*, London: Saqi Books.

29 R.W. Connell (1987) *Gender and Power: Society, the Person and Sexual Politics*, Palo Alto, CA: University of California Press; (1995) *Masculinities*, Cambridge: Polity Press; (2000) *The Men and the Boys*, Cambridge: Polity Press; and (2002) *Gender*, Cambridge: Polity Press.

30 Some commentators have argued that focusing on masculinities (who men are) has tended to divert attention from gender relations, and they prefer the term 'male practices' to highlight the importance of what men do. See, for instance, J. Hearn (1996) 'Is masculinity dead? A critique of the concept of masculinity/masculinities', in M. Mac an Ghaill (ed.), *Understanding Masculinities*, Milton Keynes: Open University Press.

31 R. Morrell (ed.) (2001) *op. cit.*

32 M. Kimmel (2000) *The Gendered Society*, New York and Oxford: Oxford University Press.

33 R.W. Connell (1987) *op. cit.*

34 'Hegemonic masculinity' is a concept that draws on the ideas of Gramsci. It refers to the dynamic cultural process that guarantees (or is taken to guarantee) the dominant position of men and the subordination of women. See R. Connell (1995) *op. cit.*

35 B. Pease and K. Pringle (2001) *op. cit.*

36 R.W. Connell (2000) *op. cit.*

37 M. Rashid (2002) 'Giving men choices: a Rozan project with the police force in Pakistan', in J. Lang (2002) *op. cit.* www.oxfam.org.uk/what_we_do/issues/gender/gem/

38 S. Frosch, A. Phoenix, and R. Pattman (2002) *Young Masculinities*, Basingstoke: Palgrave Macmillan; M. Mac an Ghaill (1994) *The Making of Men: Masculinities, Sexualities and Schooling*, Buckingham: Open University Press.

39 I. Novikova (2000) 'Soviet and post-Soviet masculinities: after men's wars in women's memories', in I. Breines, R. Connell, and I. Eide *Male Roles, Masculinities and Violence: A Culture of Peace Perspective*, Paris: UNESCO.

40 M. Flood (2001) 'Men's Role in Achieving Gender Justice', available on www.xyonline.net/Mensrolesingender.shtml

Transforming our interventions for gender equality by addressing and involving men and boys: a framework for analysis and action

Michael Kaufman

Among NGOs, governments, and international institutions such as the United Nations, there has been a tremendous surge of interest in the last few years in the subject of men and boys. This interest reflects several overlapping perspectives. There are those who understand we must reach men so that interventions for women and girls are not derailed by male resistance. There are those who see the quest for gender equality as being enhanced by specific initiatives aimed at men and boys, such as awareness campaigns to end gender-based violence. And there are those who realise that meeting certain needs of men and boys will actually enhance an equity and equality agenda (and vice versa). This chapter endorses all these approaches, and therefore rejects the competing view that the rush to improve the lives of women has resulted in males being ignored or even harmed – this assertion simply doesn't bear scrutiny.

My concern in writing this chapter is two-fold, firstly that this new-found interest in the lives of men and boys doesn't become a passing fad, and secondly that we analyse the lives of men and boys and develop appropriate programmes in the context of achieving gender equality, equity, and social transformation. I believe it is only the latter approaches that will ensure that the focus on men and boys is an enduring one. Only if organisations see the productive results of men and boys taking co-responsibility for gender transformation will new approaches for men not only gain a lasting place in the development world, but also maintain a transformatory edge.

This chapter will discuss a framework for such approaches, drawing on some examples from the White Ribbon Campaign, a campaign that aims to engage men and boys in the struggle to end men's violence against women.

Leaving out boys and men: a recipe for failure

This interest in masculinities, in the lived realities of men and boys and in the capacity of men to play a positive role in challenging sexism and patriarchy, has been cultivated by over two decades of work by a small number of individuals and organisations around the world. We have seen ourselves as allies with the women's movement and the struggles led by women.[1] It is not surprising, however, that a widespread acceptance of our approach has been slow in coming. After all, our work has developed within a critique of patriarchy, the very system that has given undue power and privileges to men. As a result, many women have been concerned that any attempt to include men and boys in working for gender equality would not only redirect scarce resources back to men (who, worldwide, already monopolise resources), but would also rob women of hard-fought social and political spaces. Meanwhile, many men and male-dominated institutions resist our initiatives for the same reasons that they resist equality work led by women: many men feel threatened by direct challenges to their own definitions of manhood, and some share the concerns raised by some women.

There is validity to such concerns. However, these fears arise from an assumption which is, at least partially, false. The goal of our work to promote women's empowerment is not only a matter of *directing resources to* women and girls but, in a broader sense, is also aimed at *meeting the needs of* women and girls.[2] By this I mean not only immediate needs, but also what we might think of as women's transformatory and strategic needs within a framework of their empowerment. This is one place where men and boys fit in. To cite but two examples: programmes aimed at men in order to increase fathers' involvement in day-to-day parenting and domestic tasks may be money spent *on* men, but it is part of the process of gender transformation to the benefit of women and girls. Similarly, money supporting a men's organisation to carry out awareness programmes with men and boys to end men's violence against women and girls, is not money spent *on* women and girls, but is money spent to meet the needs of women and girls.

Another way to approach this issue is to ask what will be the consequences of not addressing and involving men and boys. There are a number of reasons for such an omission being a recipe for failure.[3] Most obvious is the fact that men are the gatekeepers of current gender orders and are potential resistors of change. If we do not effectively reach men and boys, many of our efforts will be either thwarted or simply ignored. At best, male leaders will pay lip service to the goals of women's rights, but these goals will not be fully integrated into local, national, and international priorities. In addition, if we don't involve men we are *de facto* removing men from the gender equation. In doing so, we effectively marginalise women and women's struggles. It should be no surprise, then, that our best efforts are thwarted in moments of national or international crisis or in the midst of economic cutbacks, or that they are virtually ignored at the highest levels of social, economic, and political decision making.

Ultimately, gender is about relations of power between the sexes and among different groups of women and men. Although practical programmes to empower women are one part of changing these relations of power, there also need to be systematic and systemic efforts to change the lives of men and boys if we are to change power relations at their root.

In contrast to these negative consequences, there are potential positive outcomes of addressing and involving men and boys. Such efforts could:

- create a large-scale and broad social consensus on a range of issues that has been previously marginalised as issues of importance only to women, when in fact they are often also issues for men;

- mobilise resources controlled by men and mobilise the social and economic institutions controlled by men. In other words, such efforts could result in a net gain in resources available to meet the needs of women and girls;

- develop effective partnerships not only between women and men, but also between a range of institutions and organisations, some representing the interests of women and girls, and others *de facto* representing the traditional interests of men and boys;

- increasingly and patiently isolate those men working to preserve men's power and privilege and the denial of rights to women and children;

- contribute to raising the next generation of boys and girls in a framework of gender equity and equality and respect for the human rights of all;

- by changing the attitudes and behaviour of men and boys, improve the lives of women and girls in the home, the workplace, and the community;

- result in new and perhaps unexpected insights into current gender relations and the complex forces that promote discrimination against women and prevent gender equality;

- result in new insights into other social, cultural, and political issues. For example, we can deepen our understanding of fundamentalist religious movements by understanding the insecurities of men within societies which have defined men as powerful.

These, however, are only potential gains. I will return in a moment to the question of how to turn this potential into reality.

What men and boys will gain from gender equality and equity

Talk of the potential for men to gain from women's equality has often been mired in generalities about men's lot in life and, in some cases, from faulty analyses that men are the real victims and losers in our current systems of gender relations – faulty for the simple reason that such analyses play down the real benefits men enjoy from patriarchy. I believe, though, that we can develop a cogent understanding of these issues by rooting our analysis in the notion of men's contradictory experiences of power; that is, the relationship of men's power and what, in shorthand, we can call 'men's pain'. It is not simply a matter of saying that men experience both power and pain as a result of gender relations. Rather, it is about the link between the two. Specifically, it is the ways in which we have constructed our dominant definitions of masculinity, the institutions of patriarchy, and the relations of power among men and with women which are, paradoxically, the sources of disquietude, pain, fear, insecurity, and alienation for many men.[4]

Let me give an example. Men have defined childcare as 'women's work'; they have devalued such work, and have made sure that they do not have to spend much time doing it. In a sense this is a privilege, because it means that most men have only one job compared with most women, for whom work never seems to stop. It means fathers are able to relax at night, or pursue work or sports. And yet, how often do we hear older men talking about having worked their whole lives for their families, but that now they are retired, with their children gone, they don't even know them. The very thing that was a source of privilege has become a source of alienation and emotional pain.

Although men will actually benefit from a world of gender equality and fairness, this should be seen only as an outcome, and not necessarily a motivation to gain men's support. In societies where men's power and social hegemony remains largely uncontested, or where the day-to-day privileges that men enjoy far outstrip those of women, we are unlikely to convince many men that they will gain from sexual equity. In such societies, the balance between men's power and men's pain is decidedly tipped in the direction of men's power.

On the other hand, in societies where there has been an ongoing challenge from women to the domination of men, or where economic or social changes have eroded traditional forms of men's privilege and control, then the balance begins to tip the other way, so that the experiences of personal loss occupy an ever-greater place in men's experiences. In itself, this doesn't automatically lead to a pro-feminist consciousness. In fact, as men grasp the straws of religious fundamentalism and conservative political ideologies, a backlash against feminism is more often the case. My point is that the challenge to men's power opens a huge new space for an anti-sexist discourse among men. Finding ways to enter and exploit that space successfully must be one of our objectives.

The White Ribbon Campaign

In 1991 in Canada, a small group of men started the White Ribbon Campaign (WRC). The campaign engages in public education in order to end men's silence about men's violence against women, to raise awareness among men and boys, and to mobilise them to work for change through their schools, workplaces, and communities. To our surprise, the WRC received tremendous attention in the media. This was, in part, because of our strategy of asking prominent Canadian men from across the social and political spectrum to add their name to the founding statement. WRC quickly became a national institution and has spread to over thirty countries around the world.

Various features, some of them unique, define the approach of the WRC. The campaign focuses on men's violence against women. In some countries, it does this in the context of using explicit language about supporting women's equality; in others where a belief in gender equality is widespread among men, its messages focus on ending physical and sexual violence. WRC embodies the belief that, in most countries, the majority of men do not use physical or sexual violence; that we have been silent about that violence, and through the silence have allowed the violence to continue. The campaign uses the white ribbon as a symbol of ending this silence and as a public promise by a man never to commit, condone, or remain silent about violence against women.

The campaign is politically non-partisan, including and reaching out to men across the political spectrum. Working together, we agree to disagree on many important issues, including some issues relating to feminism. We work closely with women's organisations (and, in some cases, white ribbon campaigns have been started by women's groups). In many countries, WRC campaigns raise money for women's programmes.

Organisationally, WRC is very small – we see our role as being catalysts for action. We strive to encourage schools, corporations, trade unions, religious institutions, sports clubs, youth groups, governments, and non-government organisations to hold their own white ribbon activities. That way we know we can reach hundreds of millions of men.

In most countries, the annual focus of the campaign is between November 25, the international day for the elimination of violence against women, and early December, although educational activities take place throughout the year. Groups distribute ribbons and leaflets in schools, workplaces, and markets. Some groups sponsor advertisements in newspapers or on television and radio, using donations from advertising agencies and the media. They distribute posters and hold public meetings. In some countries, they also hold events around Father's Day to highlight more nurturing roles for men as part of the long-term solution to ending men's violence.

WRC is a decentralised campaign, choosing to act as a catalyst and example to other men and boys. While such a decentralised approach could create problems, it is also the factor that is responsible for the rapid spread of the campaign.

The AIM framework

As noted above, the gains from addressing and involving men remain only potential. There still lurks the problem that programming for men and boys could cause a net drain of resources away from the needs of women and girls. I have suggested that we need a strategic approach, with a goal that goes beyond working with males *per se*. Rather, we need to envision new initiatives, or develop new components of existing programmes to mobilise men and boys to work in partnership with women and girls in order to transform destructive masculinities, end oppressive gender relations, and to promote gender equity and equality and human rights.

The framework I have suggested for this approach is based on a number of conceptual tools, and a series of principles to guide the development of programmes and interventions involving men and boys.[5] These principles, with some examples from the White Ribbon Campaign, are:

1 **Whatever we do, the primary aim should be to work to end discrimination against women and girls, to achieve gender equality and equity, and to promote the human rights of women and girls.**
   Otherwise, we risk undermining the efforts of women, and we fail to transform the very system of patriarchy that is at the root of the problems we address. For example, in some countries the messages of the White Ribbon Campaign focus on the links between men's violence and the discrimination women suffer. Campaigns work to establish links with women's organisations, to support those groups, to develop joint initiatives, and to encourage men to listen to the voices of women.

2 **Successfully reaching men requires constantly navigating through men's fear.** We should never underestimate the huge individual investment some men can make in maintaining power and control. Our approaches must find ways to appeal to some of the very values we are ultimately challenging. An example is reaching men and boys with the message, 'You have the power to end violence against women in your community'. White Ribbon posters attempt to affirm the positive.

3 **Strive to use the language of responsibility rather than blame.** Similarly, we need to avoid using generalisations and stereotypes when discussing men. Generalised blame reduces sexism to individual relationships and individual identity, rather than understanding patriarchy and sexism as also being systemic and institutional. Nor is blame pedagogically useful. Language that leaves males feeling responsible for things they haven't done or for things they were taught to do, or feeling guilty for the sins of other men, will alienate most men and boys and promote backlash. Rather, we challenge men and boys to take responsibility for change, and we focus on the positive benefits to all. One example is a Canadian White Ribbon poster which has been widely translated. It has the headline, 'These men want to put an end to violence against women' followed by a number of lines. Some lines are 'pre-signed' by prominent men from that country, the other lines waiting to be signed by men and boys when the posters are put up in schools or places of work.

4 **Successful approaches depend on creating and nurturing groups of men.** This is not only so that men will be organised to take action, although it is important. It is also that in challenging patriarchy, men working in such groups begin to shift their relationships with other men. Looking around the world, such new organisations tend to develop a supportive and non-competitive environment, and often include support groups and close informal ties with other men. Although some groups maintain links with 'old boys' networks,' the direction of their work is to challenge the institutions of patriarchy. White Ribbon groups take pride in being supportive and co-operative, relying as much as possible on collective leaderships.

5 **Men's and boys' voices have an important place. Men assess their masculinity through the eyes of men, boys measure their masculinity through the eyes of other boys and men. It is critical to mobilise the voices of males to speak to other men and boys.** We must also involve them to help to design the message to their peers. Of course, many men who come to feminism do so because of the impact of women in their lives, but if we are to reach large numbers of men, men themselves must take responsibility. The sheer diversity of white ribbon activities in Canada alone is a good example of this, with each school or union or sports team itself deciding what it will do to reach the men or boys in their community.

6 **Create a politics of compassion, and work with men and boys to develop their emotional life and a language of emotions.** In our work to end the oppression of women, we must not shrink from compassion and empathy with men and boys. This means never losing sight of the negative impact of

contemporary patriarchy on men and boys themselves, even though they gain many privileges as males. Although the White Ribbon Campaign itself is not a service provider and does not work directly with men who use violence, some of our supporters do such work. Many of them approach this work by insisting that men take responsibility for their use of violence, but combine this with compassion and a desire to create spaces for these men to change their lives. To cite another example, where WRC works on issues of the greater involvement of men in fatherhood, we do so in part because we know that through nurturing, individuals develop strong emotional ties and need to develop a language of emotions.

7 **Reaching particular age groups requires finding specific entry points.** To be effective, we must understand what are, at different ages, the specific links of men and boys to gender issues. Speaking to teenage boys about domestic violence is important, but speaking with them about building healthy relationships is an even more effective way to make the same points, for it actually speaks to their most pressing concerns. The participatory model of WRC facilitates this by encouraging specific groups to design their own campaigns.

8 **Find ways to measure men's attitudinal and behavioural changes and the effectiveness of new initiatives aimed at men and boys,** as much of our work in recent decades has been rather intuitive and impressionistic. In Canada, for example, at the time of writing, WRC is beginning an evaluation of its educational materials.

No panaceas

Such a framework, together with the emerging practices of organisations around the world, gives us a set of tools that will help us advance our interventions and avoid many pitfalls.[6] There is no one model of 'correct practices' that fits all societies or age groups or arenas of intervention. However, I do believe that one framework can help to create and nurture diverse approaches.

Putting such a framework into practice requires examining our past and present activities and future plans in the light of a series of conceptual tools such as the ones I referred to above (although not elaborated there), and the type of guiding principles briefly presented here. For many organisations, an internal process is needed where spaces for discussion are created, so we are able to challenge ourselves in supportive environments. This may require workshops and discussions aimed specifically at involving men as partners for change, and participatory evaluations of gender relations within the organisation. It requires ongoing scrutiny and evaluation to ensure that our work is meeting its goals including, of course, supporting the efforts of women. Ongoing vigilance, and discussion with women's organisations and women at the community level will be the best guarantee that our efforts to address and involve men and boys do not work against the interests of women and girls.

Without such measures, resistance is inevitable. This can come either from those men who still feel threatened by the prospect of change, or from those men and women who see efforts to achieve gender equality as work only for women, or from those women who remain suspicious of men's capacity to be respectful partners for equality.

Luckily, however, there is an increasing number of organisations and individuals on all continents and in most countries who are working together, as women and men, to achieve gender equality and gender equity, social justice, and an end to destructive gender definitions and relations.

Notes

1   I refer to 'we' and 'our' to signify my own participation within organisations, campaigns, and activities aimed at addressing and involving men and boys.

2   This and other sections of this chapter are based on my article, 'The AIM Framework: Addressing and Involving Men and Boys to Promote Gender Equality and End Violence Against Women,' (M. Kaufman 2003, a paper originally prepared for UNICEF, and available online at www.michaelkaufman.com/articles).

3   See M. Kaufman (2003) *op. cit.*

4   See M. Kaufman (1993) *Cracking the Armour: Power, Pain and the Lives of Men,* Toronto: Penguin/Viking (available online in pdf format at www.michaelkaufman.com), and M. Kaufman (1999) 'Men, feminism and men's contradictory experiences of power,' in Joseph A. Kuypers, (ed.) *Men and Power,* Halifax: Fernwood Books, pp. 59–83. An earlier version of this article appeared in Harry Brod and Michael Kaufman (eds.) (1994) *Theorizing Masculinities,* Thousand Oaks: Sage Publications. Available online at www.michaelkaufman.com/articles

5   M. Kaufman (2003) *op. cit.*

6   See M. Kaufman (2002) 'The White Ribbon Campaign: involving men and boys in ending global violence against women' in Bob Pease and Keith Pringle (eds.) *A Man's World? Changing Men's Practices in a Globalized World,* London: Zed Books, (also available online at www.michaelkaufman.com), and M. Kaufman (2003) *op. cit.*

Masculinities: resistance and change

Benno de Keijzer

This chapter is part of a long-term joint research effort in Mexico, focusing on men's violence,[1] and a more personal analysis of men and change carried out for a doctoral thesis.[2] It is the outcome of a first distillation of findings from practical work carried out since the early nineties. The chapter focuses on the relationship between change, continuity, and resistance in the context of a slow transition towards gender equity with women in Mexico, and begins with an analysis of how masculinity is constructed and the risks involved in the process.

The main body of the chapter seeks to explore the dialectics of change and resistance: the *sources* or *catalysts of change* in men, the *levels* and *processes* of change itself, and the *contexts* in which change is happening or is actively promoted. Concrete examples will be drawn from the experience of Salud y Género (Health and Gender), a Mexican non-government organisation (NGO) formed by men and women for the promotion of gender equity through educational and advocacy activities in sexual, reproductive, and mental health; and through personal contact with other programmes, mainly in Latin America.

On men and masculinities

Why should men change? Masculinity as a risk or limiting factor

Many health, education, family planning, and development programmes targeting women in various parts of the world find that men are an important obstacle – and often the main one – to women's participation and to a project's success. Addressing key issues with men can have a significant impact, in preventing the problems they sometimes create.

The need to work with men on issues such as reproductive health, sexuality, violence, addiction, self-care, or other aspects of well-being has been clear to the core team of Salud y Género since the early 1990s.[3] That men, as perceived beneficiaries of a patriarchal social structure, would respond to this initiative was not so clear. But the experience of the organisation has shown that many men do respond, at least partially, overcoming different kinds of resistance.

Salud y Género's approach to working with men arises from working with women on various health issues, mainly sexual and reproductive problems, mental health, and domestic violence linked to alcohol abuse. It is increasingly clear how 'hegemonic masculinities' (dominant forms of masculinity, see Introduction, page 8) affect the lives of women and children in these areas.

This approach to health issues is based on Kaufman's violence triad,[4] a model of the relationships between various risks for men, in which the most visible axis is the risk towards women, while the other two sides represent the risks to other men and the risks to oneself. Men remain relatively unaware that many masculine traits (seeking power, being unemotional, competitive, uncaring, and rule-breaking) also have highly negative effects on their own lives.[5] For example, life expectancy for men in Mexico is 6.5 years less than for women (although women face specific risks related to reproduction), a gap that has grown during the last century.[6]

Understanding how men are socialised

We can't think about how to change men's behaviour until we have a developed understanding of how masculinities are constructed in a given culture. In a country like Mexico, many of the principal characteristics of 'hegemonic masculinities' are a strong influence on the ways in which most men are socialised. Salud y Género's work with men has led us to analyse the construction of male identity as a way of understanding, deconstructing, and modifying it. We have reflected on:

- the beliefs about power that we grew up with as men, concerning our essential 'authority' over women, and the sense of our cultural entitlement to services we 'should' receive from them;

- the way in which men handle emotions (especially the censored ones such as fear or sadness), which are often transformed into anger;

- the social and cultural validation of violent responses, often seen as a legitimate 'correction' of female behaviour;

- the different costs of hegemonic masculinity in various aspects of health, sexuality, and family life.

Salud y Género's methodology relies on promoting and achieving change towards health from a gender-equity perspective, drawing on Paulo Freire's theories of consciousness raising and participation in education.[7] However, a necessary balance to Freire's optimism is Pierre Bourdieu's theory, which explains why change is so difficult.[8] As socio-culturally constructed beings, we function though an array of representations, thoughts, and feelings. All these are structured in what Bourdieu calls the 'habitus': structures of perception, thought, and action that last over time and are adaptable to different situations.[9] These structures tend to be reproduced in the socialisation of others though an educational process instilled by authority (for example, by parents, teachers, the church, the military).

For men, this habitus, structured from early childhood largely by the family and the school, determines the way in which we perceive the world, and understand and act in it. By the time boys arrive at adolescence, most have learned the main lessons that shape masculine behaviour and identity and that limit certain forms of emotional expression and encourage others, such as anger and violence. These patterns have a clear influence on sexual behaviour and reproductive health, often leading men to ignore or violate women's rights. This development of restrictive masculinity makes it difficult for many men to be flexible and sensitive as partners and parents.

As adults, men's privilege leads them to believe they are entitled to greater rights and authority, and services from women from cradle to tomb. If these are denied or questioned, violence in various forms may be the consequence. Meanwhile, within a traditional culture, women also internalise their subordination. Thus the concept of habitus is not only about individual and collective masculinities, but the construction of the culture as a whole.

Relationships between men are established through demonstrations of power and through competition, as men strive to appear strong and invulnerable. Elizabeth Badinter characterises men's socialisation as taking place along a straight but very narrow path, and men fear to fall on one of two sides: the fear of being seen as female (which may lead to active misogyny), or of being seen as gay (which may lead to homophobia).[10] Men are submitted to this gender policing from early childhood far into the adult years. From this perspective, masculinity, and the denial of femininity, is something that men have constantly to demonstrate, both to women and to other men. By denial, we mean not only recognising the possibility of being different from women, but also the active rejection of everything that is perceived as feminine.[11] In Mexico, it is still common for schoolchildren to run quickly when one of them shouts, 'the last one there is … *vieja*' (an old woman). Among adult men, we find homophobic crimes in many parts of the country, where homosexuals are harassed, raped, and even killed by gangs of men. This homophobia could also be partly responsible for an increase in late diagnosis of prostate cancer, due to men's fear and embarrassment of physical examination by medical personnel. Some men even joke, 'so many years preserving my virginity, to lose it with the urologist!'

Women are often viewed by men (and by women themselves) as having a negative influence on men's socialisation. Male participants in mixed workshops sometimes say accusingly, 'What are you women complaining about, if you are raising the new generation of machos?' But although women play a central role in socialisation, they shouldn't be blamed for all its consequences, which they generally suffer. Women carry out child rearing under the weight of generations of tradition. They are often supervised by men or by older women, who are dedicated to upholding male superiority. So although teachers, mothers, sisters, grandmothers, and aunts bring up children, the process is embedded in a social system that changes slowly and that supports the persistence of patriarchal values.[12]

Boys becoming men: can we promote 'right rites'?

Change is part of the life cycle – the different stages a person passes through from childhood to adulthood. Transition rites for boys and men are important in simultaneously marking differences with women and with younger boys, en route to becoming a 'real man'. In many societies, these rites are rigidly established and are generally performed by older men. They can involve a great amount of physical and emotional pain, instilling both violence and power. Boys tend to accept these rites as inevitable, and they hold out a promise of a change in their social status. But as with rites for girls (the most appalling being female genital mutilation), boys are not asked whether they want to participate. 'I wanted a bike!' shouts Rafael, when remembering how his older relatives took him to a sex worker for his sexual initiation when he turned thirteen.

Similar differences in the responses of individual men can be seen in the experience of many young men who witness domestic violence, and see in this suffering the promise of them being powerful in their turn when they eventually become adults and head a family. In processes not fully understood, other young men who undergo the same experience develop in the opposite direction and reject domestic violence.

In urban settings, transition rites may appear to be absent, but are actually diversified, and still observable in certain landmark experiences that are central in men's lives on their path to manhood. In any workshop with men in Mexico we can ask, 'When did you feel you were a man for the first time?' The men will highlight a wide range of events: graduating from high school or starting work, having sex or getting drunk for the first time, becoming a father, or migrating to a major city or to the USA. The challenge is how to assist young men to advance through life stages such as these without risks, and without reinforcing gender inequalities, thus developing a healthier and more equitable adulthood.

The dialectics of change and resistance

Transformation in men occurs in the wider context of shifts in gender relations promoted mainly by women. In the rest of this chapter, we will analyse four aspects of this changing context, and review the sources, the dimensions and the contexts in which men are changing.

A 'crisis' for hegemonic masculinities, and gender transition?

During the last fifty years in Mexico, gender relations and relations between men have been influenced by several direct and indirect factors. Traditional ideas and beliefs about masculinity have been called into question by changes in policies, institutions, and families. One of the main influences for change is the continuous struggle of women towards gender equality in all spheres of society. This is linked to social change,[13] such as the huge rise in the numbers of women in the labour market (mainly in services and manufacturing); the acceleration of levels of poverty associated with falling wages; increasing urbanisation and rural migration to the cities and to the USA; an increase in women-headed households; an increase in step-families; and a reduction in family size (as a result of 30 years of family-planning programmes).[14]

In this context, the male role of exclusive provider and family authority is eroding, and men are confronting new needs and demands that reconfigure family arrangements. As for every crisis, this should be seen as both a risk and an opportunity. Men who are in a state of surprise and confusion argue or negotiate with women, and even with their children, who expect something different from them. As a woman in a Nicaraguan workshop put it, 'Men are looking for women who don't exist *any more* and women are seeking men who don't exist *yet*'.

This tension, often poorly handled by many men, serves as a common male 'justification' for problems like domestic violence, unemployment, and alcohol abuse. While increasing numbers of men are involved in child rearing and domestic work, many are not ready to address deeper inequalities in relation to critical issues such as the administration of money; more subtle forms of domestic violence; alcohol abuse; and the ways in which decisions are made. One of the most difficult areas is that of couple relationships and sexuality, where feminists sense that the 'hard core' of men's gender power and discrimination is alive and well.[15]

Gay and lesbian movements are having an increasing impact too, although they are not advancing in linear fashion. Could there be a more complete change in a man's life than to 'come out' to men and women in his immediate social network? In Mexico, to defy heterosexuality, one of the mainstays of dominant forms of masculinity, remains a very radical statement.

Many men who have sex with men, however, maintain misogynistic and even homophobic attitudes in public to cover up their clandestine homosexuality. Some of the leaders in the Mexican gay movement recognise the need for gay men to reflect on the construction of their masculinity. As in other countries, gays in Mexico have been the first men to openly oppose hegemonic masculinity and sexuality in an organised way. This movement is also questioning existing gender norms, as is the reality of the HIV/AIDS epidemic, which has revealed, among other things, the male-male sexual practices of heterosexually identified men.[16]

Pro-feminist men (individually and in small groups) have been reflecting and theorising on masculinity since the 1960s and 1970s in Europe and North America,[17] and men in Latin America started to do so in the early 1990s. Men react to the propositions of gender equality in various ways, ranging from open opposition (based on religious or biological considerations) to public support. Between these opposites we find a whole range of reactions, including passive resistance, adaptation, and even a chameleon-like approach among some men who adopt the discourse of equality – but not its practice.

The 1994 Cairo conference on population and the 1995 Beijing World Conference on Women[18] were catalysts for work with men for gender equality in Latin America and the rest of the world, multiplying the changes already brought about by the gender change and feminist movements. But although we have programmes and sectors of the population (including a minority of men) moving towards more equitable attitudes in the family and the workplace, conservative movements are trying to drive women 'back home', as a strategy to curb social problems (such as poor schooling results, substance abuse, delinquency), particularly among adolescents. Such conservative forces are represented in parts of the current administration in Mexico, as well as in the USA, and in many Muslim countries. The main driving force behind it is the desire to impose a renewed religious hegemony over sexuality and gender and over family relations.[19]

The seeds of change

In this section, we review some of the ways in which change enters the lives of men: in their socialisation, through the influence of women, when they are in crisis, and when they come into contact with change programmes.

There are many sources of transformation in people's lives; for men, change can happen through first experiencing love and sex, during a partner's first pregnancy, or on learning to be a parent. Change is a very ambivalent process for men, however. Many men seem interested in the possibilities provided by more equal gender relations, having suffered the consequences of hegemonic masculinity in their relationships with their fathers, brothers, or other men. At the same time, they may enjoy or appreciate the advantages of being a man in an unequal society. Men who have been socialised differently, with gender-equity messages conveyed by strong women and (less frequently) sensitive men, find relief in our workshops, saying that they have finally have found a space where they can express themselves. For a large part of their lives they have felt that they do not match up to the model of hegemonic masculinity, and they have frequently witnessed and suffered the consequences of it.

Positive influences for change can also come from schools, peers, or older men. Sergio, a mechanic in his forties, who was a member of the first groups reflecting on masculinities, and who grew up in a violent neighborhood, put it like this:

> *'You saw a lot of violence there, especially between the guys. A lot of fighting, and you had to make yourself strong because otherwise the other guy would eat you alive [abuse you], that's the truth. If someone attacked you, you had to respond and he had to know you could respond anytime to anyone.*
>
> *I was about 17 when I got to know my sister's boyfriend, a tranquil person, very calm, who was from somewhere else in the city. He was one of those who would negotiate before fighting. I remember that, at first, we thought he was a fag or scared. But no, the guy had the opportunity to show he could [fight] also, but he always started negotiating. I learned a lot from him about being nice that I had never had learned at home: how a man should be kind, especially to women. But also to men ... he would always arrive with the words, 'How are you friend?' – everyone was his friend even if they didn't know him.'*[20]

This coincides with the perspective of the organisation Promundo – a partner of Salud y Género – in its work in Brazil, which demonstrates the importance of building on the aspects of gender equality that are already present in some men.[21] Rather than focus on how the reproduction of hegemonic masculinity generally occurs, Barker explores why certain men emerge with non-violent and more gender-equitable attitudes, even though they come from violent backgrounds (see Barker, this volume). Based on ethnographic research in Brazil and the USA, he notes that these young men have, for instance, observed the costs of traditional masculinity; been victims of or witnesses to domestic violence and reflected upon it; had the opportunity to reflect on their own violence; had contact with positive male models; experienced alternative peer groups (through culture, music, or the church); or become fathers.[22]

Change also comes about through migration – a major issue for Mexico and other Latin American countries. A great proportion of migration to the USA is by men from rural areas in Mexico, who risk entering the country illegally to find work and to support their families. The way they have been socialised can lead them to take extra risks, and many violent deaths occur, linked to accidents, violence, or drugs. The spread of HIV/AIDS in rural Mexico is similarly related to migration, as these men increasingly have unprotected sex on the other side of the border.

Research by Rodríguez and de Keijzer in the state of Puebla identifies two interesting trends among men who stay longer in the USA.[23] Some learn to adapt to more equitable gender norms, sharing housework with their wives and being less abusive, knowing that the laws on violence in the USA are stricter, and actually enforced. Yet when these men come home to Mexico each year, they soon reassume the dominant form of masculinity and accommodate themselves once again to be attended to by 'their' women, starting with their mother. The other trajectory is of men who genuinely adopt long-term gender-sensitive ideals and practices towards their wives and daughters.

'Please tell our husbands' The role of women in change

Women play a central role in the promotion of gender equality, not only through what they are slowly and painstakingly achieving for themselves, but also by their direct influence on the men who are related to them. Though a significant proportion of feminists are ambivalent about the possibilities and results of working with men, a majority of women at community level ask for and support these initiatives.

In over ten years, Salud y Género has encountered this engagement time and again in rural, urban, and institutional settings in Mexico, Central America, and Peru. 'We understand' or, 'We already know, please tell our husbands' is the common response of women to the promotion of work with men. These women may be family members (wives, mothers, daughters) or colleagues in government and civil projects. Sometimes it is women leading health, education, or development projects with other women who realise the need to inform or sensitise men, or neutralise their opposition to women's progress. Most of the men we work with – men who are 'sent' (and even sponsored) by their partners, men who are curious or sincerely interested in our work – come as a result of this transition among women.[24]

Women are also promoting change at various levels, mainly in relation to critical issues like domestic violence and reproductive health. In the report of the Cairo population conference, men appear as an important part of the problem, and working with men is included in the recommendations.[25] This international movement, mainly led by women, has helped to produce the social conditions for men to start organising and responding to public and private initiatives from a gender perspective. From the late 1980s and early 1990s, research and action projects were established in countries like Mexico, Brazil, Argentina, and Nicaragua. During the same period, major UN agencies (WHO, UNICEF,

UNFPA, and others) and private foundations and institutions (such as MacArthur, Ford, IPPF, and EngenderHealth) have promoted men's involvement in initiatives on reproductive health, gender-based violence, and fatherhood. In this area too, women with a gender perspective have played a critical role (see chapters by Mehta *et al.* and Lang and Smith).

An example of personal and institutional change in Mexico can been seen in the women's organisation called Lillith, an NGO with a focus on domestic violence, based in Tecate. When the first male perpetrators of violence against women asked them for help, it seriously challenged the organisation. Lillith's discovery of the need for and the potential of working with men was so profound that it even changed its statutes. Lillith's director, a female lawyer, said, 'We never imagined how our vision would change towards working with women and men'.[26]

The long route: hitting rock bottom

In many cases, men have to face a serious life crisis as a first step to transformation. This is well known from the experience of Alcoholics Anonymous, and seems to be the case for many men who are abusive in their family relations: aggression that goes 'too far', combined with the possibility (or reality) of their partner leaving them, is a frequent trigger for men to seek help. The situation often arises from the consequences of, say, a heart attack, an accident, substance abuse, or other health problems. Many men hit rock bottom when unemployed, upon retirement, after a divorce, or on the death of someone significant to them.

The clarity that comes with facing a personal crisis is sudden: Miguel, a white-collar worker in his thirties, is part of a Salud y Género programme on domestic violence, and was present as a child while his mother was beaten. He relives the scene from the other side:

'My father came in drunk and yelling, as always, and I remember he pulled my mother towards the sink and was going to beat her. My mother grabbed a knife [raising his voice] and I stood up – I swear I was three or four – and saw that, and he turned to see me and then let go of my mother, and that scene remained in me ...

When I was fighting my wife it was like reliving that time when I saw that my Dad was going to beat my mother ... [lowering his voice] my daughter saw me and she crept under the bed. I never forget that, never, never. It is something that helped me share it [with the reflection group].'[27]

This kind of experience leads some men to seek help. Yet a significant proportion of men cannot face being confronted through programmes designed to help them control and understand their own violence. Some even manage to negotiate a reunion with their partners using the assistance of the programme as a way to obtain it. In the USA and Mexico, it is only a minority of men that goes though the process and emerges with a substantially more equitable attitude and practice.

When the reality of men's health is revealed in our workshops, starting with the analysis of their own and their peer's experiences, men tend to see themselves as victims: 'our situation is worse than women's'. We stress that the idea is not that they should feel they are the new victims of the twenty-first century. Instead, addressing men's health is an important opportunity to analyse their situation, and provides a convenient strategy for men to work with.

Promoting change

In the last decade many programmes have been developed which target men. Salud y Género has constructed a methodology for working with men and women in different age groups, drawing inspiration from various sources, including Paulo Freire´s theories, and mental-health and feminist approaches.[28]

The work of Salud y Género is based on three basic educational tools: dialogue, experience sharing, and reflection. We have learned that it is necessary to provide spaces where men and women can share experience and negotiate alternative ways of relating. An initial period is necessary when the men and women in the group work apart, and we carefully seek ways of bringing them together, fostering communication rather than conflict. The men who participate in our activities join voluntarily, or are contacted through institutions and networks in most states of Mexico and in some countries in Central and South America. Over the last seven years, Salud y Género has worked with around 500 men every year, in workshops that range from a half day to a full diploma course over a year.

Every workshop tends to unsettle a significant number of participants. What happens after this shake-up depends very much on the support or resistance encountered at home from partners, extended family, peers, and co-workers. This dialectical relationship between individual and collective change has, at times, both disappointed us (when hoped-for change hasn't come about) and surprised us (when change does occur unexpectedly). Change seems more assured when it is collective – when it occurs among groups of men and women who support each other during the process, and who seek to expand on the experience in their work and their primary relationships. This process can also be enhanced when there is strong and explicit institutional support for gender equity. We are still seeking to understand these processes in a more profound way.

ReproSalud in Peru promotes such change by combining educational activities with various communication strategies aimed at shifts in culture towards a respect for women's rights and reduced tolerance for violence against women.[29] The same applies to the work with young men of Promundo and Program H associates (see Barker, this volume).

Peers are often reported to be an obstacle to change. A man who is changing his life is a threat to other men, who will criticise or ridicule him as unmanly, as dominated by his wife ('his chicken orders him around'), or as a 'sissy'. Although he begins to see the advantages of change, this criticism works on his own understanding of masculinity and may undermine his resolve. This occurs with problems like alcoholism or violence, and also in the reproductive decision making around vasectomy. Some men have 'covert' vasectomies, getting them done in their annual vacation as a way to hide the operation from family and peers, who might question the men's masculinity and sexuality. The organisation Coriac has labeled certain kinds of men 'closet tenders' because they are affectionate with their children in private, but never in public (something seen as unmanly for an 'important' man).

Men are increasingly drawn to attend our workshops through the influence of peers who have already participated in some process of reflection. If this process lasts long enough, and a new network of peers can be constructed, transformation is on more solid ground. Eventually there should be an increasing number of men moving in the same direction. They become potent agents of change, because they have credibility with other men. This has clearly been the case for men struggling with alcohol abuse and violence in their lives, but it can also happen around reproductive issues: in the traditional state of Coahuila, Mexico, a group of factory workers overcame criticism of their decision to undergo vasectomy, reaffirming their action by forming the 'Pistols Without Bullets' group, which promotes vasectomy through factories and associations.

Finally, change can be elusive. The old, dominant concept of masculinity has become confusing and ambiguous, because it is a stereotype. Most men wouldn't dream of calling themselves 'macho' now (a concept that was valued until the 1970s), but their actions may still reflect those persistent attitudes. To fail to recognize that the 'Neo-macho' man continues to wield power, albeit in different guises than before, means that we miss out on opportunities to understand what is happening.

The dimensions and process of change

Although many women are expecting and promoting change in the men close to them, it is clear that change is a complex process. First of all, transformation has to do with the *desire* to change. Men who only attend workshops as a result of partner, institutional, or peer pressure will eventually drop out. The stages of change are not necessarily sequential. During the initial phase, change is more perceptible in men's discourse, especially in urban settings. In rural settings, change in practice can come about in a more direct way. Time must elapse between desire for change and practical change.

Men's discourse is a manifestation of the process of collective reflection between men, rehearsing and disseminating a different way of narrating their own experiences, and later even confronting sexist jokes or the comments of other men. An example of an initiative focusing on this first step is the White Ribbon Campaign (see the chapter by Kaufman in this volume), in which the white ribbon a man wears provides the opportunity for him to publicly reject violence against women. But this level of discourse is inadequate if it does not lead to practical results. Women are especially sensitive to men who incorporate new discourse as political correctness *only*, the skin-deep adaptation of a chameleon.

Workshops and reflection groups lead men to share and question the way in which they have been socialised. To have a group of men talking about their experience and listening to others in an emotional way, without competing or being drunk – that is a little miracle in Mexican culture. This reflection may or may not lead to the appreciation of new possibilities for living and relating. As a middle-aged man in a Tijuana *barrio* puts it:

> *'To have information, to know that there are other alternatives is very beneficial, because one can break with the daily routine, break with a lot of things, a model ... a traditional mould.'*

Men learn to be more aware of their emotions and the masks they use to cover them. In the experience of an adult male health promoter in the same city:

> *'I always used a mask or something, because I was afraid I would be rejected if I were vulnerable with everyone around me: my family, my parents ...'* [30]

In men's workshops, Salud y Género works directly on self-esteem. Low male self-esteem is sometimes overlooked, owing to the influence of the assumption that men already think more than enough of themselves! Frequently, however, the male attitude of bravado and confidence is no more than a mask – though one which men are extremely reluctant to remove. In our experience of working with men, only twice have participants voiced the desire to work on self-esteem. They bravely expressed this wish in front of their peers in a prison near the city where Salud y Género is based.

Through the workshops, men become more sensitive to how they are present (or not) in their family relationships. Their awareness of the nature of their contact with their children increases. Dealing with couple relationships can be more challenging, and workshops frequently uncover problems that had existed for some time. To identify these problems and to start working on them is generally easier for women than for men. According to a Tijuana health promoter:

> 'We were reared to be macho, to show manhood to disseminate respect and to win respect. And in certain ways to be always above the weaker sex ... women. In these sessions we have learned to mend, in many cases, the mistakes and vices we have carried since childhood, and to apply other ways to the ones who come behind, our descendents, our children.'

The real proof of change is practice – that men will progressively emerge with attitudes tending to gender equity, family democratisation, and a coherence in what they say and what they do in their institutional and community work. This process is not linear. Men can begin under pressure to change, or the stimuli can come unexpectedly, as part of an institutional programme. After a time, these men develop an acceptance of gender-equity perspectives, and a minority even become role models for other men. However, we also know men who start to change, but find it too stressful because of internal or external pressures and later fall back into previous attitudes and privileges.

This conflictive process can also have psychosomatic repercussions. A man in one group dealing with violence said, 'She was the one with colitis. Now I'm the one suffering it'. Stopping a violent reaction leads to the question of what men should do with the accumulated tension, some of which can rebound on themselves. In many cases, this anxiety is a necessary component and motor for change; as Freire puts it, a learning process charged with emotions. This stress, malaise, or suffering has to be voiced in order to help transformation.

In the experience of ReproSalud in Peru with rural and indigenous men, many men no longer want to be labeled *machista*, but lack an alternative model, while being suspected by others of being 'hen-pecked'. As in other contexts, the fear arises of roles reversing, and women bossing them around. One can only guess at the size of men's accumulated guilt that leads to this fear of women taking an equivalent gender revenge. But some men have learned to laugh it off, particularly because there is a collective process going on. A male community worker in Ucayali described his experience:

> 'They might see you cooking and they say "Hey! Saquito" (diminutive for saco largo or hen-pecked). Before, men used to get mad, they could tell you to go jump in a lake, but not now, they all joke with each other.'[31]

But change also has to happen at the level of programmes, and eventually, of public policy. The process of change at this level often begins with initiatives taken by civil society organisations in their local area, and may lead in the end to the slower process of institutional change. Many public institutions in Mexico are increasingly open to campaigns and programmes that address and include men in issues like fathering, reproductive health, and domestic violence. This is slowly leading to an increasing public awareness of these issues.

And what about the volunteers and trainers? It is clear that a gender perspective has to influence us as well – participants, the trainers we train, and ourselves as trainers – and must affect our lives deeply to be meaningful. Otherwise it will be nothing more than political correctness.

Areas of change

We will briefly examine thematic and problematic fields or areas where change is happening or being promoted. These could also be considered 'fields' in Bourdieu's sense: areas where competing theories and strategies develop for addressing issues like sexuality and reproduction, violence, fathering, and youth.[32] Some of them have attracted more attention and resources (such as reproductive health and violence), while others (fathering, for example) appear to have the potential to engage larger numbers of men. Change in one of the areas could promote change in others, for example, many men dealing with their own violence have reported that they have started to drink less (or stopped altogether) and that they have developed richer relationships with their children. But this change is far from widespread or automatic, as shown by the example of men who try to be more involved fathers, but do little to improve their relationships with their partners. Very often it is divorce that leads men to intensify, and even compete in, their relationships with their children.

Reproductive and sexual health

A great deal of effort has been invested in 'male involvement' or 'male participation' programmes in this sector, many of them growing from family-planning programmes, and validated by the international conferences in Cairo and Beijing. This has led to programmes in Mexico and in other countries developing initiatives to work with men as a way to improve women's health and situation.[33]

One of the first, and frequently the only, windows of male participation in reproductive health has been the promotion of vasectomy. Many government health institutions in Latin America have limited their strategies for men's involvement to this area, and have only recently started to envisage other opportunities. Though the percentage of men in Latin America having a vasectomy has increased, it still lags behind the number of sterilization procedures for women. But the impact of this practice on women's equality in reproductive health issues is complex: a vasectomy can be undertaken by a man as an egalitarian act ('She has had two caesarean sections already – it's my turn'), but research shows that some men decide on it as a way of controlling their partner's sexuality, ('If she gets pregnant, I will be sure it was not me'). Other men deflect criticism or suspicion about their masculinity by asserting themselves with humour as 'sacharinos' ('we sweeten without fattening').

Some controversial initiatives are successful in reaching men, but lack a gender perspective that sensitises men and empowers women. Slogans directed at men, as in the Zimbabwe campaign ('You are in control!'), or in Mexico ('Are you really so macho? So plan your family') openly reinforce patriarchy. If a campaign like this contributes to a backlash for women, it is better to eliminate such strategies.[34] Many other programmes and campaigns have found creative ways to promote reproductive goals from a gender-equitable perspective.

Other sexual health issues for men have not been addressed to the same extent, though initiatives have emerged in the last decade as a result of the recognition that men are 'driving' the HIV/AIDS epidemic. The need for a holistic approach has been clear from the early development of strategies against the epidemic, when information giving alone proved to be ineffective. The incorporation of safe-sex strategies has been effective among the gay community (after an appalling number of deaths), and the use of such strategies appears to be increasing among the younger generation, many of whom use them from the time of their first sexual experiences.

Fathering

In Mexican culture, especially in urban settings, many men (particularly young men) play a greater role in child rearing than previous generations did. This is a logical consequence of the entry of women into the labour market, although the extent of men's participation in childcare and domestic work is still limited compared with that of women.

Fathering seems to be a useful entry point to start working on with many men. Discussion of fatherhood can elicit men's beliefs about authority and negotiation, domestic work, discipline and violence, emotions, and reproduction. In Brazil, PAPAIs work with young fathers and adolescents has stressed that taking care of others (a partner or children, for example) is perfectly compatible with being a man. This can lead to thinking about caring for oneself and about risk taking.[35] Other Brazilian initiatives link the health sector with civil society organisations, addressing fathering by creating 'Fathers Week'.[36]

In an effort to celebrate Father's Day in a new way, Salud y Género worked with schools to ask fathers, mothers, and children (in separate groups) to draw a life-size picture of a father with children, and to write down anonymously what they liked and disliked about fathers. The exercise culminated in the exhibition of three mega-drawings, observed by everyone. The drawings acted as a reflection of men's relationships, and helped them to become aware of the reality of them.

Children today play an important role in men's transformation into engaged fathers, especially in middle- and upper-class communities and in urban settings. Reflection on the importance of fatherhood in children's development is well established, but the role of children in their father's development is still to be studied in depth.

How do men learn to be fathers? Sometimes it is only through the experience of having been their father's sons. In Salud y Género workshops, if there is enough time and openness, we access and work on our experience of having been children as a way to understand our attitudes as fathers. This exercise has lead to some of the most intense and interesting workshop experiences.

It is hard for many men to talk about fatherhood, because of their own negative experiences. The father figure in a family is often missing or rejected. The father can be the breadwinner, but emotionally isolated from the rest of the family; rarely, the father can be a warm and friendly guide. Affection and everyday commitment are more rare. Men may indeed dispute the validity of the traditional father figure as being repressive, violent, drunken, and womanising. But they also point out that this was the model handed down to them, the way they were taught to be men – they know no other way. Fatherhood is not as visible as motherhood is. Thus, men construct their own roles as fathers using fragments of their own previous experience.

A significant proportion of men in Mexican culture are not able to change their attitudes as fathers, and only become involved in caring when they are grandfathers, often to the surprise (and jealousy) of their own children: 'Look, my Dad is changing diapers; or crying; or playing with my children!' It seems that these men not only retire from work, but are also able to retire to some extent from the masks and obligations of patriarchy, easing into a more flexible role. Of course, more involvement of fathers is important, but it is the quality of this involvement that can enrich the lives of men, their partners, and their children.

Men and violence

In no field is change so critical and necessary as in the prevention of violence against women. Although the perennial nature–nurture debate on violence is still alive, in the view of Salud y Género, everyone is capable of violence. Human culture can produce both Ghandis and Tysons at the same time, and if the capacity to be violent can develop, so can the potential for respect and negotiation.

In the methodology we use, men who attend the group voluntarily are encouraged to become aware of their expectations of their own authority and the services they expect from their partners and families. Through the examination of specific cases, many of the men are surprised by the different ways in which violence and control are present in their intimate relationships. They slowly recognise the costs of violence, and they come to understand how it develops in them, as part of a strategy to get them to hold back before expressing anger. Learning to retreat from a heated discussion is a feat that can take several months, and is a prerequisite for reflecting on the origin of these reactions in early life, and acquiring the tools to negotiate conflicts.

The two main forces for change are the understanding of power dynamics in relationships and contact with emotions. Men may have been emotionally limited by cultural tradition, commonly restrained from expressing fear, sadness, and tenderness. The process of addressing these feelings, men's power, and the services men feel entitled to, is unexpected to many, and leads to a high drop-out rate in voluntary programmes. Many men eventually return to a programme after being involved in a subsequent conflict.

Some interesting approaches to addressing men's violence have been developed over the last decade. For example, the White Ribbon Campaign can be a first step for many men to breaking their silence and speaking out against violence against women (see chapter by Kaufman). The challenge of redefining messages for men in a positive and creative way has been taken up by the US organisation 'Men Can Stop Rape', with an excellent example of the redefinition of the concept of strength.[37] The campaign's emphasis is on men's strength to listen, to negotiate, to ask, and to accept a 'no'– so simple and yet so difficult for most men.

Youth and change

Like other organisations, Salud y Género gives great priority to work with young men – a sector that is largely ignored. It is crucial to work with younger men and adolescents at a stage when many aspects and practices of their identity as men are forming. Boys are easier to reach at an early stage than later, especially if they are out of school.

Yet the challenges are enormous. We need to acknowledge the growing difficulties faced by young people, particularly those from a working-class or rural background. Opportunities to continue studies and to find a job get more difficult every day. The high death toll due to HIV/AIDS, violence, and drugs is leading to a decreasing adult life expectancy in many countries. Many researchers have identified changes in attitudes among young people in these situations. Among young men in urban areas of South Africa and Brazil, and young rural migrants in Mexico, the idea of a short, but intense and risk-taking, life may appear attractive in contrast with the lives that older relatives have led, which may have resulted in imprisonment, alcohol abuse, or diseases such as tuberculosis. Nevertheless, our aims and expectations for young people remain high, particularly in the light of the initial results from the Program H initiative described by Gary Barker in this book, in which Salud y Género is actively participating.[38]

Conclusion

Although men as a group have been omnipresent in all aspects of culture, it is only recently that they have been subjected to analysis from a gender perspective. Viewed in this way, hegemonic masculinity can be identified as a risk and limiting factor for both women and for men themselves. Most men are relatively empowered during the process of their socialisation, only to find the costs of masculinity in their later life. Thus, for many analysts and development projects, men are often seen as a major problem. This chapter has tried to picture men as part of the solution.

We have reviewed some of the processes, contradictions, and opportunities that occur when men approach change or, more often, when change comes in their lives. A process of change will not necessarily result from an educational activity, but opportunities for change can be a consequence of significant life events.

In Salud y Género we believe that work with men can and should meet both women's and men's needs from an equity perspective. Women can certainly benefit from programmes with men on alcohol abuse, or from strategies aimed at sensitising men to domestic violence, sexuality, and reproductive health issues. A surprise for many programmes like ReproSalud in Peru is the way in which men get involved, moving from being obstacles to being passive acceptors and even to being active collaborators. These programmes have tried to be very careful that this male participation doesn't limit women's empowerment. Many women feel vulnerable when men actually do get involved in family relations, child rearing, and even in domestic work, especially when men do so in a competitive way.

The potential areas of male participation are not free of conflict. Working on the idea of men's rights is threatening to many women struggling for their own rights. This is especially true when the focus is on sexual and reproductive rights. It is more useful to talk of men's involvement and participation in sexuality, reproduction, and family relations, and approach men's rights in a relational context – considering them vis à vis women's rights, and in the light of women's reproductive responsibilities.

Salud y Género's experience has shown us that working with men must include dealing with the emotions and the pain involved in the processes we initiate. Understanding these emotions can enhance the development of what has been called 'emotional intelligence', as opposed to the supposedly typical male 'rational intelligence'. Successful work with men should also include questioning the ways in which we establish different types of power relations with women and with other men.[39] It must also include an assessment of the costs of masculinity to men's health and to the lives of others, and the potential gains in changing, not only for women and children, but also for men.

Acknowledgements

I wish to thank Salud y Género, the MacArthur Foundation, the Open Society Institute, and the University of Columbia for their continuous support of the development of ideas and strategies for work with men. I also thank Sandy Ruxton, the editor of this book, for his patient harassment so that this article would be on time.

Notes

1   This project, developed by CRIM (Regional Center for Multidisciplinary Research) at the National University, Salud y Género and CORIAC (Men for Egalitarian Relationships Collective), seeks to understand the social factors linked to male violence and the processes of change and resistance among men attending the two latter institutions' workshops.

2   A significant proportion of this chapter draws on two prior papers: the Salud y Género case study ('Constructing new gender-equitable identities: Salud y Género´s work in Mexico', in IGWG, 'Involving Men to Address Gender Inequities', Washington, DC: Population Reference Bureau, 2003), and B. de Keijzer, *Sexual-reproductive Health: What About Men?*, forthcoming 2004, New York: Columbia University and the Open Society Institute.

3   Salud y Género, 2003, *op. cit.*

4   M. Kaufman (1987) *Beyond Patriarchy*, Toronto: Oxford University Press.

5   B. de Keijzer and G. Ayala (2003) 'Hombres Construyendo Democracia en las Relaciones Familiares', UNDP and INMUJERES, Mexico.

6   The mean gap in Latin America is 5.2 years more for women, and it tends to grow parallel to the degree of development (see T. Valdés, 1995, *Mujeres Latinoamericanas en Cifras, Tomo Comparativo*, Instituto de la Mujer, Spain, and FLACSO, Chile). In Latin America, men accounted for 62 per cent of deaths in the 5 to 19 age range in 1950–55; this percentage increased to 70 per cent or more in the 1990s. Violent deaths, including homicide, accidents, and suicide, together with reduced risk to women associated with reproduction, account for these differences. The costs of the HIV/AIDS epidemic are also part of this toll – the ratio of AIDS cases in men and women was six to one in Mexico during the 1990s (see INEGI, 2001, *Mujeres y Hombres en México*, Aguascalientes, Mexico). Since then the proportion of women with AIDS has grown, due to heterosexual transmission from their partners. It is an acknowledged internationally that men, many of them young, are driving the epidemic (UNAIDS, 2001, available from www.unaids.org/worldsaidsday/2001/EPIgraohics/EPIgraphic1_sp.gif).

7   See P. Freire (1970) *Pedagogy of the Oppressed*, New York, NY: Continuum.

8   P. Bourdieu (2001) *Masculine Domination*, Stanford University Press.

9   Bourdieu sometimes includes emotion and bodily attitudes as part of this construction – the embodiment of class and gender difference as power and privilege that appears as 'natural' to most men and many women.

10 E. Badinter (1995) *XY: On Masculine Identity*, New York, NY: Columbia University Press.

11 N. Fuller (2001) *Masculinidades: Cambios y Permanencias*, Lima: Pontificia Universidad Católica del Perú.

12 Salud y Género (2003) *op. cit.*

13 B. de Keijzer and G. Ayala (2003) *op. cit.*

14 Up to a fifth of households in Latin America were headed by women in the early 1990s (see Valdes 1995, *op. cit.*). The fertility rate has dropped in Latin America in the period 1950–95 from 5.9 to 3.1 children per woman (with extremes of 5.4 in Guatemala and 1.9 in Cuba). Mexico has gone from 6.8 to 3.2 in that period, and was 2.6 by 2000 (Ministerio de la Mujer, 1995 and INEGI, 2001), with over 70 per cent of couples using some contraceptive method in 2000.

15 G. Rodríguez and B. de Keijzer (2002), 'La Noche se Hizo Para los Hombres', Edamex and Population Council, Mexico.

16 B. de Keijzer (2003) *op. cit.*

17 V. Seidler (ed.) (1991) *Achilles Heel Reader: Men, Sexual Politics and Socialism*, London: Routledge; M. Kaufman (1993) *Cracking the Armour: Power, Pain and the Lives of Men*, Toronto: Viking; M. Kimmel and T. Mosmiller (1992) *Against the Tide: Pro-feminist Men in the United States 1775–1990, A Documentary History*, Boston: Beacon Press; R. Connell (1995) *Masculinities*, Cambridge: Polity Press.

18 The International Conference on Population and Development, 5–13 September 1994, Cairo, Egypt; the Fourth World Conference on Women, 4–15 September 1995, Beijing, China.

19 K. Clatterbaugh (1990) *Contemporary Perspectives on Masculinity: Men, Women and Politics in Modern Society*, Colorado and Oxford: Westview Press; E. Brusco (1995) *The Reformation of Machismo: Evangelical Conversion and Gender in Colombia*, Austin: University Of Texas Press.

20 Quotations drawn from the research report of R. Castro (CRIM), B. de Keijzer and G. Ayala (Salygen), and R. Garda and E. Liendro (Coriac), 'Factores Sociales Asociados a la Violencia Masculina Contra las Mujeres en México', ('Social Factors Associated with Men's Violence Towards Women in Mexico') forthcoming, 2004.

21 G. Barker and I. Lowenstein (1997) 'Where the boys are: attitudes related to masculinity, fatherhood and violence toward women among low income adolescent and young adult males in Rio de Janeiro, Brazil', *Youth and Society*, 29(2): 166-96.

22 Studies in Chile show how a young man can have a legitimate excuse to leave the *barra brava* (local soccer hooligans) upon becoming a father (see H. Abarca and M. Sepúlveda (2000) 'El Feo, el Sucio y el Malo: Un Estudio Exploratorio Sobre Masculinidad y Violencia entre Varones de dos Barras del Fútbol en Chile', mimeo, Rio de Janeiro: Fundación Carlos Chagas).

23 G. Rodriguez and B. de Keijzer (2002) *op. cit.*

24   B. de Keijzer (2004) *op. cit.*

25   The concluding Action Programme of the 1994 Cairo conference calls for special efforts emphasising men's shared responsibility and promotion of their active involvement in responsible parenthood; sexual and reproductive behaviour; childcare and education from the earliest ages; shared control of and contribution to family income; health and nutrition; and the recognition of the equal value of children of both sexes. It also stresses the prevention of violence against women and children.

26   Salud y Género (2003) *op. cit.*

27   R. Castro *et al.*, forthcoming 2004 *op. cit.*

28   Salud y Género (2003) *op. cit.*

29   Movimiento Manuela Ramos (2003) 'Opening Our Eyes: A Work Experience with Men on Gender Issues and Sexual and Reproductive Health', Lima.

30   These testimonies come from the evaluation carried out by Salud y Género of a Medicina Social Comunitaria project with men in the region of Tijuana, Mexico.

31   Movimiento Manuela Ramos (2003) *op. cit.*

32   P. Bourdieu (1984) *Distinction: a Social Critique of the Judgment of Taste*, London: Routledge and Kegan Paul.

33   The Alan Guttmacher Institute (2002) *In Their Own Right: Addressing the Sexual and Reproductive Needs of American men*, Washington.

34   B. de Keijzer (2004) *op. cit.*

35   Project H: Instituto Promundo, Papai, ECOS, and Salud y Género (2002), *Working with Young Men* series, Rio de Janeiro.

36   V. Branco 'Masculinies, Reproductive Health and Public Policies', presentation to the Conference on Reaching Men to Improve Reproductive Health for All, Interagency Gender Working Group (IGWG) Dulles, Va., USA.

37   In their Strength Campaign the mottos always start with: '*My strength is not for hurting, so when she said no, I said OK; so when I wanted to and she didn't, we didn't; so when she wanted me to stop, I stopped; so when I wasn't sure how she felt, I asked*'. Men Can Stop Rape (2003), the Strength Campaign, presentation to the Conference on Reaching Men to Improve Reproductive Health for All, *op. cit.*

38   This joint project with Instituto Promundo, Papai and ECOS (all Brazilian organisations) creates and implements interventions to engage young men in the promotion of gender equity, addressing problems such as sexuality and reproduction, prevention of HIV/AIDS, gender-based violence, mental health, and fathering.

39   M. Kaufman (1999) 'Men, feminism and men's contradictory experiences of power', in J. Kuypers, (ed.) *Men and Power*, Halifax: Fernwood Books.

Bibliography

Barker, Gary (2000) *What about the boys?*, Geneva: WHO.

Barker, Gary (2003) 'The Status of Men in Sexual and Reproductive Rights since Cairo: Obstacles, Partners or Subjects of Rights?', Power Point presentation at the Conference on 'Reaching Men to Improve Reproductive Health for All', Interagency Gender Working Group (IGWG) Dulles, Va., USA.

De Barbieri, Teresita (1992) 'Sobre la Categoría género: Una Introducción Teórico-metodológica', in 'Fin de Siglo: Género y Cambio Civilizatorio', Ediciones de las Mujeres, no. 17, Santiago, Chile: Isis Internacional.

de Keijzer, Benno (2000) 'Reaching men for health and development', in *Questions of Intimacy: Redefining PopulationEeducation*, Hamburg: UNESCO Education Institute.

de Keijzer, Benno (2001) 'Hasta donde el cuerpo aguante: género, cuerpo y salud masculina', in Cáceres, *et al.*, *La salud como derecho ciudadano: perspectivas y propuestas desde América Latina*, Lima, Peru: Universidad Peruana Cayetano Heredia.

Gutmann, Matthew (1996) *The Meanings of Macho: Being a Man in Mexico City*, Berkeley: University of California Press.

Kimmel, Michael (1997) 'Masculinity as homophobia: fear, shame and silence', in Harry Brod and Michael Kaufman, *Theorizing Masculinities*, Thousand Oaks: Sage.

The things they don't tell you about working with men in gender workshops

Maree Keating

Working with predominantly male groups, however enthusiastic they are, raises specific challenges for aid and development agency staff facilitating gender mainstreaming in programmes.

At the beginning of a gender workshop, male and female participants alike will often list among their 'fears' potential conflict in the group, or 'being unable to say what we really think', even in programmes where gender equality has been an accepted and acceptable topic of discussion for years. The fear of tension and conflict is clearly related to the gender divide, although other issues to do with power relationships – such as the position and length of service of the participants within their organisations, their status in the community, and their caste – also naturally play a role in limiting people's openness in a group. Common fears expressed in workshops, though, include, 'Will men be able to say what they think without being "attacked" by the women?' and 'Will women be able to express their experience without being "belittled" by the men?'.[1]

Given these apprehensions, which arise from people's repeated experiences in volatile, confusing, or poorly facilitated mixed-group discussions on gender, is it better to avoid the sensitive discussions of power, and focus instead on practical issues? This article examines why I believe it is critical to discuss and make visible power and equality issues in gender workshops, even when we are working with predominantly male groups, and the terrain seems difficult. It also offers reflection on some of the difficult issues that make many facilitators decide to avoid the subject of male power, and on my own experiences running workshops where these issues have arisen. I conclude that advisers and trainers are better able to give teams the tools to improve overall programme development by facilitating open discussions of what constitutes male power, especially with predominantly male groups.

The vexed issue of gender and power

Kamla Bhasin writes of working with men for gender equality, that in mixed groups 'many participants get extremely upset when, drawing on their data, we conclude that we have to look at power relationships within the family', and that often ' ... men who very deftly and passionately analyse caste and class as a system ... are too afraid and resistant (and intellectually dishonest?) to consider patriarchy as a system.'[2]

Similarly, facilitators – including myself – often prefer to avoid exploring the issue of power in a workshop, in order to maintain group cohesion and agreement about how to address the practical needs of men and women. Colleagues have often stated that when they run workshops they can often manage a discussion of poverty in such a way that the group comes to conclusions about the ways in which rigid views about gender relations inhibit economic capacity, without the facilitator having to take on the ensuing discussion about challenging and changing social and family norms. Many facilitators prefer to steer discussion away from a deeper debate about the basis of social rules around women's exclusion and the implicit power men have over women as a result of these rules. However, my experience has been that if the power issues are not specifically addressed, then the outcome of the workshop can raise more questions than answers, and either leave people frustrated or secure with the notion that it is too hard to change these things.

For example, in a regional gender workshop I recently co-facilitated in Ghana, the group had no overt problems agreeing on the links between gender and poverty, and the ways in which gender discrimination leads to poverty. There had been agreement about the need to challenge attitudes which prevent girls and women from having access to basic services, such as education. There had been discussion about whether practices such as early marriage, keeping children out of school, cutting rituals, and circumcision could be violations of both male and female children's rights and lead to poverty and to health problems. However, we needed to dedicate some time to developing a shared analysis of whether socially accepted and unquestioned male dominance of the family and social hierarchy plays a role in maintaining women's disadvantaged and therefore vulnerable position.

A critical moment of tension in a workshop gives facilitators several choices. Do we step in and spell out our organisation's position on the issue? Do we move quickly on to safer ground, and talk about how to address practical needs and achieve equal participation of women? Do we leave everyone to their own interpretation of what equality might mean in the particular context in which they work? Or do we give people the time to work through their ideas about power in a semi-structured discussion?

We decided in the Ghana workshop that the session following the plenary discussion would be spent in small groups, defining the issue of power in relation to our gender from a personal rather than an organisational viewpoint.

As we had started the workshop with a small-group discussion of 'How gender has affected you and your family', people returned to these original groups to discuss 'How does gender and power affect you in your life?'. This was an opportunity to re-establish the programme discussions we had been having within a personal framework, and it allowed the issues to be explored in a less potentially confrontational manner. As a result, the issues raised in the feedback session were powerful. One woman, who had not spoken at all before then, gave a personal testimony about a forced marriage. Several women and men talked about the impact of male–female power relations on their sexual rights within their relationships. They discussed the power dynamics within their own families, for example, who was able to make decisions about the future, and who had economic, land, religious, legal, and family rights. A very attentive group then talked about the ways in which power can be used with, against, or over others, and from there the meeting continued smoothly on to the next scheduled activity, which was to look at how practical development programmes can simultaneously address inequality between men and women, and women's participation.

Despite the fact that the discussion had commenced with some tension, overall, this session received excellent feedback from participants, who felt that they had learned something important in separating out different kinds of power. Emotion had entered the workshop, and as a facilitator I learned that this was not a bad thing. It did not lead the men or women in the group to feel undermined or wrong, and it did not damage the friendly atmosphere. An underlying discomfort had been present in the room, and it had been addressed.

Allow time for exchange

I often hear it said that it is difficult in gender workshops to get men to acknowledge the power-related dimensions of gender roles. And yet once outside a workshop environment, men often seem as intensely interested as women in discussing changes in gender roles and gendered power in their personal lives. In informal settings between or after sessions, where people have the opportunity to talk about their families, their own upbringings and influences, and their hopes for their children, some of the barriers that exist in people's working lives come down. Conversations can take on a very different tone, and give people a chance to learn about each other's lives, hopes, and aspirations. When facilitating a workshop, it is important to know the group you will be working with, in order to bring some of this more open style of listening and sharing into a workshop atmosphere to attain a better result. Often, the way in which a facilitator introduces arguments and ideas into the discussion will provide male and female participants with tools to use within their families and networks afterwards.

In gender workshops, men often refer to the pressure they are under from other men to conform to the masculine stereotypes of being controlling and powerful leaders in the family, despite whatever private arrangements they have with their wives and daughters. For example, at the beginning of one gender workshop in Democratic Republic of Congo, everyone gave an example of one man and one woman they admired and the admirable qualities they had. Several men spontaneously spoke about their esteem for men who had non-traditional and respectful relationships with their wives despite the pressure they came under from their fathers and their friends. When we discussed it in more detail, it seemed that most of these men had come to agreements with their wives that their arrangement stay a private one, and that in public the man could still play the traditional role of autocrat and leader in the family. Given the frequency with which this pressure is mentioned, working in predominantly male groups can be an opportunity for facilitators to help participants to develop arguments to use in their own conversations with each other.

In the same workshop, participants provided a brief poverty analysis, and people listed common root causes of poverty, including exploitation, war, colonialism, corruption, abuse of power, exclusion of groups from representation, control of resources, wealth, and land. Later in the workshop, most of the men said that it was inevitably bad for families and communities if women had control of money, because they would then seek independence, or even divorce from their husbands; I reminded them of the sorts of things that they had said about colonialism, and about the ways in which exclusion from control of resources and decisions kept communities poor. We then shared several examples of the ways in which rigid adherence to gender roles had entrenched or deepened poverty in their own families and communities. In the evaluations of the workshop, many of the men reported that their most profound learning was in making the link between the language of colonisers and the language of men who wished to retain control. They said they would use this insight when challenged in their families, and it would be a useful way for them to respond to criticisms.

In one discussion I facilitated in Nigeria, there was a very lively debate about the roles of men and women.[3] 'Could women climb trees to get sugar?' 'No!' roared the men, 'Yes!' roared the women – giving personal stories of doing so when they were teenagers, and of mothers and grandmothers who did so into adult lives. 'Could men manage money?' 'No!' roared most of the women – and some of the men as well. And yet as the discussion progressed, one by one men stood up and told stories of responsible men and unmarried men who seemed perfectly capable of doing so.

One member of the support staff had expressed the fear that if he let his wife earn an income, she may subsequently wish to be head of the household. We analysed a range of situations in different countries where war and socio-economic change had forced families to go through a painful process of reassessing the respective economic roles of men and women. Was it always bad for men when these changes took place? One of his male colleagues responded to his concerns by saying that reducing adversarial approaches to leadership and the household economy is also good for men. 'Think,' he said, 'about how much energy men expend in maintaining power at home – and how much we lose from the damage we do to our personal relationships'. He equated maintenance of male dominance in the family to a situation of war, where people are always tense, and must be ready to assert their dominance. The conflict analogy appeared to have a powerful effect on the men in the group, and afterwards men and women commented individually that the session had given them some good ideas about how they could challenge colleagues and partners on their rigid attitudes to men's and women's roles.

Facilitating discussion when women's rights are not seen as human rights

When people have emerged from war, or have been through long periods of chronic conflict where human-rights abuses are commonplace, existing inequities in society can appear normal – and therefore invisible – in people's social analysis. Through all the trauma, it can be difficult for people to distinguish abusive behaviours resulting from the accepted and feared hierarchical systems to which they have learned obedience. Powerful men from powerful families often have unlimited access to resources, and people do not challenge them. In addition, the daily abuses documented by NGO staff in villages may not be raised with village heads because they are often resolved unsatisfactorily. Such was the case in Cambodia, where the gender officer for an INGO reported that a widow was being preyed upon by a man who would come to her house each night and rape her. When the village head was informed of this situation, the woman was forced to marry her rapist. Clearly, in this situation male and female staff of NGOs need to develop ways of preventing, challenging, and addressing such gross violations of women's human rights.[4]

I co-facilitated my first training on mainstreaming gender equality in 1999, in Cambodia. Most of the participants were men, because the majority of staff and partners were men. By the middle of the second day, the workshop had covered sex-role stereotypes, case studies of how gender discrimination influences the direction of development programmes, and a gender and poverty analysis of the country. We then began to talk about CEDAW[5] and women's human rights. The group saw discrimination against women as a big obstacle to development and a big contributor to poverty. Participants were extremely enthusiastic about the training material, and there was a comradely spirit of learning together in the room. However, the notion of equal rights posed a dilemma for participants, most of whom had not challenged the cultural norms that put women essentially below men in the social hierarchy.

On the question of whether male violence against women is acceptable, some unconvincing responses arose from the group, including, 'The UN says it is not OK' or, 'The INGO says it is not OK'. Eventually someone said, 'It is bad for the children to see it'. Another ventured, 'It is embarrassing for the neighbours to hear it'. No one described the violence as a violation of women as human beings. An influential male staff member then announced that in his view, it is acceptable to hit your wife, and that he himself did so. In fact, he said, he would recommend that men hit their wives in order to ensure that they are obedient and behave correctly. Others were asked to respond to this comment, and a woman from the Ministry of Women's Affairs concurred that if a woman was disobedient time and again, it was important for a husband to hit her to show her the right way to behave. For example, if a woman did not manage money well, did not keep the children clean, and did not prepare meals on time, her behaviour needed to be sanctioned seriously. A young man, also a staff member, was then brave enough to stand up and say that, in his view, if this man hit his wife, he was a perpetrator of violence. He said he had grown up in a family in which his father respected his mother, and the children were taught to do the same. He was able to challenge his colleague and the senior official in a way that female staff in the room were probably not comfortable to do. It was a brave act on his part, given the power and prestige of the man he was challenging.

It is probably the nightmare of many facilitators to have these sorts of personal views aired by members of a team in a workshop. How does one deal with the fact that many of an organisation's staff or partners may openly tolerate or themselves perpetrate violence within their families, or even promote it as appropriate? Despite the tension of the moment, the incident proved to be a powerful catalyst for learning. It brought out into the open the fact that many people who have survived long and brutalising periods of war do tolerate violence of all sorts on some level, even though they do not necessarily like to see it. It also helped us to discuss the issue of male collusion and the fear of reprisals surrounding interventions in violence against women; issues which participants may not have been able to articulate otherwise.

After the situation just described, a few participants acted a role play of a real situation they had encountered in a village, which had led to domestic violence.

What came out most strongly was that although participants may not have personally agreed with domestic violence, they themselves felt at risk of hostility (particularly the men) if they intervened or challenged the practice. For this reason, the men argued, it was safer for women to raise the issues of domestic violence with men in the village. Also, because women were seen to be 'morally superior' to men in some way, many participants felt that women would be listened to more readily than men. However, they all eventually agreed that although women staff may be listened to at the time, the violent behaviour did not necessarily change in the long term, and that male staff had to find a way to address the issue as well.

By contrast, in 2003, in a workshop in the eastern Democratic Republic of Congo, a reasonably senior workshop participant stood up after a woman had explained the high incidence of rape during the conflict, and said that he did not agree that this was rape. It was simply a man 'relieving himself', which was natural. Every man in the workshop vehemently objected to what the man had said, arguing with him and expressing their outrage at his views. The peer group clearly disagreed with the man's point of view, and the co-facilitator did not have to do anything but insist that views be put respectfully. It seemed to be a shock to the participant that all his male colleagues rejected his viewpoint. Once people had said their piece, I steered the conversation back to women's experiences of harassment and trauma during the conflict. The women said that although men are often killed outright, at least then it is over. After rape, a woman has to live with the consequences for the rest of her life. This brought a flurry of defensive responses from the men. As a facilitator, I intervened in the discussion only to say that conflict and war naturally traumatises every man woman and child, and that one cannot easily describe one form of suffering as worse than another, but that as development workers we need to listen to and understand the differences in people's experiences in order to take them properly into account in our work. At this everyone agreed, calmed down, and went back to a discussion about our public health programme, and how we could address the issue of sexual violence.

I have outlined the progress of this discussion to show that flash points constantly arise around women's human rights in mixed groups, especially with regard to sexual violations and domestic violence. Men's rights 'over' women are being called into question fundamentally in these fora. Men and women can learn from having a well-guided discussion, in which women can express their experiences without being belittled, and men can express their opinions without being silenced. But as a facilitator, I have found that it is crucial to manage the group in such a way that participants can find points of common belief, and disagreements can be aired without having to destroy a safe environment.

Using identity for leverage

Like some other gender trainers, such as Kamla Bhasin,[6] I have not found that being female has necessarily interfered with the quality of workshop outcomes when working with men in groups. However, that is certainly not to say that it does not play a distinct role in the dynamic. As a white, unmarried woman, facilitating gender workshops in many different cultural environments with predominantly male groups, I have found that it is essential to set up the training in such a way that neither the facilitator nor the participants slip into defending their gendered positions. But it is obviously not just my gender that is being noted by men and women in the group. My colour, religion, familiarity with the language, and the context all contribute to or detract from my credibility.

When I was running a workshop for a team in Afghanistan, I heard that a female, Muslim trainer had run a session with the same team, and that a male staff member who might have been thought of as being 'resistant' to gender equality responded very positively to the ideas she raised. Her familiarity with Islamic ideas and beliefs was obviously part of her success, particularly her ability to quote Quranic scripture as evidence.[7] However, her Asian appearance and age were probably also very relevant. Interestingly, in the session I ran, the same member of staff was hostile to the suggestion that women's rights could ever be addressed at the policy level in Afghanistan. He said that we should not even be discussing women's position, because 'if you challenge the Qur'an you will die'.[8]

In this workshop, I asked people to reflect in small groups on the gender-role changes that they had seen take place in their own families since their grandparents' time, and to suggest why they thought these changes had come about. My co-facilitator, an Asian man who had grown up in Afghanistan and had lived for many years in the UK, joined one of the groups. In the feedback session, his group said that they had learned interesting things about various kinds of families in Britain, and wanted to learn more, in order to think about alternative approaches to gender through exposure to new ideas. My colleague informed me afterwards that he had told the group about lesbian couples raising children in the UK. He attributed the genuine openness of the group to the fact that his identity permitted him to raise the issue without it seeming to them to be a challenge.

Our identities always matter. Am I able to raise gender and power issues in the particular ways that I do, precisely because to men from developing countries I am an outsider, a single, white, middle class female? Are they behaving in ways they think I would like to see? When I work with predominantly male groups, how do I know for sure that I am not simply providing an opportunity for men to indulge in a pretence of commitment, and to display their fluency in the new idiom of gender politics in front of their teams? I have started to suggest to country programme managers that in some of the meetings of my follow-up visits, we invite the wives of male staff to join in, in order to ensure that discussions about power relations in the family are reflecting the whole picture accurately, to provide an opportunity for husbands and wives to communicate their views in front of each other, and to break down the barriers between a workplace analysis of family and community power structures and our personal lives. If I am providing an opportunity for showmanship, then that could be a creative opportunity for everyone to step outside the familiar and to look differently at things. The important thing is to find ways in which this can be translated into action later on.

Does mainstreaming gender equality mean we barely have to mention it?

Of gender-equality training, Chris Roche reflects that 'Personal exploration must be buttressed and complemented with intellectual argument'.[9] This is why it makes sense to start gender workshops with a discussion of the causes of poverty, and the different kinds of poverty that exist for different groups of people. However, I have seen gender trainers tie themselves (and their audiences) in knots by using efficiency arguments for gender equality. In some cases, the economic arguments for maintaining gender inequality seem to win hands down! And our trainees often know those arguments well.

Using efficiency arguments can be very useful, however. For example, some colleagues told me of their facilitation process in a workshop on livelihoods. A group of livelihoods staff and partners are led down a path of enquiry such as:

'What are all the sources of income in a household?'

'How are they acquired?'

'Who does what?'

'What are the most lucrative forms of activity?'

'What are the constraints to maximising income?'

Men's and women's roles are not specifically mentioned by the facilitators at this point. The group is led into a discussion about how livelihoods opportunities are maximised in the household. Participants eventually come to the conclusion independently that gender inequality is a major factor curtailing the potential for income generation in the household, and as such is an obstacle to the achievement of sustainable livelihoods. The group realises that attitudes, beliefs, and practices around gender inequality need to be challenged and changed if communities are to achieve sustainable livelihoods. Approaching the issue of gender equality through a discussion of economic prosperity seems to provide one solution to the facilitator's dilemma of how to facilitate, or even avoid, the critical moment of resistance or tension in a group around issues of power and gender equality, and yet still allow participants to make the links between poverty and gender inequality.

My experience is that even when gender inequality is seen as an obstacle to prosperity, it does not mean that (largely male) staff and partner organisations will be able to challenge it. That is a stage of thinking which requires focused and overt attention, and it is hard to imagine how it can be done without some personal reflection and modelling of good behaviour. What behaviours do the norms of male power maintain within communities and households, and what empowerment could both men and women gain in exchange for the surrender of men's control over resources, decisions, and even women's bodies? What are the risks faced by men and women in challenging male power and control, and what strategies can we adopt, what stories can we tell, what examples can we give to decrease fear and resistance?

Most facilitators would dearly love to be able to avoid the tricky issue of gender relations and power. It makes running gender-mainstreaming workshops so much easier if we do not have to steer a path through these potential risk areas. However, if we do not take up this challenge, we are missing an opportunity to offer examples and strategies to staff, and to provide a model for finding ways through the objections and fears that they themselves will face in the field in the implementation stages of mainstreaming gender into a programme.

A key issue here is the sex of the facilitator. Milton Obote Joshua, a gender trainer with experience in Africa, says of trainees, 'Gender training offers men a perfect opportunity to assert their control over women trainers.'[10] He states that while male trainees will challenge the notion of women's subordination with a female trainer, they do not with a male trainer. While it can therefore be easier for men to facilitate male or mixed groups on gender equality, there can also be a tendency for male trainers to avoid the critical issues. And training sessions run by a man can often be hijacked by the use of abstract conversation or polemic about the inequality or vulnerability experienced by men.

Is this possibility of hijacking stronger because male facilitators often use their privilege to bond with male participants from the start, and so cannot uncover the difficult issues later on without breaking this male-to-male bargain? If so, to be successful in gender training, male facilitators need to have a clear understanding of gendered power dynamics themselves, be aware of their own gendered behaviour, and identify and address the male–male bargain in the early stages of the workshop. Otherwise, power remains ambiguously referenced only, and the gendered status quo is not touched.

Provoking across the enemy line: getting past the battle of the sexes

An experienced female colleague recently told me that in mixed groups, women are often the ones to raise personalised and provocative points, using the opportunity of the forum to express all their grievances about men's failure to understand women's position. It is important right from the beginning of a gender workshop to set clear ground rules to ensure that these situations do not become corrosive, and that participants are guided away from defending gendered positions towards analysing power, its manifestations, and its impact. Chris Roche refers to women's resistance to men entering into gender discussions and debates by saying of male gender advocates that 'men who wish to undertake this role must accept that, in the eyes of some, they can never win. If they succeed ... this will simply confirm that the institution listens to men rather than women. If they fail, critics will say that they lack true commitment.'[11]

Kamla Bhasin argues that when working with all male or predominantly male groups, 'The problem is how to respond to men's oppression seriously and sincerely without at the same time depoliticising or diffusing the issue of women's subordination.'[12] This is a delicate issue, and one which many facilitators are loathe to touch. It will inevitably arise in any mixed-group discussion of power, and perceptions of power. If we do not manage these discussions carefully, women can leave feeling that men have had another chance to demean their experiences, and men can leave feeling they have been blamed again (despite their goodwill).

I am reminded of a workshop I ran recently for a number of organisations in Nigeria, with six men and five women trainees. From the beginning, the participants described their repeated experiences in mixed workshops in which discussions had turned into heated arguments between men and women. I told them I would help them to ensure that did not happen in our workshop, as long as they were prepared to be aware of the potential as well, and we would work together to get through the difficult moments.

My strategy was to build a structure from the start in which we identified the types of experiences that leave people vulnerable to poverty (including marginalisation, isolation, lack of representation, exposure to violence, lack of protection), and moved on to discuss the impact on people of internalising negative role descriptions of themselves (dumb, incompetent, weak, powerless, inarticulate, uneducated, or unworthy). While we discussed women, we also discussed other categories of people who experience marginalisation and social exclusion. We concluded, as a group, that one of the side effects of negative role casting is that people start to feel isolated and to believe that they really do possess all of those negative attributes – and they even act out the behaviour expected of them and pass on the negative ideas to their own children.

On the second day of the workshop we were discussing programme strategies to address gender inequality. One man suddenly declared that he had been systematically working for women's equality for many years and had even lobbied for women's representation on local councils. However, he said, women are their own worst enemies, because they do not organise. They complain that men do not do anything, and then they themselves do not even come to the planning meetings and support the process for their own equality! Predictably, the women started to respond angrily, accusing the man of not seeing how much work women do all the time for equality, and how frustrated they, too, feel. The disagreement was about whether women perpetuated their own situation, or were caught in a system which was set against them.

This was obviously one of the situations the participants had predicted, and so I reminded them of their own ground rules. We returned to our earlier list of the negative effects of exclusion and discrimination. We agreed that we have to be aware constantly of the personal and social impacts of disadvantage and discrimination, which often militate against the development of group cohesion, leadership, and the confidence to change things. As an activist, it can feel perfectly reasonable to be frustrated with this, yet it can sound supremely arrogant to the members of the disadvantaged group. We discussed black and white race issues in relation to this issue in order to distance the debate from the gender battle that was bubbling just below the surface, and people soon saw each other as allies in a struggle again, rather than enemies.

Conclusion

I have attempted to reflect on why I think it is vital that aid and development agencies should discuss and confront power issues in work to mainstream gender – especially with predominantly male groups, even though there may be deep resistance to the idea. If we do not, we miss the opportunity to help people to develop the crucial tools they need to discuss gender equality beyond the workshop. Women in the group feel frustrated, and men believe it is unnecessary or too difficult to be expected to change the status quo.

Allowing emotion to enter a workshop will not necessarily be seen by participants as a bad thing. Men in the group are sometimes looking for ways to argue in defence of non-traditional approaches to masculinity with friends and family. They can learn from the debate with each other, if it is well facilitated and respectful.

Making a link between power, race, colonisation, ethnicity, and oppression can help to break down resistance to clear and critical gender analysis. Although male groups can usually agree that gender discrimination leads to poverty and suffering, the notion of 'equality' is one that must be unpicked carefully to enable them to view critically the cultural norms that put women below men in the social hierarchy.

Predominantly male groups will probably respond differently to female and to male facilitators. If the bargains and relationships we enter into as facilitators are not identified openly at some point, the possibilities of the agenda being hijacked and of showmanship without commitment to gender equality is greater.

As facilitators in development agencies, we create spaces for much needed debates with staff and partners. Talking about gender equality in predominantly male groups requires an awareness of the pitfalls and the possible areas of conflict. I believe that we owe it to participants of workshops to model techniques and analyses that will provide them with greater confidence to interrogate male power. It is not enough to argue that communities are better off when women participate in development activities, or that household economics are better sustained if women are given more freedom, although these are important points. For agency staff and partners, the question so often is, how do we raise these issues with others, and how do we avoid alienating communities with the challenges inherent in questioning male authority? We need to suggest ways of doing this in our workshops, not by avoiding the issues, but by respectfully allowing views to be tabled and examined.

Notes

1   These were some of the fears expressed at workshops run in eastern Democratic Republic of Congo and Afghanistan.

2   K. Bhasin (2001) 'Gender training with men: experiences and reflections from South Asia', in C. Sweetman (ed.), *Men's Involvement in Gender and Development Policy and Practice: Beyond Rhetoric,* Oxford: Oxfam GB.

3   It is important to note that the majority of the views expressed here are those of security men, and not programme staff.

4   Practical guidelines are readily available, such as UNHCR's 'Sexual and Gender-based Violence Against Refugees, Returnees and Internally-displaced Persons: Guidelines for Prevention and Response', available in pdf format at www.unhcr.ch/

5   UN Convention on the Elimination of all Forms of Discrimination Against Women (1979).

6   Bhasin (2001), *op. cit.*

7   There are many examples within Islamic teachings and many training devices which can help groups to challenge inequality. Due to a generally low level of understanding of Islam, many groups are often only familiar with the teachings that seem to consolidate women's subservient position, in line with cultural norms.

8   Interestingly, in a subsequent workshop I ran, this man responded very favourably to notions of gender mainstreaming, but agreed with me that the team needed specific coaching on Islamic arguments against violations of girls' and women's dignity and rights. His hostility had vanished as his understanding of the challenge grew.

9   C. Roche (2001) 'Middle-aged man seeks gender team', in C. Sweetman (ed.), *op. cit.*

10   M.O. Joshua (2001) 'Gender training with men: experience and reflections from East Africa', in C. Sweetman (ed.), *op. cit.*

11   C. Roche (2001), *op. cit.*

12   Not everyone agrees that men as a group can suffer from oppression. Rather, it can be said that men may experience constraints on their lives, or suffer harm as men, or carry particular burdens due to their roles as men. See K. Bhasin (2001), *op. cit.*

'How do you eat between harvests?' and other stories: engaging men in gender and livelihoods

Thalia Kidder

Introduction

Local economic development projects often fail to reach their potential because promoters pay little attention to the gendered attitudes and behaviour that underlie livelihoods strategies. When project managers analyse gender relations in livelihoods activities, they are often limited by a narrow focus on women's roles or on social factors, and leave aside both men's roles and economic factors.

This chapter identifies men's roles and beliefs while exploring gendered economic issues in livelihoods work. Engaging men in discussions and action on gender and livelihoods can facilitate work to overcome inequalities for women, and can address ways in which gender stereotypes may disadvantage some men. Examples are provided of approaches and questions to spark men's interest and involve them, from the experience of Oxfam GB's livelihoods team. The chapter's conclusion highlights the limitations of focusing solely on women, and provides pointers for developing this work in future.

Gendered livelihoods: more than 'women on the committee'

A ' livelihood' refers to the capabilities, assets, and strategies that people use to make a living; that is, to achieve food security and income security through a variety of economic activities. For Oxfam, 'sustainable livelihoods' are those that allow people to cope with and recover from shocks, to maintain quality of life over time, and to provide the same or better opportunities for all, now and in the future.

When people believe that certain roles and activities are only appropriate for men or women, it can have negative consequences for the success of livelihoods initiatives. For example, project managers may rely on and entrench static definitions of men as 'breadwinners' and producers, and women as 'carers' and service providers, making it harder to improve the traditional livelihoods activities in which families engage.[1] Likewise, gendered beliefs and roles can limit the efficiency and equity outcomes of local economic development projects.

When project managers undertake a gender analysis,[2] the easiest factors to identify are often the social ones. A frequent starting place is to look at the relative participation of men and women 'on the committee', in the design and decision making of economic projects. Other factors such as gender inequalities in literacy, numeracy, and training may affect production and marketing activities. Projects may also address the inheritance laws and marriage traditions that influence the ownership of assets. All of these non-economic issues are critical obstacles to gender-equitable, successful livelihoods. Yet this 'social' analysis is insufficient – initiatives also need a gender analysis of the economy, whether the national economy or the household economy, and men's and women's behaviour and roles in it.

The 'economy': what's missing in our picture?

The way people think about 'the economy' is itself gendered. For example, although they need to consider the production of all goods and services, they usually include only those products that are sold in the cash market. They don't think about 'backyard production' for home consumption, nor food products made for family meals. When these activities are left out of consideration in 'economic' development plans, these production activities may be excluded from investments, training, or tools provision. It is a gender issue, since men and women do different amounts of cash and non-cash production. In workshops, the Oxfam livelihoods team has used both a conceptual approach and a practical approach to interest men – and women – in these missing areas.

We have used visuals to add strength to a conceptual discussion. We draw a picture of 'employment' or 'production' that the local economic project seeks to improve and monitor, focusing on the 'usual' (cash) markets (see figure 1). Then we draw new circles that fill up blank areas of the page with unpaid work in agriculture, business and natural resources, and subsistence production. The 'complete' picture is strikingly different (see figure 2). Our experience suggests, however, that even if participants consider it interesting to 'see' unpaid work and non-market production, they still believe it is a minor part of the economy.

Exercises done by participants themselves are often more powerful, because they surprise people with their own words. In Haiti and Malawi, working with groups composed mainly of men, we introduced the session as 'household economy' – no mention of gender (see figure 3). Facilitators asked participants to list the 'things' a local household needed to feel 'well-off'. Their list started with food, water, clothing, a good house, furniture, education, health, entertainment,

Figure 1: The local economy
Where do people work? What needs investment?

Figure 2: The economy
Where do people work and what needs investment?

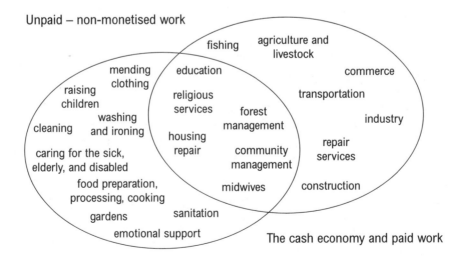

and so on. When facilitators asked further questions, participants expanded the list, adding washed clothes, cooked food, a clean and repaired house, and services for the elderly and ill, all as essential items. The discussion continued by exploring which aspects of household maintenance, education, etc. were bought with cash, and which were provided by the State, gathered from the environment, bartered, or undertaken by family members. Finally, participants used colours on the chart to identify activities by gender. Seeing the extent of the red colour representing women, one Haitian co-operative manager joked appreciatively, 'So that's why my daughter says she works so hard!'. As participants affirmed the importance of these activities and constructed the visual representation themselves, the significance of unpaid, domestic, and women's work in the economy was undeniable.

Figure 3: The household economy
Who is responsible for providing these goods and services?

List	bought	natural resources	State	social/family networks	household work	hire others
Housing	●	●		○	●	
Food production	●	○		◉	○	●
Cleaning	●			○	○	
Education			○	●	○	●
Health			●	○	○	

Key
○ Women
● Men
● No gender division

In an impact evaluation exercise in Nicaragua, we asked male farmers to draw an image of a calendar year with their household sources of income. Cash-crop harvests and the sale of cattle were noted in certain months. The farmers easily answered the question about the use of harvest income; it was spent on repairs, debts, school fees, and production inputs. The question 'how do you eat between harvests?' produced a silence. Then slowly, the household-income calendars filled with 'new' sources of income – from women's activities – such as taking in ironing, or selling eggs, tortillas, cakes, cheese, fruit, and sweets.

'So what?' The consequences of seeing gender in the economy

If certain aspects of the economy remain relatively invisible due to gendered ideas about what the economy is composed of, these activities may not receive sufficient investment or time from families or from local economic development programmes. Using the example above, fruit or cheese businesses might not be prioritised because no one has examined their production, consumption, or marketing. And a family might make more sensible choices about how to use credit, buy tools, seek training, and use their time, if both men and women are well-informed about all the family income sources – fruit, cheese, and cakes, as well as cattle and corn.

When men become more aware of the significance of women's participation and value women's contribution to household and local economies, the dynamics of decision making in families can be improved.[3] If men and women are aware of relatively equal (but different) contributions to the household economy, more daily decisions might be made on relatively equal terms. Yet, if a husband and wife believe that the husband is the 'provider' and the wife produces little and earns only 'pin money', decisions or veto-power on many issues may tend to stay with the man, even if these beliefs do not reflect the reality.

Furthermore, when people identify and address economic gender roles, the equity, efficiency, and effectiveness of a community's livelihoods projects can increase. Some men are motivated to overcome the barriers and discrimination faced by women 'because it's more equitable'. Yet, when a group is struggling hard to build a successful production or marketing operation, the viability of the business comes first. Equity concerns may be sidelined or postponed. In the experience of Oxfam's livelihoods team, therefore, it is crucial to identify how projects may be less *effective* if gender stereotypes are not challenged. When we identify the *economic efficiency* of addressing gender inequality, some men may find these arguments more acceptable, as well as motivating.

'Both men and women work here – what's the problem?' Gender-segregated jobs in production

Women and men might increasingly work in the same sector – for instance, in export manufacturing or financial services – but researchers of global trends have found that they 'work essentially in different occupations, although the specific jobs [men's and women's] do vary both by region and over time'. This affects the status accorded to particular jobs. For example, working as a secretary might be considered a 'male' job in some countries, as it has been historically in others; but in the places where it now tends to be defined as a 'female' job, being a secretary has arguably less status – particularly for many men who feel that their masculinity would be undermined by doing 'women's work'. When jobs and employment status are stereotyped by gender, there are often negative consequences for the quality of 'women's' jobs, pay, benefits, and security.[4] Because of these problems, many livelihoods initiatives encourage women to develop new skills and take on new occupations. What is the incentive for men to support these efforts?

First, facilitators can point to equity issues as a reason to challenge gender-stereotyped jobs. Project leaders can encourage awareness-raising by casually referring to 'her' when proposing new positions. 'You mean this technician has to be a woman?' questioned one Nicaraguan farmer. The response 'she could be, couldn't she?' led to a useful agreement that women should be encouraged to apply. At the best, these discussions can identify gendered barriers to certain jobs, debunking myths (for example, that women shouldn't drive tractors!), and addressing real issues like working hours, safety considerations, transport options, and childcare responsibilities.

Second, projects and organisations can be encouraged to consider economic efficiency as a reason for not recruiting staff by gender. One can point out that, in theory, gender-stereotyping means that a project may not get the best person for the job. In practice, Oxfam's livelihoods staff have found it necessary to use context-specific and utilitarian arguments to convince directors and boards to start a process of change around gendered jobs. With projects in El Salvador and Albania, project managers discussed problems of sustainability if women candidates were not recruited as accountants, trainers, or managers. In each country at that time, young men were being 'lost' to migration, and turnover in these positions was an organisational risk. The directors agreed that it was more practical to recruit some women for these jobs.

In a programme evaluation in Senegal, men interviewed affirmed self-interestedly that when women were 'allowed' into more viable or lucrative areas of production, this reduced the burden of responsibility on men to support their families during a difficult economic situation. Clearly, the intention is not to shift more work on to women. The idea is to open up debate, to question traditionally gendered roles or opportunities in order to generate income for the family. The practical implication may be that if wider options are to be sought by women, it is likely that men will be required to do some or more of the domestic work.

Whereas some men have gained significantly in power and wealth from the development of the global economy,[5] others have been marginalised by societal norms and by their own beliefs about the jobs appropriate for men. In industrialised countries, when heavy industries have closed, male miners and ship-builders have found themselves 'out of work' and depressed, while their wives have taken up 'female' jobs in telemarketing and services. In developing countries, studies carried out in towns near export processing zones have documented the impact on unemployed men and families as women go into predominantly female factory workforces. An Oxfam study of the situation in the UK concluded that, 'Education and training programmes are no panacea for the problems created by economic restructuring in recent years. Nevertheless, they have a place in helping men to adjust to changing circumstances'.[6]

'Why don't women ever sell chickens?' Beyond production, to marketing

Changing gender-stereotyping in jobs and production roles is a long, difficult process, but in the experience of the Oxfam livelihoods team, many projects are addressing this issue. However, few livelihoods initiatives go beyond the production sphere to identify and address gender segregation in marketing. Although the products and services considered 'female' differ by locality, the divisions are often considered 'natural', rather than socially and culturally defined. It is assumed in some contexts, for example, that only women sell fruit, goats, and sewing services, and only men sell grain and cattle, or repair bicycles. In other contexts, men sew, and women are responsible for cattle.

Markets are also gender-segregated by location, scale of operation, and time-frame: women often trade in perishable food crops, in small amounts, locally. Men take larger stocks and cash crops to regional or national markets. National trade policies that prioritise cash crops over food crops may have a negative gender-equality outcome for women, who tend to be concentrated in the latter sector. The outcomes of this gender-segregation are usually neither efficient nor equitable. In terms of economic efficiency, the whole community may face problems if certain markets for food products are not functioning well. Through the lens of equity, women's marketing activities tend to be risky, more vulnerable, less diversified, and have lower profit margins than the market roles assigned to men.[7] Livelihoods staff have often found that loan funds struggle not because of poor loan collection, but because of the limited business activities women are 'allowed' to engage in.

The Oxfam livelihoods team has opened debate about gendered marketing by asking questions that lead participants to challenge the 'traditional', 'natural' divisions using their own words. On a visit to a microfinance partner in Bamako, we asked, 'What are the most profitable trading activities?' followed by listing the common ones for men and for women. When we asked, 'Why don't women ever sell chickens?' (a profitable activity) the question was greeted with laughter. A few men tentatively responded that it was because of women's 'lack of working capital, need for a market stall, less technical knowledge', and then acknowledged that *some* women traders did have these resources. Gently we probed, '*Could* they sell chickens – has a woman ever tried?' Apparently one had, but male chicken-sellers had pressured their relatives not to patronise her business.

The support of a few influential men may be required to change these traditions. In Nicaragua, a women's furniture store had to persuade the mayor and his brothers to identify themselves publicly as customers in order to break a similar, unofficial, boycott. Larger, regional market institutions have needed to reserve stalls for women and to promote women's committees to overcome barriers put up by the 'old-boy networks', which provide traders with crucial market information, credit, transport, and other resources.

'Are women better repayers?' Men's gender issues in finance

Microfinance initiatives around the world have raised awareness about women's traditional exclusion from credit and their lack of collateral, thus such projects target women with loans. Nevertheless, the livelihoods team has found that many of the participants in microfinance training workshops maintained the traditional wisdom, 'finance is money, and money is not gendered'.

In microfinance and gender workshops, we were increasingly creative in presenting 'gender frameworks' but this made little difference to the participants' awareness of the relevance of gender issues. Finally, we stumbled on a magic question in a workshop of male credit-fund managers in Santo Domingo. After a debate about poor loan repayment, one facilitator asked, 'Are women better repayers?' and followed the resounding 'Yes!' with 'Why so?' The men all spoke up, 'Women manage money more carefully, they think ahead; men take too many risks, men spend on themselves too much, men don't save. Women put it under the mattress, or buy jewellery or animals.' The 'gender' issue had been entirely turned around. Often such discussions focus on women's supposed deficits, such as poor numeracy, lack of ability to manage loans, and lack of collateral. Instead, in this case participants had identified men's gendered attitudes and roles in household finance, and changes for men (in terms of patterns of savings and investment) as critical for successful microfinance initiatives.

This question found similar responses – and laughter – in Senegal and Indonesia, and was effective in engaging participants in a compelling gender analysis of financial services. In an exercise similar to the one on the household economy above, participants listed needs for lump-sums of money – economic projects, weddings, education, illness, furniture, travel – and identified whether families tended to borrow, save, or use remittances for these needs. They then discussed multiple ways of borrowing and saving according to gender. In the end, the groups had identified obstacles and difficulties for both men and women in carrying out their gender-defined roles in household finance. From this, the microfinance groups could devise targeted financial services and training to address these issues; interventions that might not have been identified through a discussion of 'generic' financial needs.

It is important, however, not to generalise about men and women and savings behaviour or risk analysis. Anecdotes may point to gendered differences in financial behaviour, yet the cause is not simply gender socialisation. We can promote discussion about attitudes to household finance and financial roles linked to individuals' experiences of reserving resources for hard times, his or her time horizons for economic planning, the division of caring responsibilities, or being assigned the role of 'social safety net' and guaranteeing the family will be fed. All of these may be gendered, but differ between contexts.

A more rigorous analysis of household finance and financial services requires looking at the sources of *income* controlled by men and women, and the responsibilities for *expenditure* which relate to these and are assigned to each. A study in Kenya found that demand for different savings and loan products varied according to gender. Men did save, but in larger, less frequent sums linked to harvests and sales of large animals and destined for the purchase of assets. Women made use of savings services that allowed frequent, small deposits linked to daily or weekly trading income, which were destined for smaller purchases such as household necessities, or small assets and personal expenditure (such as clothes).[8]

This same study identified that some young men were disadvantaged and excluded from financial services, in part because of gender stereotypes. The research found that shame operated as a social sanction to deter female borrowers from defaulting on payments, and thus enabled women's groups to be effective. This social sanction didn't work as well for men, and their groups were less likely to operate effectively. By comparison with older men, young men were less likely to have collateral for loans or cash crops through which they could gain access to formal financial systems. These young men therefore also lacked access to informal financial systems, since men's groups were far less common than those for women. One strategy a young man could employ if he had a sufficiently good relationship with a woman who trusted him, was to join a women's group as a ghost member, with the woman actually taking his contribution. In the Oxfam livelihoods team's discussions with microfinance organisations in Haiti and Indonesia, women's groups were not open to having any male members, in part because of the perception that men were not as responsible with loan payments.

Dolls and baseball teams: gendered models of efficient economic organisation

Why do many livelihoods projects promote *micro*-enterprise – especially for women? Micro-enterprise does generate income, and may allow families to move beyond subsistence, but tends to be risky, vulnerable, and less efficient. Sustainable economic development requires going beyond micro-enterprise to larger, more diversified and integrated economic organisations: businesses, production co-operatives, and marketing associations.

Efficient economic organisations require leadership, specialisation and rotation of tasks, co-ordination of work schedules, bargaining and negotiation skills, and effective conflict resolution. While these skills may be transferable from boys' and girls' experiences, there are skills gaps for both men and women, because boys' and girls' socialisation is often very sex-segregated. In Nicaragua, a Church-council training project for production co-operatives asked many women why it was so difficult to maintain them. One woman responded, 'When my brothers grew up, they played on baseball teams. They had to pick captains, decide what positions they'd play, and resolve arguments about whether a player was out or not. I grew up playing dolls with the neighbour girl. If we argued, each went home and cried.' Clearly, the skills of co-operation and negotiation are not gender-specific. However, these Nicaraguan women had identified gaps in their practice of role specialisation and conflict resolution that related to gendered socialisation. This analysis confirmed one strategy of the training project, which was to develop exercises to help women practice dividing up tasks, specialising in roles, co-ordinating schedules, rotating leadership, and resolving conflict.

Boys do not necessarily learn the skills and aptitudes to run an efficient economic organisation as they undergo the active negotiated process of gender development, however. Their recreational activities may be competitive rather than co-operative, often revolving around sports and physical aggression. Some institutions, such as sports clubs and boys' schools, may exhibit and exalt 'tough' manifestations of masculinity in their organisational culture. And it is sometimes argued that the absence of men from childcare may create later pressures on boys to suppress characteristics that could be considered 'feminine', including caring, trust, and collaboration. Factors such as these may underlie the relative lack of patterns of solidarity and interdependence among men compared with women, which has often been a disadvantage in microfinance organisations. Engaging men in discussions about behaviour in 'teams' and 'clubs' may be a useful starting point for identifying the strengths, weaknesses, and changes required in current patterns of leadership and collaboration in livelihoods projects.

Conclusion

Livelihoods programmes are more effective, efficient, and equitable when they address gendered roles and behaviours. Yet gender analyses of livelihoods are often limited – the easiest factors to identify are social ones, and the focus is usually on changing women's gender roles. This analysis is important but inadequate, and misses the ways in which household, local, and national economics are gendered as well. We need to clarify the nature and consequences of the economic roles, attitudes, and behaviour assigned to (or assumed by) men and women.

'Why engage men?' As argued by many chapters in this collection, involving men in working for gender equality in livelihoods initiatives has the potential to support efforts to overcome barriers and discrimination for women. Raising men's awareness about gender roles in household economics may also change the dynamics of household bargaining and decision making by improving men's perception of women's economic contribution. There are potential advantages for men, too, from gender equality: fuller, more balanced work and home lives; a greater sense of co-operation; and a contribution to social justice. The whole household or community may be better off economically, as well as socially, from these changes in gendered economic roles.

Although men's economic attitudes and roles may benefit them as a group, certain men may be disadvantaged by gender stereotypes and roles in economics. As examples above have shown, when economic restructuring eliminates industrial jobs, men may suffer unemployment rather than take up 'women's jobs'. Likewise, some young men can be excluded from solidarity-group finance because of the gender stereotypes about 'irresponsible men'; and in some contexts, men's gendered attitudes about savings and risks can be problematic for microfinance projects. Socialisation experiences may inhibit the development of the skills of co-operation or trust that are crucial for running effective economic organisations. These examples can be employed usefully in discussions with men to broaden the understanding of the consequences of gendered economic roles and behaviours, and to go beyond the myth that gender work just 'helps women'.

Men and mixed-sex organisations may be engaged more readily if the focus of discussion is around the practical benefits of eliminating gender segregation in jobs, or the efficiency reasons for challenging traditional, gendered roles in production and marketing. Although the Oxfam livelihoods team has always affirmed the equity arguments, economic efficiency reasons are useful and compelling in promoting processes of change. Saying 'this business could be more sustainable and profitable if these gender roles were changed' is a powerful argument indeed, and thus efficiency arguments are worth identifying. Once men, as well as women, begin to be aware of the 'gendered economy', they may be more likely to pursue a wider range of skills through retraining, to create forums for continuing discussion of gender equality, to publicise successful programmes, and to understand the incentives for men to play a stronger role in caring.

How can livelihoods programmes begin to engage men in working for gender equality? The experience of Oxfam's livelihoods team has offered some lessons. Visual images, and new ways of looking at economies and livelihoods are effective. The striking realisation of 'what's missing in the picture' may stay with workshop participants long after the concepts and words have been forgotten. Men may engage more fully if a discussion is titled 'household (or local) economy', and the gender analysis emerges later. It has been particularly effective to create participatory exercises that surprise (men) with their own words and conclusions, challenging their ideas about what is important in the economy or livelihoods. Conceptual frameworks have not usually worked as a way to begin change: in each theme and context, the livelihoods staff has searched for key questions, even funny ones, that jolt men – and women – into thinking and acting differently, based on their own experiences. From the experiences so far, Oxfam's team is confident and enthusiastic that it will find many more creative, fun, and effective ways to engage men in working for gender equality in livelihoods: we have just begun to explore how change happens.

Notes

1   For further information, see
www.oxfam.org.uk/what_we_do/issues/livelihoods/introduction.htm

2   Gender analysis explores inequalities in gender roles and responsibilities in society, and identifies the practical needs and strategic interests of men and women. It asks key questions such as 'who does what?', 'who has what?', 'who decides?', 'who gains?', and 'who loses?'
It examines the impact not just on men and women in general, but on particular groups of men and women, taking into account diversity according to, for example, age, race, class, ethnicity, disability, and sexual orientation.

3   See, for example, S. Bradshaw (2001) *Dangerous Liaisons: Men, Women and Hurricane Mitch*, Managua: Puntos de Encuentro.

4   R. Mehra, S. Gammage (1999) 'Trends, Countertrends and Gaps in Women's Employment', *World Development*, 27 (3): 533–50.

5   R.W. Connell (1998) 'Masculinities and Globalisation', *Men and Masculinities*, 1 (1).

6   S. Ruxton (2002) *Men, Masculinities, and Poverty in the UK*, Oxford: Oxfam GB.

7   S. Baden (1998) 'Gender Issues in Agricultural Liberalisation', BRIDGE development and gender, Institute of Development Studies Report No. 41.

8   S. Johnson (2003) 'Analyzing the Role of Gender Norms in Financial Markets: Evidence from Kenya', seminar paper given at Institute of Social Studies, The Hague, 17th November 2003, mimeo.

Mainstreaming a male perspective into UK regeneration: the experience in South Yorkshire

Cinnamon Bennett

Introduction

'Objective 1' is a European Union funding stream that helps Europe's poorest areas, those with fewer businesses and jobs, to regenerate their economies and to create employment. Along with other European regions in receipt of this funding, South Yorkshire is attempting to mainstream a gender perspective into regeneration programmes as a condition of its project funding.[1] The South Yorkshire Objective 1 programme has defined a gender perspective in regeneration work as one which pays attention to women's and men's experiences and relative resources, while retaining a commitment to alleviate gender inequality. Hence, there is a need to understand the complex issues facing men who are living in poverty – to include a male perspective.[2]

Analysis of the South Yorkshire labour force has shown that there is a significant minority of men who require assistance: male unemployment is almost four per cent higher than in the rest of England. Moreover, nine per cent of all men of working age in South Yorkshire – around 36,000 people – are economically inactive due to poor health and disability, compared with only six per cent of men in England as a whole.[3] This chapter describes how funding has been allocated in the South Yorkshire programme to support projects that aim to assist men back into education, training, and employment (alongside other project activities mainly aimed at supporting women). It analyses how the programme was designed, the kinds of projects that are being developed to fill the gaps in provision, and highlights key issues relating to masculinity and to men's role in a changed labour market, which have to be addressed if interventions are to be successful.

South Yorkshire's context and Objective 1 status

In the UK, the 1980s and 1990s were a period of economic restructuring from a reliance on heavy industry to a service-based economy. South Yorkshire's experience typifies this change. The reduction of coal and steel production and the closure of manufacturing plants meant significant downsizing of traditional employment sectors: over the last decade around 203,500 women and 158,800 men lost full-time manufacturing jobs.[4] Evidence of a widening pay gap between women and men in South Yorkshire and their counterparts in the rest of the UK meant that the sub-region qualified for Objective 1 Structural Funding for economic regeneration from 2000 to 2006.[5] South Yorkshire's programme has the dual aims of creating 35,000 sustainable, high quality jobs, and of transforming the economic base to include high technology growth areas. Programme activity is grouped into three areas: developing people's skills, developing businesses, and improving physical infrastructure.[6] Central to all activity is a commitment to social equity, to assist those at greatest disadvantage to re-engage in the world of work, and to connect the most deprived communities to the processes of economic renewal.

Gender mainstreaming in regeneration work

In 2000, new pan-European regulations came into force, requiring all regions in receipt of such funding to mainstream a gender perspective throughout their programmes. In South Yorkshire, the programme has contractual targets for gender. For example, activities focusing on training and education have target numbers of women and men to assist, and some activities have targets to increase the number of companies in the sub-region with improved equal-opportunities employment practices. In addition, the South Yorkshire programme is unique among the four UK programmes[7] in creating a positive-action funding stream to tackle gender imbalance in the labour market. This focus was inspired by the past failure of the public sector in the UK to deliver equal-opportunities objectives; policy commitments often become 'tokenistic' when resources are not made available to effect action and change.[8] The Gender Measure, a discrete funding stream within the Objective 1 programme, accounts for approximately 1.45 per cent of the entire programme funding, and can be used for training and education projects in the context of economic regeneration.[9] Of this amount, 0.35 per cent has been allocated to innovative projects which are attempting to develop a male perspective in their work. The strategy of the Gender Measure is to mainstream the lessons learned through the work of the innovative projects into the design of other relevant programme activity.

Programme design: incorporating a focus on men

Following common practice across the programme, an advisory group has been formed for the Gender Measure, with a remit to put together a detailed funding-allocation strategy. The Gender Advisory Group has a further role to monitor the progress of gender mainstreaming across the programme as a whole, following the examples of activities funded by the Gender Measure. The group is composed of experts in gender studies and the delivery of equal-opportunities policies and gender sensitive training. Its members work in academia, women's voluntary organisations, public-sector administration and employers' organisations. The group has met quarterly since 2000, successfully tackling its remit by outlining the funding strategy, checking the profile of projects funded, and holding management to account through its representation on programme-management structures.

Factors underpinning the success of the group have been the choice of a chairperson with a clear understanding of the theory of gender mainstreaming and gendered labour-market segregation, supported by practitioners from a range of employment sectors who are able to suggest ways in which the strategy can be translated into achievable actions. Many members of the group are motivated by a strong personal commitment to achieving greater gender equality. This shared motivation produces consensus at meetings and a high level of attendance and consistency of membership over time.

In devising the funding-allocation strategy, the group started with the description of the Gender Measure outlined in the region's application for Objective 1 status.[10] This outline defines the purpose of the measure in feminist terms: to tackle gendered labour-market segregation by addressing the educational, aspirational, and domestic barriers facing women, as well as the structural barriers presented by inflexible employment practices. Analysis of employment trends in South Yorkshire during the 1990s revealed that, contrary to popular perception, women rather than men had suffered the majority of full-time job losses.[11] Consequently, the Gender Measure identifies 85 per cent of its potential beneficiaries as women. The group drew on its collective expertise and knowledge of relevant UK policy initiatives to structure the strategy into four strands of activities to be supported:[12]

- initiatives to tackle women's and men's segregation in the labour market;
- activities to assist employers to improve their employment opportunities through the adoption of work–life balance practices;
- intervention to re-engage men into training, education, and employment;
- activities to assist women's progression into senior decision-making roles.

The approach is to build up a gender infrastructure in South Yorkshire through the development of gender networks, databases, case-study organisations, policies, and records of better practice, as well as increasing the gender expertise of individuals and organisations.

The male re-engagement strand of the funding-allocation strategy reflects national efforts to address the 'under performance' of boys at school[13] and the 'crisis' of male economic inactivity brought about by the demise of heavy industry and the increase in female employment.[14] There are indeed real concerns regarding the position of some groups of men in the UK, especially those who are unemployed or economically inactive. The statistics show, for example, that men living in the most economically deprived areas of the UK have far higher than average rates of mortality. Nevertheless, the overall trends still show that women are the majority of those living in poverty.[15]

The impact of these trends on gender relations is also evident. Within disadvantaged communities in South Yorkshire, for example, there is evidence that women continue to provide the bulk of care within families, although they are more often in paid work than formerly. Meanwhile, many men still cling to the 'breadwinner' ethic, even in circumstances where they are not able to provide. This renders their position in the family problematic, putting pressure on both women and children.[16]

A lack of gender-disaggregated statistics for South Yorkshire at the time when the programme was applying for funding, meant that a broad definition of 'beneficiary' was adopted. The male re-engagement funding strand can assist 'older men' who have suffered dislocation from their traditional labour-market sector due to economic restructuring or ill-health, and 'younger men' with few qualifications and poor employment records and prospects. Clarity will be provided by an updated gender profile of the labour market to be published in 2004, based on the 2001 census of population data. Initial findings suggest that educational under-achievement and economic inactivity are significant issues for some men living in certain districts, and that economic and educational disadvantage is compounded by ethnicity.

The inclusion of a funding strand focusing solely on men was influenced as much by political concerns, as by the extent of the problems some men were facing in the sub-region's labour market. Resistance to and resentment of women-only programmes in the UK public sector has been documented.[17] Given the male-dominated nature of South Yorkshire's economic base, historically rooted in steel and coal production, the Gender Advisory Group were keen to avoid the Gender Measure being perceived only as a programme of funding for women, for projects run by feminist and women's organisations. They wanted to give a clear message that gender equality was relevant to men as well as to women, that it would potentially benefit both groups, and that all organisations could apply for funding.

Project development to fill gaps in provision

To facilitate the development of gender projects, the South Yorkshire programme has established a gender manager post, currently held by the author of this chapter. This post acts as a resource for the Gender Advisory Group to implement the funding strategy and to support applicants for funding. A key responsibility is to set up awareness-raising conferences and seminars in order to build expertise and to attract applications. These activities were especially important in attracting the first applications to the male re-engagement funding strand. In particular, they helped to identify agencies and organisations with the expertise and interest in working with a male perspective, and to seek their input on the types of initiatives for men that were missing from existing support for unemployed and economically inactive people.

A conference was held in November 2002 in which case-study projects were presented, run by organisations which were not the 'usual' regeneration funding partners. They included a football club, a health-service organisation, a local radio station, and the YMCA.[18] Each project had developed successful methods and structures for working with men. The objective of the conference was to inspire similar organisations in South Yorkshire to consider developing comparable activities. Feedback from the event suggests that this approach worked. Attendance exceeded expectation (especially from health and social services practitioners), and the majority of delegates were men. Nearly a third of the attendees went on to participate in a follow-up seminar to prioritise areas for funding, and most of them submitted project ideas once the funding-allocation framework had been endorsed by the advisory group.

Discussion at both events raised some pertinent issues which are relevant to other contexts. First, delegates asked for recognition from the funding bodies that work to re-engage men in the labour market requires long-term intervention, and cannot be achieved cheaply, rapidly, or with a guarantee of high numbers of successful beneficiaries. Funding bodies therefore need better sex-disaggregated data in order to set realisable objectives.

Second, participants suggested that projects working to re-engage men need to develop a holistic approach that starts with each man's personal situation and educational level, and provides an environment in which a range of support agencies can provide assistance. The need to build men's self esteem and confidence is critical. Implicit in requests for confidence-building activities is the opportunity for men to re-evaluate 'traditional' masculine roles in the context of a changed labour market; this may involve rethinking what they can achieve for themselves, and how they can contribute to their family's upkeep.

The importance of reassessing traditional concepts of masculinity was reinforced by the delegates' insistence that there are not enough male project workers working in the regeneration field at grassroots level. It should be added that it is not enough simply to have more men in these roles; it is also essential they are aware of the gender issues in men's lives, and are prepared to model non-traditional forms of masculinity. Many delegates used themselves as examples: one described how he had lost his job in the steel industry and after using support services as a beneficiary, had then considered a career in the health and social care sector. He had brought with him an understanding that services were insensitive to men's needs, and ideas about how they could be changed to attract more men to use them.

Schools and parenting-support services were the third area that delegates highlighted. They identified the need for activities to challenge conventional images of fathers as 'breadwinners' and 'non-carers'. Such assumptions result in teachers and associated professionals unintentionally excluding men from involvement in their children's development, as well as serving to perpetuate traditional gender roles in relation to their children. A similar concern about stereotyping was expressed in relation to employers: notions of the 'school leaver' as the ideal recruit mean that employers often overlook the advantages of appointing older men. Recruitment strategies therefore need to take both gender and age into account, and to be aware of what different groups of men have to offer.

One of the central issues of the conference was how to attract men back into an educational context when they had ceased to think of employment as an option in their lives. Delegates were emphatic that the only way to re-engage these men is to offer activities which interest them – in other words, stereotypical 'male' activities, such as sport, technology, or construction and home improvement. The marketing of new initiatives needs to be tailored to the 'traditional' man in order to be effective. As one delegate explained, men were failing to pick up his organisation's leaflets about services because they offered 'support', something that a 'macho' culture compelled men to shun. As soon as the wording was changed to 'information' the situation was reversed.

As a result of these contributions the following areas were included in the funding-allocation framework: employer-led projects offering training to men, linked to job vacancies; projects to engage men in innovative ways through their interests or their circumstances; and projects to develop a male perspective in service delivery. Five projects have been selected so far, from a strong field of applicants; two projects are still being considered for funding. Examples of projects proposed include:

- a brokerage service to match men with employment vacancies in small and medium-sized businesses in sectors which reflect men's hobbies and pastimes, such as fishing, home improvement, sport, and mechanics;

- fast-track training for employment opportunities in gas fitting and plumbing for those men who fall below industry qualifying standards, due to personal or educational difficulties;

- a community-based environmental construction project to build local playgrounds and decorative sculptures, focusing on increasing men's confidence and interesting them in acquiring skills in construction;

- a sports and leisure scheme offering a variety of activities and courses to mixed groups of men, to encourage mentoring between men of different ages;

- short courses to build self-esteem, aimed at men who are economically inactive due to poor health and who have been referred by their health practitioners;

- and activities with childcare providers to develop positive employment opportunities for male carers through improved employment policies, support networks, and information for parents.

An evaluation of the methods used by projects, as well as the experience and achievements of their beneficiaries will be undertaken in September 2004, as the projects end. Dissemination of better practice will then take place to an audience of practitioners in South Yorkshire, and a judgement will be made on a further funding allocation from the Gender Measure.

Implications for mainstreaming a male perspective

According to a European Commission definition, gender mainstreaming is a process of ' ... mobilising all general policies and measures specifically for the purpose of achieving equality by actively and openly taking into account at the planning stage their possible effects on the respective situations of men and women.'[19] This is not as simple as it appears, as the Commission itself concedes.

In the process of mainstreaming gender, a number of concerns needs to be addressed. First, there is a need to be clear about what is meant by a gendered approach. Fundamentally, such an approach is intended to produce policies or programmes based on accurate knowledge of the different circumstances, resources, and responsibilities of women's and men's everyday lives. At a deeper level, it also encompasses a commitment to change; an understanding that greater gender equality can only be advanced by challenging gender stereotypes and creating non-traditional opportunities.

All projects funded under the male re-engagement strand have adopted a 'male perspective' in the sense that project staff know which men are targeted, and have experience of addressing their particular situations. What is less apparent is whether projects are committed and able to challenge restrictive or oppressive notions of masculinity in their work. An obvious difficulty, highlighted above, is that to attract South Yorkshire's poorest men to consider new opportunities, projects must acknowledge the men's aspirations, which are usually based on traditional stereotypes of 'men's work' and their position in the family. This suggests that marketing materials and project environments should be designed accordingly. Only after men have been recruited can issues be broached relating to male roles and the construction of masculinities. Practitioners have advised that this is best done indirectly. Projects may be able to undermine stereotypes through discussions of men's employment options, particularly in relation to job prospects in a changed labour market, to self-esteem and confidence, and to supporting the family through wages instead of through state benefits. The outcomes are not guaranteed, however, as entrenched attitudes and behaviour can prove hard to shift.

Second, one of the early criticisms of gender mainstreaming is that it can dilute action to achieve gender equality by emphasising general rather than targeted strategies. In response, the European Commission has stressed the need for a dual approach:

> *On one side [is] the systematic application of gender impact analysis and its continuous monitoring and evaluation of all community policies and activities. On the other side, the continuation, and when feasible, strengthening of the specific positive measures which are currently being applied.*[20]

Positive action is needed to build expertise and infrastructure (sometimes called 'capacity') which then facilitates the process of mainstreaming a gender approach.

In our work in South Yorkshire, we have attempted to adopt this dual approach in the Objective 1 programme design and delivery. The Gender Measure, gender manager, and Gender Advisory Group represent positive-action resources to change the values and processes which underpin project development and funding allocation. The projects are intended to act as 'flagships' or good-practice examples, demonstrating the difference that having a gender perspective can make to the outcomes achieved by beneficiaries. The interaction of the gender manager and members of the Gender Advisory Group with programme staff and programme partners has the effect of spreading information and increasing awareness about the gender approach. The events and conferences are an opportunity to provide information and consolidate knowledge, as well as to build networks of interested individuals and gender specialists across the sub-region.

This attempt to implement a dual approach hinges on two extraneous factors, which mean that it may not be replicable in every context. First, the gender 'conditionality' (the obligation to include gender within programme design and delivery) demanded by the European Commission in relation to Objective 1 funding has prompted programme partners to consider gender outcomes from the outset. It has also provided justification for ring-fencing resources to deliver targeted actions. Conditionality helps to ensure that active resistance is removed and reluctance can be challenged. The second factor is the presence in South Yorkshire of individuals with expertise to implement the Gender Measure from within the programme, and to monitor its impact on wider practice. Their experience and vision has so far ensured that the gender perspective is being pursued in its fullest sense.

While gender mainstreaming is safeguarded at the programme-management level, advocates for a male perspective at project level may face greater resistance as they attempt to influence service providers and employers. Contractual obligations to the European Commission relating to gender are one step removed. Moreover gender-mainstreaming methods suggested by the Commission, such as gender-impact analysis, have been developed for policy makers rather than for managers running businesses, or delivering services. Oxfam GB's UK Poverty Programme is one of only a few UK initiatives which has trialled these techniques with organisations, and included within them a focus on men.[21] This experience has shown the importance of having experts to administer the tools, if they are to diagnose the gender issues correctly and to suggest improvements. Rather than promoting the use of specialist gender tools, practitioners at project level may have greater success using the 'stick' of recent UK equality legislation and the 'carrot' of the business case for equal opportunities. As unemployment in the UK continues to fall, and services and employers find themselves recruiting from 'hard to reach' groups, the arguments for considering men's and women's diverse needs and abilities will become more pertinent.

Conclusion

The European Commission has championed gender mainstreaming since 1995, as an approach to equality which builds and extends past practice.[22] Mainstreaming relies on legislation or conditionality to prompt action and to overcome tokenism by holding programmes to account. If necessary, positive-action measures can be used to increase expertise and infrastructure, which in turn support individuals within organisations to plan confidently and routinely for gender differences. The focus on gender equality rather than on women's development is also significant. It can elicit support from feminist practitioners as well as their non-feminist colleagues, who may feel less threatened by an approach which appears more balanced, since men's concerns are also addressed.

In the South Yorkshire Objective 1 programme, mainstreaming a male perspective aims to further the achievement of gender equality in two ways: firstly, providing training for disengaged men to move into paid employment closes the gap between the economic positions of different groups of men in South Yorkshire. Secondly, it may assist the women related to male beneficiaries by improving their financial security and personal opportunities. Offering training to men in non-traditional employment challenges gender stereotypes of 'women's work' and 'men's work', and may contribute in time to undermining pay differentials and sectoral segregation.

Work to assist disadvantaged men in South Yorkshire back into employment, and to develop a male perspective in service delivery is in its early stages. As practitioners have stated, progress will be slow, and funding needs to be sustained over a considerable period. The projects underway are already raising a number of delivery issues. Projects need gender-aware male workers to assist men to explore the new opportunities and identities available to them in a changing labour market. But to attract men to participate, projects have to appeal to their aspirations, which may be based on traditional notions of masculinity and 'men's work'. The South Yorkshire programme intends to evaluate how successful project staff think they have been in resolving this tension and in extending gender awareness among fellow practitioners. In 2004, it is planned to facilitate discussions between these projects and a number of positive-action projects working solely with women, to explore the similarities and differences in their practice with the objective of identifying what 'good' economic regeneration based on gender analysis consists of at the project level.

Notes

1   South Yorkshire is a sub-region of Yorkshire and the Humber. It consists of four districts: Barnsley, Doncaster, Rotherham, and Sheffield. The total population of the sub-region is 1.27 million, with a working-age population of 800,000 women and men.

2   Throughout this article we use the phrase 'a male perspective'. We believe this phrase is valuable, as it points to an approach that starts from the experience and understandings of men themselves. However, we also acknowledge that it can be problematic to talk about a homogenous and unified male perspective, and that men's experiences are divided by class, age, religion, sexuality, and so on.

3   Source: 'Gender Profile of South Yorkshire's Labour Market 2003', Objective 1 Directorate (2004), forthcoming.

4   *Ibid.*

5   Additional funding from the UK government and private-sector finance means that the Objective 1 programme in South Yorkshire amounts to £1.8bn overall.

6   The Objective 1 programme is divided into three areas of intervention: people, communities, and skills, business and enterprise, and development and infrastructure. Each area consists of a number of 'Measures'. Each Measure represents a discrete funding stream, focusing on achieving certain targets through a range of eligible actions.

7   The UK programmes of Objective 1 are in Cornwall and Scilly, Merseyside, South Yorkshire, and parts of Wales.

8   C. Cockburn (1991) *In the Way of Women: Men's Resistance to Sex Equality in Organizations,* Basingstoke: Macmillan.

9   The Gender Measure is European Social Funding. The Learning and Skills Council of South Yorkshire has contributed a significant amount of public-match funding, and the remainder will be provided by funding applicants from the voluntary and community and the private sectors.

10   This 'Single Programming Document' was put together by stakeholder organisations in South Yorkshire, working together as the South Yorkshire Forum. It represents the sub-region's submission to the European Commission for Objective 1 status for the period 2000–2006.

11   The proportion of both men and women in South Yorkshire working part-time hours has increased during the 1990s, compared with England as a whole.

12   Since coming into office in 1997, the Labour government has introduced a number of measures to tackle gender inequality. It set up the Women's and Equalities Unit (WEU), which has issued guidelines to all government departments on how to mainstream equalities into all policy making. The Unit has also led a campaign on equal pay for women, reinforced by the Equal Opportunities Commission. Analysis of low pay for women shows that the main causes are women's choice of low-paying employment sectors, and their segregation into lower-grade positions. Responsibility for caring for dependents means that many women work part-time hours, which compounds their relatively low position in employment hierarchies. In an attempt to alleviate the impact on earnings of caring responsibilities, the government has issued the National Childcare Strategy to increase the provision of affordable childcare, and tax breaks have been introduced to assist working parents. The Department of Trade and Industry is promoting work–life balance practices to employers to encourage them to offer flexible working patterns, which benefit business and allow employees to better meet their outside work commitments.

13   Some researchers question the notion of boys' 'underperformance', arguing that working-class boys and boys from ethnic minority groups have always fared less well than those in other social groups, and that the statistics upon which comparisons are made of the performance of girls and boys are often highly selective. See for example, D. Epstein *et al.* (eds.) (1999) *Failing Boys,* Milton Keynes: Open University Press.

14   See R. Crompton (1997) *Women and Work in Modern Britain,* Oxford: Oxford University Press.

15   See S. Ruxton (2002) *Men, Masculinities, and Poverty in the UK*, Oxford: Oxfam GB.

16   See B. Dicks, D. Waddington, and C. Critcher (1998) 'Redundant men and overburdened women', in J. Popay, J. Hearn, and J. Edwards (eds.) *Men, Gender Divisions and Welfare*, London: Routledge.

17   Historical analysis of the delivery of women's equality policies in UK local government in the 1980s reveals evidence that male-dominated hierarchies frequently attempted to sidestep or undermine their implementation, due to a lack of understanding or to personal antagonism For a full list of sources, see C. Bennett (2000) *Mainstreaming in Organisations: Strategies for Delivering Women's Equality in UK Local Government*, Ph.D. thesis, Sheffield Hallam University.

18   Young Men's Christian Association.

19   European Commission, COM (96) 67, final from 21/2/96.

20   European Commission, EQOP 02-97 rev DG V/D/5 Jan. 1997: Section 1.

21   See S. Ruxton (2002) *op. cit.*

22   C. Booth and C. Bennett (2002) 'Gender mainstreaming in the European Union: towards a new conception and practice of equal opportunities?', *European Journal of Women's Studies*, 9 (4).

Men As Partners: lessons learned from engaging men in clinics and communities

Manisha Mehta, Dean Peacock, and Lissette Bernal

Introduction

In an urban community in South Africa, a victim of domestic violence, afraid she'll be beaten again, acquiesces to the drunken insistence of her husband and endures intercourse.

In a peri-urban community in Bolivia, a mother of four secretly obtains birth control despite her husband's objection, risking accusations of infidelity, violence, and abandonment.

In a rural community in Nepal, a young married man accompanies his wife to the local health post for antenatal care visits.

Walking home from work on the outskirts of Manila, a young man discusses birth control options with his girlfriend.

In Guinea, a group of men trained as peer educators conduct home visits to local families to explain different reproductive-health issues.

The settings and specifics may vary, but scenes like these take place every day in communities across the world. In many countries, all too often men act in ways that contribute to a variety of public-health problems, such as domestic and sexual violence, sexually transmitted infections, spiralling rates of HIV/AIDS, and high rates of maternal and infant mortality. However, as these vignettes also make clear, men can, and often do, play a critical role in promoting gender equity, preventing violence, and fostering positive sexual and reproductive-health outcomes for themselves, their partners, and their families.

Spurred by the recognition that men's attitudes and behaviour can either undermine or promote sexual and reproductive health, many sexual and reproductive health organisations around the world have launched initiatives to encourage positive male involvement. This chapter describes the lessons learned by one such initiative: the Men As Partners (MAP) programme at EngenderHealth.[1] In this chapter, we present the framework for the MAP programme, and explore how it is applied to engage men in service-delivery settings and communities. We also share lessons that we have learned as a result of implementing the MAP programme in a variety of contexts and countries to address a diversity of reproductive-health issues.

The purpose of the MAP programme

EngenderHealth is a New York-based organisation working internationally on reproductive health. Developed in 1996, the original goal of the MAP programme – in collaboration with local partners – was to increase access to information and services that could contribute to men sharing the burden of disease and pregnancy prevention with women, who have shouldered this responsibility for too long. The programme currently focuses on promoting the constructive role that men can play in reproductive health, including the prevention of HIV, STIs, and gender-based violence, and in maternal care and family planning. Most importantly, the MAP programme is working actively to promote gender equity by engaging with men to challenge the attitudes and behaviour that compromise their own health and safety and that of women and children.

The MAP framework

Since 1996, the MAP programme has evolved to ensure that a critical part of its approach is an understanding of gender dynamics and the negative ways in which the unequal balance of power between men and women can play out. As a result of lessons learned from its programming, EngenderHealth realised that health-service providers and community members needed to make the link explicit between gender issues and reproductive and sexual-health behaviour, so that information and knowledge were translated into practice effectively. In addition, we found that we had to work with men to examine current gender roles, in order to increase awareness that these roles pushed them into unsafe sexual behaviour and prevented them from seeking services that could help them. In so doing, we encouraged men to develop alternative and more healthy ways of defining their own masculinity.

The MAP programme is therefore based on the following three related elements of constructive male involvement: first, that current gender roles often give men the ability to influence or determine the reproductive-health choices made by women; second, that current gender roles also compromise men's health by encouraging them to equate a range of risky behaviours with being 'manly', while encouraging them to view health-seeking behaviour as a sign of weakness; and third, that men have a personal investment in challenging the current gender order, and can be allies in the improvement of their own health, and the health of the women and children who are often placed at risk by these gender roles.

These three fundamental principles of constructive male involvement are applied by MAP in both service delivery and community settings. In the former, trainers work with service providers to ensure an understanding of gender issues and how they can affect men's and women's reproductive-health decision making, including the use of and access to health services. In work with communities, facilitators ask men to reflect on their own values about gender, to understand the power relationships that exist based on gender, to assess gender stereotypes, and to examine and challenge the traditional gender roles that can compromise an individual's health and safety.

We have found that the MAP framework can be applied in a variety of cultural settings and with different groups of men, such as men in prisons, men in the armed forces, and men in HIV-positive support groups. Based on the identities and needs of the men we work with, we adapt the framework by emphasising different cultural and gender issues, depending on the overall goal of the MAP programme in any given setting.

Before initiating a programme, MAP assesses the needs of the men with whom it is intending to work. This information is then incorporated in any subsequent programme that is implemented. In an urban setting in Nepal, for example, men may be putting themselves at risk by not going to seek health services, because they equate the use of formal reproductive-health services with being less 'manly'. As a result, many may be seeking out traditional providers if they have health concerns. In a MAP programme in such an environment, we would work with both traditional and formal-sector providers to help them understand men's needs, and we would also implement outreach work in order to help men feel more comfortable about seeking healthcare from formal-sector providers. In South Africa, when working with men in HIV-positive support groups, we might adapt the framework to emphasize gender issues related to the household and to caring responsibilities, since women bear the burden of taking care of family members who are sick, and men may see household responsibilities as being less 'masculine'.

Working with men in service-delivery settings

Most reproductive-health services offered around the world in service delivery settings such as clinics or health posts are geared almost exclusively to women. Men are generally the forgotten reproductive-healthcare clients, and their involvement often stops at the clinic door. When they accompany their partner to a facility, men may find no programmes encouraging or allowing them to participate in reproductive-health decision making with their partner, or to address their own reproductive and sexual healthcare needs.

Over the last few years, often at the behest of female clients, health institutions have realised that the constructive involvement of men in reproductive health is essential in order to reduce negative outcomes significantly, especially with respect to the HIV/AIDS epidemic. Health-service providers are now making concerted efforts to reach men both in communities and in clinics, and to offer services that address both men's and women's healthcare needs, either alone or as partners.

Facilities have faced several challenges as they try to reach more men, however: men have only brief contact with reproductive-healthcare systems; providers may not know how to interact and work with male clients; and services need to be provided for men without compromising women's autonomy or their independent access to similar services.

To address these challenges, EngenderHealth offers technical assistance to facilities and providers to help them advance the delivery of reproductive-health services to men. The MAP programme has been implemented in several countries, including Pakistan, Nepal, and Bolivia. The programme involves training using a three-part curriculum on men's sexual and reproductive health. The first part focuses on working with providers and sites to address organisational and attitudinal issues that may inhibit men from using services. The second addresses communication and counselling issues that health workers may face when interacting with men or couples. The third offers training to providers in the clinical management of men's sexual and reproductive-health concerns. At the end of the training, facilities develop an action plan that they can implement to increase men's access and use of the services. This can include the implementation of new services at the site, a change in clinic hours so that more men can attend, a separate entrance for men to come into the clinic, outreach in the community, and so on.

Service delivery and community links

Since an improvement in the type of services offered is not normally sufficient to increase their use, EngenderHealth also works with facilities and providers to stimulate demand for men's reproductive-health services within the community. In Guinea, for example, EngenderHealth brought together information, education, and communication specialists from the Ministry of Health, representatives from non-government organisations, representatives of the national media, and community members to develop messages about male involvement and maternal and child mortality. These were then shared with the community through a series of interrelated activities, including home visits by trained peer educators, mosque lectures by trained *imams* (Muslim religious leaders), roundtable discussions on radio and television, and community-wide fairs. In Nepal, EngenderHealth has trained men of all ages in the community to serve as reproductive-health peer educators to provide basic counselling to men and couples in the community. In Pakistan, barbers were trained to provide messages to male clients on family planning and other reproductive-health issues. The trainings include an exploration of gender issues to help participants understand the impact that traditional gender roles can have on the lives of both men and women.

The impact of working with men in service-delivery settings

Evaluation of MAP's work at the service-delivery level has focused on assessing whether its training efforts have led to changes in practices among service providers and community members and to a greater use of services by men, with or without their partners. Such evaluation is important in order to understand whether increasing the quality of, and access to, services for men can lead to a change in the level of demand and use of these services. Evaluations have highlighted three primary changes.

Increased knowledge, and positive attitudes among service providers and community members towards men's involvement in reproductive health

An analysis of the knowledge, attitude, and practice surveys carried out before and after the workshops conducted by EngenderHealth in various countries suggests that participants are becoming more positive in their attitudes about men and reproductive health after receiving the training. As one trained doctor commented, 'Through the training, we were able to identify specific problems for men in the centre. This helped a lot and increased the influx of patients, because awareness is greater about coming to the centre.' A nurse at another clinic observed that the training 'has been very practical. Before, I only worked with women ... [Now] I am more knowledgeable about men's illnesses and how to deal with men. It is also very surprising – I did not think it would be easy for them to talk to me or for me to talk to them.' Finally, as a doctor at one clinic explained, 'Within my community and mosque, people ask me for advice. The training has opened my relationship with my clients. I used to be very nervous ... now I put myself in the place of my clients and listen to find a solution. It has changed my relationship with my children as well – I am more open with them.'

Increased access by men and their partners to reproductive-health and family-planning services

In Pakistan, after the MAP project was implemented, the MAP sites provided over four times as many vasectomy procedures in 2000 as in 1996. In Guinea, several of the providers interviewed during our evaluation in October 2002 stated that the numbers of repeat infections in female clients had been decreasing since they had started to bring their partners in for treatment. In Nepal, providers indicated that many more couples were coming for antenatal care as a result of the MAP project.

Increased range of services offered at facilities

In Bolivia, after the MAP project was initiated, the pilot sites started offering comprehensive assessments of sexual and reproductive-health history, cancer screening, and substance-abuse and mental-health counselling. In Guinea, service sites participating in the MAP programme identified infertility as a leading concern among clients. Since then, they have expanded their diagnostic laboratory services and developed referral linkages to address this client concern.

Working with men in communities

EngenderHealth has also been working with men to respond to the HIV/AIDS epidemic and to violence against women. In South Africa, recognising the urgent need for a response to these two critical issues and the centrality of working with men to achieve this goal, EngenderHealth and the Planned Parenthood Association of South Africa (PPASA) initiated a Men As Partners programme in 1998. The MAP programme was launched in eight of South Africa's nine provinces, establishing a presence in communities across the country, including urban, peri-urban, and rural communities.

The programme addresses attitudinal and behavioural issues that negatively affect the health of both men and women. It also seeks to encourage men to become actively involved in preventing gender-based violence, and in HIV/AIDS prevention, care, and support activities. The strategy applied here builds on the long history of anti-apartheid activism, which lends itself well to an approach aimed at mobilising men, and in the process, galvanising a groundswell of men willing to take a stand to promote gender equity.

Educational workshops have been implemented with groups of men and mixed-sex audiences. Since its inception, the workshops have been conducted with groups of men in a wide variety of settings such as workplaces, trade unions, prisons, faith-based organisations, community halls, and sporting arenas. In their design, the workshops reflect a commitment to deal with the complexities of gender roles and the challenges associated with shifting long-held attitudes, values, and practices. Most workshops are a week long, and often residential. Unlike many other approaches that tend to have a single-issue focus, the MAP workshops address the complexities of how gender roles affect men's lives. They therefore simultaneously address violence, sexual and reproductive health, parenting, support and care for people living with AIDS, and, always, men's roles and responsibilities to end violence and create healthy, thriving communities. They are also beginning to include a focus on activism and social justice.

Almost all MAP activities use and emphasise participatory group approaches which have much in common with the methodology and rationale articulated by Paulo Freire in *The Pedagogy of the Oppressed*[1]. These interactive educational activities are used by the MAP trainer to train workshop facilitators and in community group work. Workshop activities constantly refer back to the subject of gender. For example, an activity about HIV will explore the ways in which gender roles can increase the likelihood that men will engage in unsafe sex, or deter men from playing an active role in caring for and supporting those left chronically ill by AIDS. Similarly, facilitators might use role-plays to examine men's attitudes towards health-seeking behaviour, and challenge the notion that a 'real man' only uses health services when he's already seriously ill. Using interactive activities that explore gender norms, participants share and discuss their attitudes towards family planning, antenatal care, and parenting, and examine the ways in which traditional gender roles restrict the choices available to both men and women. A common question that facilitators ask during the discussion of any activity is, 'how does this issue affect men and women differently?'

The rationale is relatively straightforward for conducting the work of changing men's gender-based attitudes, values, and behaviour in groups rather than relying exclusively on more traditional media-based social advocacy work. Given that men are socialised in groups (in the schoolyard, at home, in religious institutions, on the playing field, in their workplace) it makes sense to provide alternative experiences of group socialisation which challenge them. Such an experience allows men an opportunity to build connections with other men and to experience themselves differently as men. It also permits them to express their dissatisfaction with, and concern about, their habitual roles, in the company of other men.

In some of the workshops, many participants are unemployed or are employed for only short periods of time. As a result, EngenderHealth has started to tackle broader societal issues such as poverty and unemployment, since these can significantly affect men by undermining traditional male identities, leading to increased chances of risky behaviour. These issues are important to acknowledge and address, since they can reinforce traditional gender roles. The relationships between social problems and male identities are discussed in the workshops, helping men to examine how poverty and unemployment have affected their own perceptions of being men, and how these may lead to practices that can put both them and their partners at risk. The MAP programme is also building links with organisations that have more experience in areas such as poverty and unemployment, in order to share successful approaches and to build expertise in tackling other non-reproductive health needs that men may have.

Building a 'big tent' to reach larger numbers of men

Faced with the growing devastation caused by HIV/AIDS and by violence against women, EngenderHealth and PPASA have worked hard to expand the impact of the MAP programme. To achieve this they have pursued two strategies: building capacity within the NGO sector to reach greater numbers of men, and promoting community-based efforts to mobilise men in support of gender equality and social justice. In order to involve greater numbers of men, EngenderHealth and PPASA have recently succeeded in establishing close working relationships with organisations capable of reaching millions of South African men. These include the Solidarity Centre (an umbrella organisation that works with the three major labour federations representing over three million union members), the AIDS Consortium (representing 800 community-based HIV/AIDS-focused organisations), and the South African National Defence Force (with a membership of about 65,000). Together EngenderHealth and PPASA will provide ongoing training and technical assistance to a core group of staff in each of these organisations, who will in turn run workshops in their union, community-based organisation, or the military. In addition, to make sure that the MAP approach is integrated into more clinical settings, EngenderHealth works with Hope Worldwide, a national NGO specialising in HIV/AIDS prevention, care, and support, and with the Peri-natal HIV Research Unit at Africa's largest hospital, the Chris Hani Baragwanath Hospital in Soweto.

In developing these partnerships, MAP workshops have undergone a number of changes and have become more focused on providing participants with the skills and motivation needed to promote and sustain change in their personal lives, in their organisations, and in their communities. As a result, workshops are sequenced to ensure that each subsequent workshop strengthens and enhances the skills of each participant. As such, the workshops focus on the day-to-day strategies men can use to promote gender equity and positive male involvement, examining community-based efforts underway elsewhere in the world to assist in the planning of local strategies. Workshops will soon offer training in advocacy and research skills, and will include opportunities for participants to practice organising and mobilising skills in order to link their personal changes to greater community change.

The impact of working in communities

At the community level, EngenderHealth's evaluation work has focused on understanding whether the programme has resulted in a change in attitudes and practice relating to gender equity, including issues around sexual violence. The results show that the MAP approach has had significant success in shifting men's attitudes. Post-training assessment of attitudes among MAP workshop participants, interviewed before the training and again four to six months afterwards, has revealed the following.

- Before the workshop, 54 per cent of the participants disagreed or strongly disagreed that men must make the decisions in a relationship; after the workshop, 75 per cent of the men felt this way.
- Before the workshop, 61 per cent of the participants disagreed or strongly disagreed with the statement that women who dress in a sexy manner want to be raped; after the workshop, 82 per cent of the men felt this way.
- Pre-training, 43 per cent of the participants disagreed or strongly disagreed with the statement that sometimes when a woman says 'no' to sex, she doesn't really mean it; after the workshop, 59 per cent of the men felt this way.
- Pre-training, 43 per cent of the participants disagreed or strongly disagreed with the statement that a man only really becomes a 'man' when he has fathered a child; after the workshop, 72 per cent of the men felt this way.

The process of change evident in the research findings is also captured in the words of MAP educators and activists. As Boitshepo Lesetedi, MAP co-ordinator at PPASA, puts it, 'I realised it was impossible to work around issues of gender when you haven't started with yourself, because I was carrying my own baggage, my own myths and stereotypes. So it became more of my own life than work, realising how much freer I could be when I don't have to be doing what has supposedly been men's role'. MAP educator Patrick Godana describes his involvement in the following way: 'Being involved in MAP work has helped me to see the beauty of life.'

Lessons learned

We have found that the MAP framework can be applied in a variety of settings. Based on the work of EngenderHealth to date on constructive male involvement, we highlight the following lessons:

1 **Present men as potential partners capable of playing a positive role in the health and well-being of their partners, families, and communities**
   Despite gender norms that often lead to men's control of different aspects of their partners' lives, it is important to recognise that many men care deeply about the women in their lives, including their partners, family members, co-workers, neighbours, and community members. Given the opportunity and the know-how, many men are eager to challenge customs and practices that endanger women's health and are willing to participate in reproductive-health decision making that supports the well-being of

women. Approaches that view men in a positive way – as partners or allies – are especially useful in redefining men's involvement in the promotion of gender equity.

2   **Societal crisis can create opportunities for dialogue or for shifts in gender relations**
    Several crisis-related situations have led to important shifts in how programmers, researchers, and individuals view gender relationships. The HIV epidemic has led to an increased dialogue and to substantial efforts to reach men and involve them in helping to stem the epidemic in their communities, and encouraging them to participate in equal decision making on reproductive-health issues. Large-scale unemployment and poverty have fostered changes in how women participate in decision making in the household and family, as more women enter the workforce. Such factors have also helped to shape different masculinities, with some men starting to participate in traditionally women-centered domains. High levels of violence in society have prompted an increased emphasis on creating positive role models for young men, and on implementing programmes that reach young boys at an early age in order to help them develop more positive and equitable masculinities.

3   **Reach men where they are**
    Instead of seeking or creating new arenas in which to engage men, programmes should utilise the existing key venues where men congregate or can be reached. These include sports and religious events, workplaces, and social locations such as bars or cafés. All of these are important places where information and discussion on a variety of issues can be shared with men. Scaling-up a programme is also easier when working through existing institutions that can reach large numbers of men, such as unions, the military, and industries such as mining or transportation, where men predominate.

4   **Provide private spaces for men to obtain services**
    Most reproductive-health services offered around the world in service-delivery settings are geared almost exclusively to women. Having realised the importance of constructive male involvement in reproductive health, these settings have started providing facilities for men only. On many sites, these are provided within the same clinic as the services for women, but special areas within the site are designated for men, or clinic times are established only for men. This has helped to make men feel more comfortable and has encouraged them to seek help.

5   **Provide opportunities for men to share experiences with each other**
    Given that men are socialised in groups – in the schoolyard, in religious institutions, on the playing field – it is important and valuable to offer men alternative experiences of group socialisation that challenge their

traditional notions of manhood. Experiences such as these allow men an opportunity to build connections with other men and to explore different aspects of their own identities. In a safe and comfortable environment, they also allow men to express their dissatisfaction with, and concern about, these changing roles in the company of other men.

6 **Build organisational cultures that are committed to working with men**
No amount of training and capacity building is likely to be effective without the buy-in of the senior leadership within partner organisations – regardless of whether these organisations are service providers, large trade unions, or corporations. To ensure that key decision makers and managers support the MAP approach, the MAP methodology includes where possible workshops and training with senior management and key staff in each institution on the relationship between gender equity and reproductive health. In the longer-term, MAP hopes to address other aspects of organisational culture, such as recruiting appropriate staff, and more systematic training of staff at all levels.

7 **Involve stakeholders from the beginning**
In any MAP project, EngenderHealth tries to involve key stakeholders from the start to ensure participation and ownership. In Guinea, for example, the Ministry of Health, service providers, community leaders, local reproductive-health organisations, and clients were included in the process from the beginning. This not only helps to gain their support, but also encourages personal reflection and a commitment to adopting a new set of norms.

8 **Build strategic alliances with communities**
To create effective community support for activities that might affect the status quo, it is critical to obtain the support of key local community members. In Nepal, the MAP project ensured that the peer educators who were trained included key political representatives. In Guinea, the project would not have been successful without the active participation of the local *imams,* who played a valuable role as sources of information. Without their involvement and public endorsement, the project probably would not have been so successful in reaching out to men.

9 **Respond to staff needs**
Understanding the needs and roles of clinical staff is an integral part of ensuring successful provision of reproductive-health services for men. A provider's own attitude to sexuality, his or her own feelings about gender, and previous training all play a role in how he or she may interact with a male client (either as an individual or as part of a couple).

10 **Conduct research to identify how men can serve as allies**
A substantial amount of work has been done to date to identify men's reproductive-health needs in different settings and to understand how they

might put themselves at risk. However, there is still a need to understand how to encourage and support men to become allies in improving their own health, as well as the health of the women and children who are often placed at risk by traditional gender roles.

11 Integrate a strong social-justice emphasis into work with men, and build coalitions with progressive social movements where feasible

Many movements to involve men, including the growing movement to end men's violence against women, share several goals with civil rights and other social-justice movements. Working together offers many advantages. Social movements gain strength and credibility when they pay attention to issues related to gender equity, and gender-justice activists gain important understanding about activist strategies and the communities in which they work. Given their commitment to principles of equity and liberation, men involved in these movements are, in theory, likely to be natural supporters of constructive male involvement, and are more likely than most to do so actively in their personal and public lives.

12 Promote activities that go beyond education and individual change

Many of the organisations collaborating on the implementation of the MAP programme have been historically focused primarily on community education and individual change. Few have prior experience in advocacy, policy change, or community mobilisation. To ensure that partner organisations can take this work on, MAP workshops in some locations now include a focus on advocacy, community mobilisation, social norms campaigns, and policy change.

As the evaluations and learning indicate, significant progress has been made in terms of men's involvement, and changes in attitudes and practices are visible. Perhaps the hope for change is best expressed by one church leader and past MAP participant who said, 'I used to use the Bible to defend patriarchy. I now use it to challenge gender stereotypes.' Such comments remind us that men can play a vital role in helping to achieve more equitable gender relations, something from which both men and women will benefit greatly.

Notes

1   The name 'Men As Partners' has been registered by EngenderHealth.

2   Paulo Freire (1970) *Pedagogy of the Oppressed*, New York, NY: Continuum.

Taking the bull by the horns: working with young men on HIV/AIDS in South Africa

Gaetane le Grange

Introduction

South Africa is one of the countries worst hit by the HIV epidemic. This chapter describes the experiences of a non-profit organisation, Targeted AIDS Interventions (TAI), in their efforts to educate young South African men about the threat posed by HIV/AIDS and encourage their involvement in the fight against the disease. First, it sets out the hugely damaging impact of HIV/AIDS in South Africa and discusses the wide-ranging economic and social factors that have fuelled the increase in risk-taking behaviour that lies behind the crisis. Then the inadequacies of the initial responses to HIV are highlighted, which focused exclusively on educating women. This experience informed TAI's subsequent initiatives to engage young men in discussion and counselling through soccer clubs and schools. Some of these exciting projects are outlined here. The chapter concludes with the lessons learned by TAI in working with young men, underlining the importance of including men comprehensively in HIV/AIDS strategies.

HIV in South Africa: the tears of a nation

South Africa, the 'rainbow nation', is a country of contradictions. It is a nation filled with hope, endeavour, freedom, and equality, and yet a large part of the population is faced with grinding poverty, unemployment, the fear of violence, and deeply entrenched cultural structures that support the oppression of millions of women. And then there is HIV – a disease that has severely damaged this country. It is estimated that, although South Africa holds less than one per cent of the world's population, it has 10 per cent of the world's HIV-positive population, and 600 South Africans die every day from AIDS-related illnesses. The majority of these people are between the ages of 15 and 35 – parents and workers, our future. Countless children have been orphaned, older siblings having to leave school to try and provide for younger family members and care for their dying parents, and pensioners have to care for their grandchildren on very meagre earnings. An entire generation is slowly disappearing.

The province of KwaZulu-Natal (KZN), where the organisation TAI is based, is struggling under the burden of a disease which flourishes where poverty is rife, where violence is an everyday occurrence, and where low levels of education are the norm. In KwaZulu-Natal, the overall prevalence of HIV is around 19 per cent. Based on a sample of women between the ages of 14 and 40 years attending antenatal clinics in a rural district in KZN, research by Makhaye in 2002 has shown that HIV prevalence among these women is as high as 35 per cent.[1] Morrell (2001) indicates that levels of infection in the adult population of some districts of KwaZulu-Natal are as high as 50 per cent.[2]

Although there is much still to learn about this epidemic, there are some well-established facts. HIV/AIDS is not simply a medical problem; it is also a societal problem exacerbated by a range of factors. For example, poverty has an impact through malnutrition, the pressure to engage in sex work for income, and limited access to education, treatment, or resources. Stigma and ignorance prevent people from disclosing their HIV-positive status or seeking treatment.

Increasing social and economic marginalisation, family instability (often as a result of migration), and a volatile (and often violent) political environment, have also significantly altered – and in some cases, undermined – traditional male and female identities.[3] For instance, some unemployed men have taken to beating their wives or having sex with multiple partners to show that they are still 'real men'. Meanwhile, many women in poverty-stricken areas resort to sex work in order to provide for their children.

These, and many other factors, have contributed to the growing levels of gender-based violence, high-risk sexual encounters, and family abandonment that are so prevalent in South African society. This is manifested in the widespread abuse of women's rights and the extraordinarily high levels of rape in South Africa. As a woman, I wake up every day with the knowledge that one in two South African women will be raped in her lifetime, that 75 per cent of these rapes are gang rapes, and that I am more likely to be raped by between three and 30 perpetrators than by a single person, but that the rapist who acts alone is more likely to kill me.[4]

Undoubtedly, this desperate state of affairs is contributed to by distorted cultural attitudes, socially endorsed violence,[5] and discriminatory beliefs surrounding women. It may also in part reflect the hopelessness and fear that so many men feel as a result of poverty and the loss of guidance and support due to the erosion of family and traditional structures, among other factors. Although there is no justification for destructive, risk-taking behaviour, it is possible that many men increasingly feel that they lack any positive options – that they have no future.

A women's disease?

Gender inequality greatly increases the vulnerability of women to HIV infection, and is one of the main factors contributing to the spread of the disease in South Africa. This, combined with the impact HIV is having on women (there is a prevalence rate for women of approximately 30 per cent in the province of KwaZulu-Natal), informed much of the initial response to the HIV epidemic. Many HIV-prevention and care efforts were aimed at women: building capacity, supporting and empowering women, based on the philosophy that empowering women would empower the nation. An unforeseen consequence of that strategy has been that a tremendous amount of pressure was placed on women to rise to challenges that are not theirs to face alone. By failing to focus on men, the very projects that sought to 'free' women have, unwittingly, led to their further victimisation.

That was the reality faced by TAI in 1995 when implementing its Rural Women's Project in KwaZulu-Natal. The project included aspects of small-scale income generation, HIV prevention, and home-based care. It was very successful in terms of income generation and care, but as many as 90 per cent of the women who participated were unable to implement their personal decisions about HIV prevention. Many of the women were beaten and suspected of being unfaithful when they suggested using condoms to their male partners. Some were even chased away from their homes. It became apparent that, due to the norms of the prevalent patriarchal society in KZN, women were not allowed to discuss or make decisions about sexual (and many other) issues with their male partners. As one woman said,

> *'I know he has an affair with the woman who has three children from different partners. When I suggested that we should use condoms, he told me he has two other partners at the place of work. He threatened to leave me if I ever nag him again. I have since stopped worrying him.'*

The outcome of the women's project, combined with the growing recognition of men's role in the spread of HIV/AIDS, led to TAI deciding to work with men – and thus the Shosholoza AIDS Project was created in 1998 (the name is based on a popular Zulu song). The project was sponsored by the Joint Oxfam HIV/AIDS Programme in South Africa (JOHAP), in which Oxfam CAA, Oxfam Hong Kong, Oxfam Ireland, Oxfam Novib, and Oxfam Germany participate.

Culture and tradition

Before the project started, TAI critically examined the factors that increase young men's vulnerability to HIV in KwaZulu-Natal through the use of surveys and focus-group discussions. The first causal factor identified was culture and tradition. Many traditional beliefs remain influential, such as the prestige attached to men having multiple partners, women not being allowed to stipulate the terms of a sexual relationship (not even being able to decline sex or ask to use a condom), and an aversion to using condoms (especially in marital relationships, even when the husband maintained multiple extra-marital relationships). Perhaps the most alarming discovery was the pervasiveness of the myths surrounding sex, sexuality, and HIV/AIDS. These include the belief that HIV is deliberately put on condoms to spread the disease; that eating ice-cubes before engaging in sex acts as a contraceptive; that when boys have their first wet dream they must begin sexual activity or face going mad from a build-up of sperm (pimples in adolescent boys are seen as a result of sperm accumulation); that having sex with a virgin or young child can cure AIDS; and that HIV is God's way of punishing evil-doers.

Poverty

A second causal factor was the levels of poverty in the rural areas where the project was to be implemented. Poverty influences the spread of the HIV epidemic in several ways, such as limiting access to condoms and to treatment for sexually transmitted infections. Poverty has also caused the erosion of family structures, especially in situations where many men have migrated to urban centres in search of work. Once there, men often establish new sexual relationships and only return occasionally to their rural wives and families, or abandon them completely, a situation which has significantly influenced the spread of the virus between urban and rural areas. This process mirrors that described by Moodie and Ndatshe in their long-term study of labour migration to the Transvaal gold mines.[6] They describe how masculine identities were shaped by migration, apartheid, forced resettlements, and industrial change. Men's early ideals that focused on creating and providing for a self-sufficient homestead in partnership with women were gradually transformed, and the men came to value toughness, physical dominance, and aggressiveness.

Another aspect of the influence of poverty on HIV in South Africa is the ever-increasing number of children who are being forced into sex work by adults.[7] This phenomenon is predominant among young girls, but is also growing among young boys; many of the young men with whom TAI works can quote examples:

> *One peer educator talked of a man who was a shoemaker. He used to repair shoes for 10 rand [US$1.45], but if you didn't have the money you had sex [sodomy] with him and he gave you 10 rand afterwards. When young boys wanted money they used to go to that shoemaker and have sex with him for 10 rand.*

> *From one group, eight boys knew girls who had 'fallen in love' with older men for the sake of getting money, jewellery, and food. The older men promise these young girls marriage. One boy quoted a 12-year-old girl in his school, who was in love with an older man. She said that she was proud of him, as he buys her everything she wants. He used to give her money and fetch her after school. When the boy talked to this girl she did not take him seriously. She said her family was poor and this 'sugar daddy' provided her with money to buy food for the family. The boys also reported seeing a 10-year-old girl arrive at her home in the morning after she had spent the night at an older man's house.*

The fact that young children are having sex with older men (and women) for financial support is extremely disturbing, especially in light of the fact that HIV is highly prevalent in the adult age group.

Absence of fathers

A third causal factor is the large number of boys who have been left without a father in a culture that is strongly patriarchal. Women-headed households are often looked down upon by the community, and this has serious implications for a child's socialisation, how 'acceptable' the child is within his or her community, and for the development of their self-esteem. When TAI asked young men about what it meant to lose their father, they said,

> *'The mother may not be able to discipline a boy without the father. Some mothers fail to tell their children if they are wrong. The child grows up not knowing between right and wrong. The children can be unruly and don't respect men because there is no man at home.'*

> *'My father is working and living a five-star life in Pretoria [a major city in South Africa] but he is not supporting us. I feel bad about him. I have developed a negative attitude towards him. I'm also thinking of paying revenge by killing him.'*

This skewed socialisation and lack of self-esteem contribute to increased high-risk sexual encounters. If you are worth nothing in your own eyes, why should you care about your future or that of others? In this context, risking HIV infection and death is a gamble that is easily explicable.

Tradition and culture, poverty, inappropriate socialisation, and a multitude of other intricately interwoven issues (such as power transactions within relationships, religious beliefs, economic control, and societal norms) all contribute to a level of violence against women in South Africa that is deeply rooted and socially acceptable. This is further supported by a baseline survey of 102 young men (12 to 25 years old) that was conducted by TAI in 2003.

Seventeen of the respondents had either threatened or beaten their partner, and out of the 35 sexually active respondents, three admitted to forcing a girl to have sex against her will.[8]

Based on the dynamics described above, and with the frustrating knowledge that we could not tackle all the issues, TAI decided to focus on several key areas in its work with men:

- providing accurate information about puberty, sex, and HIV/AIDS;
- discussing gender-orientated issues relating to culture, beliefs, and perceptions of masculinity (with the aim of promoting gender awareness);
- and personalising the risk of HIV infection.

Shosholoza: keeping hope, moving forwards

The Shosholoza AIDS Project (as initiated by TAI in 1998) is a project based on peer educators, targeting young men between the ages of 15 and 18. A baseline survey of 100 young men was done to ascertain the values, beliefs, and possible risk-taking behaviours of this group. The results showed that 95 per cent of the boys had never used condoms; all those who were sexually active had more than one current sexual partner; and only three per cent said that a woman has a right to say 'no' to sex. None of them believed that either they or their partners could be infected with HIV.

After much consideration, it was decided to use soccer (South Africa's most popular sport) as a means of mobilising and motivating the participants. Due to the high public attendance at soccer matches, it was felt that stadiums were perfect venues for participating peer-educator teams to promote HIV awareness. In addition, soccer players are often seen as role models in communities, making them both at high risk of HIV infection due to their popularity, and highly influential in terms of HIV prevention due to their prominence. TAI realised that soccer competitions could be used to encourage participation because, for many young men in KZN, soccer is as much a passionate way of life as it is a sport!

The South African Football Association (SAFA) was approached and asked to identify eight of their affiliated teams for training. After a process of consultation, teams were selected and underwent a three-day training workshop, which concentrated on issues such as sexuality, puberty, sexually transmitted infections (STIs), HIV/AIDS, communication skills (including decision making and negotiation skills) and project planning. Time was given for the peer educators to first come to terms with HIV in their own lives, during which group discussions of prevention strategies and sexuality were held.

When the groups felt prepared, they began to implement small projects within their communities: holding training workshops for neighbouring soccer teams; organising HIV-oriented soccer events; engaging spectators at matches; distributing condoms; and holding personal sessions with friends.

The Shosholoza AIDS Project was very enthusiastically received, and the trained groups' outreach programme for other soccer clubs saw an estimated 2000 men trained in basic HIV information and prevention (the result of the efforts of 80 very determined peer educators). In addition, the peer educators were encouraged to involve their partners and to discuss HIV and prevention. As a means of verifying that this had taken place, TAI conducted a survey of 44 female partners. In this study, 93 per cent reported that their partner had spoken to them about HIV/AIDS. One hundred per cent of the female partners could cite three reasons for using condoms (prevention of HIV/AIDS and STIs, and pregnancy). TAI felt that the evidence produced by this study indicated that these young men had taken the HIV message to heart, and were trying to protect themselves and their loved ones.

Despite the committed efforts of the peer educator groups, TAI realised that, as a result of their early sexual debut[9] (between 14 and 16 years), many of the boys could already be HIV-positive. In fact, according to a study by the Planned Parenthood Association of South Africa, more than 70 per cent of South African teenagers are sexually active by the age of 14.[10] A strategy had to be developed to encourage a delay in the onset of sexual activity, to promote abstinence, and to provide accurate information about prevention methods to those who decided to become sexually active. Thus TAI resolved to work with an even younger group of boys (11 to 15 years), and the Inkunzi Isematholeni Project was initiated in 2001.

Inkunzi Isematholeni: taking the bull by the horns

Inkunzi isematholeni is a Zulu idiom, which when literally translated means 'how the calf is raised will determine the quality of the bull'. This summarised the spirit of the project, which was to help guide boys and young men away from the violent and destructive behaviour that had become predominant in KwaZulu-Natal, and to support their development into good fathers and sexually responsible partners.

TAI approached 20 predominantly rural schools in the province to take part in the project. It was felt that schools provided an ideal environment for projects involving very young people, as there are many support structures available to them, including teachers, principals, school governing bodies and the school's facilities. School principals were contacted, the project was introduced to them, and their potential involvement outlined. Their permission to implement the project was obtained, and one committed teacher from each school was selected to guide the process. These teachers were tasked with selecting 10 participants from their school. For each school's peer-educator group, a mixture of extroverted students (for public speaking) and introverted students (for personal discussions) was encouraged.

The Absa Group (South Africa) sponsored the Inkunzi Project, and a staff complement of six involved 200 boys and young men in three main sets of activities. First, three-day training workshops were conducted, which focused on providing correct and relevant information on puberty, sexually transmitted infections, HIV/AIDS, and condom use. The workshops encouraged reflection on issues such as culture, masculinity and femininity, personal HIV vulnerability, and prevention strategies. Firm emphasis was placed on encouraging participants to think for themselves, asking questions like 'Where do you want to be in fifteen years?', 'What will your house look like?', and 'How many children would you like to have?', and then asking 'How do you think becoming HIV-positive will influence your dreams?'. Creativity was encouraged, and many issues were explored through the use of role-plays, case studies, and other thought-provoking exercises. It was felt that it was important to develop certain skills in the participants, such as

- communication skills to enable them to talk about these very sensitive and difficult issues;
- project-management skills, which would enable the groups to implement and manage their own initiatives when they began reaching out to their fellow students and community members;
- negotiation skills, as there seemed to be some resistance to using condoms or abstaining from sex on the part of female partners who had low levels of knowledge concerning HIV and its transmission.

Second, TAI co-ordinators regularly visited the groups to reinforce the training. These visits served the purpose of allowing the participants to discuss issues facing them, their personal decisions, and questions they had been asked and were unable to answer. Further relevant information was also provided during these sessions.

The third activity focused on promoting caring behaviour, and involved the establishment of vegetable gardens in all 20 schools to provide food for children in need (identified by the peer educators and the principal). A programme to plant indigenous trees was also initiated, and peer educators were entrusted with caring for young trees.[11] These activities introduced the participants to aspects of caring for and supporting others, something which is not culturally encouraged among men in KZN. The aim of these activities was to encourage greater involvement of boys and men in caring for those infected and affected by HIV.

TAI conducted targeted training workshops for the groups' guiding teachers and several selected school governing bodies (SGBs). This training aimed to help the teachers and SGB members understand the scale of the HIV epidemic, its impact on the education system, and their own role in curbing the spread of the disease. As a control, some SGBs were not trained, in order to assess the impact of the training of SGBs on the peer-educator project. This aspect of the project is still under evaluation.

TAI also engaged the Inkunzi peer educators in a variety of exercises aimed at further strengthening the project and maintaining interest, including

* exchange programmes between participating schools;
* a weekly discussion of themes such as rape and child abuse;
* making posters;
* producing HIV-related drama, poetry, and *scathamiya* (Zulu dance).

Schools were encouraged to host debates on subjects such as 'Women are to be blamed for the spread of HIV'. The debate at one school had many strong-minded contributions, not only from the female audience, but also from the male peer educators who were arguing against the statement, with the eventual conclusion that both men and women are responsible for the spread of the disease.

Effective, or just a load of bull?

Various research activities were conducted to assess the impact of the project. These included preventative counselling, focus-group discussions, and message development. These exercises provided a real insight into the thoughts and feelings of the young men.

The preventative counselling took the form of one-on-one sessions, in which a trained facilitator distributed a questionnaire. Peer educators from five regions of KwaZulu-Natal took part in this study, the majority of the 173 participants having joined the project two years earlier. At the time of the study, 37 per cent of the participants were sexually active, and it was found that most of these boys had had their sexual debut between the ages of 14 and 15 years, before they had joined the project. Of the remainder who were not yet sexually active, 45 per cent were between the ages of 14 and 15. In the age group in which most boys become sexually active, the majority of our participants were remaining inactive. We feel that this indicates that our project has had a positive impact in delaying the sexual debut of the participants, with many of our peer educators 'sticking to their guns', despite being teased about their choice to abstain, and some even having their masculinity questioned.

The focus-group discussions concentrated on several broad issues such as gender, violence in our communities, parental influence, caring, and social or environmental factors. The discussions gave the peer educators a chance to share and reflect on their personal beliefs, as well as allowing us to evaluate our project. On issues of gender, peer educators showed a growing awareness of women's rights, as indicated by the response of the peer educators to the question 'what is women-abuse?'

> *'The common abuse in our areas is women-abuse. This form happens more regularly when men are not aware that they are abusing. Men will stress that certain chores are women's work, not considering that women are being overworked. If you are in love you divide work.'*

Some boys reported knowing of incidents in which girls were dragged into the bushes when they refused sex to boys (in the community) who propositioned them. The majority of peer educators felt that, even if the girl was their girlfriend, they had no right to force her to have sex.

The research on message development also provided inspiring results. The peer educators were given materials to make banners displaying various themed slogans. When asked what the benefits of using condoms are, one group wrote, 'Listen if I tell you to use a condom, because we are trying to reduce the increase of orphans'. The advantages of delaying sexual debut included, 'Let us wait, so that we shall rejoice tomorrow and acquire knowledge from the elders' and 'If you have a partner, you should know her better, not sexually. Understanding one another makes a good relationship.' Some sad notes were written to a father who had died of AIDS, such as, 'Daddy, you left us when we were enjoying your company the most. Your death has opened our eyes. We will educate others and also care for the sick.'

Working with these boys and young men is a very rewarding experience. The project has become self-sustaining after the initial training sessions. Many co-ordinators arrived for their follow-up visit to find that, as in one example, the initial group of 10 had now swelled to 16 very eager members. We were also surprised to learn that Inkunzi Isematholeni has recently acquired a group of female peer educators in one of the schools. Due to the pressure the girls were exerting, the boys felt it would be prudent to include them. In retrospect, the main problem encountered during our work with young men has not been trying to get them involved, but rather trying to find the resources and energy to keep up with them!

Conclusion

Although the task of responding to the challenge posed by HIV/AIDS is long term and requires action on several fronts, we believe the project work of TAI is making a significant contribution to combating HIV/AIDS and addressing gender inequality. We ascribe our practical success in engaging these young men to several factors.

1   We have tried to be **empowering** and not dictatorial in our approach. TAI tries to encourage peer educators to develop and implement their own strategies to prevent the spread of HIV in their schools and communities, with only minimal guidance from TAI. This creates a participatory environment, which makes peer educators feel that they are in control of their project.

2   The project is seen to have a certain '**coolness**' factor, and it is almost prestigious to belong to the group. This is probably due to the use of soccer to interest the boys, inter-group competitions that are held with prizes donated to the group or school (trophies are much coveted), and the distribution of incentives (including t-shirts, small financial contributions, catering at meetings, etc).

3   TAI structures its activities so as to provide a platform for young men to **express themselves** and talk about topics that are sometimes very painful and rarely discussed within their families and culture. Conducive and comfortable environments are created where trust is imperative. The group establishes a code of conduct, which includes rules stipulating the confidentiality of what is discussed in the group. The times for discussion are greatly valued by the peer educators, with many of them remarking on how relieved they feel to be able to talk freely about sex, sexuality, and the traumatic experiences they have had.

4   Last, but by no means least, the element of **fun** is vitally important when working with young men. Although HIV is a serious topic, there should be plenty of opportunity to laugh, joke, and just generally horse around. Activities should be culturally specific (in the case of the Zulu culture, these include singing, dancing, acting, and handcrafts) and encourage creativity.

These factors, combined with innovative project ideas and dedicated staff, have resulted in our peer educators realising that there are options for them. They have the abilities and knowledge needed to protect themselves and the ones they love. They can make a difference within their communities by informing others and by caring for those in need. They have a future worth fighting for. By being a part of this project, we hope that these remarkable boys will not only become worthy men, but human beings who value and respect the rights of others (especially women) and who contribute positively to this rainbow nation.

Notes

1   G.C. Makhaye (2002) 'HIV Infection and Factors Influencing Risk in Antenatal Clinic Attendees in Rural KwaZulu-Natal', Masters thesis, not yet published.

2   R. Morrell (ed.) (2001) *Changing Men in Southern Africa*, London and Durban: Zed Books/University of Natal Press.

3   Unemployment was estimated at 37 per cent in 2001. See *CIA – The World Fact Book*, www.odci.gov/cia/publications/factbook/print/sf.html (accessed in February 2004).

4   www.speakout.org.za (accessed in February 2004).

5   Many men feel that it is part of their traditional role to 'discipline' their wives. In fact, many South African women consider being beaten as part of 'normal life'.

6   T. Moodie and V. Ndatshe (1994) *Going for Gold: Men, Mines and Migration*, Johannesburg: Witwatersrand University Press.

7   The participants in these activities (both the children and adults) do not believe that they are involved in 'prostitution'. Often the adult is well known to the child, and takes on the role of 'benefactor' to the child and his/her family in exchange for sex. Often these relationships have the 'consent' of the child's parents.

8   As previously noted, it is widely believed in certain South African cultures that men are obliged to 'discipline' their partners and that female partners do not have the right to refuse sex. As such, it is likely that this is an underestimate of the actual levels of this abuse, as many young men would not have considered their actions as 'abuse' or 'rape'.

9   All references to sex and sexual debut relate to penetrative sex.

10 Planned Parenthood Association of South Africa (2003) 'Teen Parent Programme: A Baseline Survey and Needs Assessment for Adolescents and Teen Parents in South Africa', final report, November 2003.

11 Vegetable gardens sponsored by McDonalds Seeds (South Africa), and indigenous tress donated by Sappi (South Africa).

12 The age-group breakdown was as follows: 27 per cent younger than 13 years; 29 per cent between the ages of 14 and 15; 21 per cent between the ages of 16 and 17; and 23 per cent older than 18 years. Twenty-seven per cent of the participants lived with both parents; 39 per cent lived with their mothers; 19 per cent lived with grandparents; five per cent lived with their fathers; and 11 per cent lived with others, such as uncles and aunts.

Fatherwork in the Caribbean: examples of support for men's work in relation to family life

Janet Brown

This paper is a review of fatherhood initiatives reported within the Caribbean region that support men's positive participation in the lives of their children and within their families. It gives a brief description of the gradual move away from 'role-deficit approaches' which have tended to measure men's family participation against ideal images of fatherhood and then set out to 'fix' men. These approaches have usually reflected women's needs in relation to the family, or political or institutional agendas seeking to involve men in specific ways. The more recently acknowledged need for men to reflect and debate on approaches to family life that derive from their own experiences and perceptions as well as the needs of their partners, has encouraged the development of initiatives which more directly address men's own issues and their roles as fathers.

'Fatherwork' in the title of this paper was coined by Dollahite, Hawkins, and Brotherson[1] as a more user-friendly term for 'generative fathering', itself an application of Erik Erikson's concept of 'generativity' – caring for and contributing to the life of the next generation. Snarey's foreword to the Dollahite and Hawkins edited collection *Generative Fathering* suggests that 'generative adults create, care for, and promote the development of others, from nurturing the growth of another person to shepherding the development of a broader community'. Translated as 'fatherwork', the term also implies that becoming a positive influence in a child's life is *developmental,* not only for the child, but for the father. Rather than holding up 'ideal' images of fatherhood against which men are measured (as almost inevitably inadequate), 'fatherwork' suggests that men can and do *work* at transforming their desire to be a good or better father into reality over their lifetime; that fathering is a set of skills and behaviours that can be learned, improved, and changed as demands or circumstances change, and that temporary failures are not the whole of the realities of fathers' relations to their children and partners.

This perspective is a more helpful one in analysing work with fathers generally, and specifically in the Caribbean, where role-deficit perspectives of men as fathers are deeply embedded. In the developing economies of the region, the primary expectation of men as fathers has been in the role of *financial provider,* and the related role of *protector.* With large segments of the region's populations unemployed or under-employed, this narrow role definition relegates many men to a marginal existence within and outside their families. Add high rates of conjugal instability and strong cultural expectations that a son should support his mother and siblings financially, and the cultural support for this deficit framework becomes glaringly apparent. In Jamaican parlance, men are 'given basket to carry water'.

This paper will briefly describe some initiatives that aim to support men's fathering in a more developmental way in the Caribbean. The shadows of deficit thinking about Caribbean fathers are not absent from these approaches, but the projects are selected because they seem to signal a movement by programme interventions and by men themselves in the direction of *fatherwork* as a conscious developmental task, rather than as a defensive response to portrayed inadequacies. The programme examples illustrate some of the central issues which are being addressed:

- how to ensure men's participation in the development of programme approaches which articulate and support their needs as fathers and partners;[2]

- how to address and reduce the tensions which often exist between mothers' and fathers' perceptions of their respective roles in relation to their children;

- how best to take the needs and perspective of the child into account in addressing these issues; and

- how to build bridges that bring men and women together to find mutually acceptable solutions to long-standing issues of gender inequity, and which serve the need of children for healthy models for future roles and relationships.

It is hoped that highlighting the Caribbean experience will provide ideas for those in other regions who are struggling with similar fatherhood and family issues.

The first section of this chapter will briefly review Caribbean fatherhood in the research literature. The second section will list a few regional, national, and community-level activities, introducing the main players in fatherhood projects and initiatives. Finally, some of the major lessons learned will be outlined, with related recommendations for future Caribbean fatherwork.

Fatherwork in the literature

In the Caribbean, the earliest research noting men's roles in the family is found in literature examining the roles of women. These studies take into account the historical and cultural factors which influence Caribbean families and which differentiate them from the large body of research on North American families.

Caribbean family studies describe the common life-cycle changes in union status of the majority of the population. Only 16 per cent of Jamaican women in their childbearing years are married; this is a common pattern throughout the African-Caribbean populations. The vast majority of first-born children are born into 'visiting' unions of young, unmarried partners. Later in life, many of these parents move into common-law unions, and may eventually marry their partners, sometimes after their children have grown. Children are not infrequently sent to live with other relatives for parts of their lives. Therefore, women and men may have children from one or more unions who may or may not live with them.

The family units both in and outside conventional marriages were the starting point for identifying the positions and roles that Caribbean men assume over their lifetimes in relation to their partners and children. Early studies, using perspectives influenced by North American literature, described Caribbean family forms as largely 'dysfunctional', because they are not nuclear within the context of marriage. More recently, researchers have begun describing the *functional* aspects of these long-standing patterns that in fact aid survival, child protection, and family advancement in the context of poverty, sacrifice, and high levels of in- and out-migration. This research provides strong impetus to the need to better understand the role of men in Caribbean families.

Research on identifying and promoting healthy child-rearing practices gave subsequent impetus for examining Caribbean fatherhood. Early Caribbean family research focused mainly on the matrifocal nature of the family and the strong mother–child bonds, often within female-headed households. In the late 1980s, a survey of education, health, and social services and programmes for young children by the University of the West Indies (UWI) Caribbean recorded a strong call from practitioners for help with parenting-education supports.[3] Of particular concern was the 'non-involvement' of fathers in their children's lives. This call, and the tenor of public discourse on the 'irresponsible', 'absent' Caribbean father kick-started ten years of research and related programme interventions by UWI's Caribbean Child Development Centre (CCDC), examining fatherhood and the gender socialisation of children. Close collaboration in this research was maintained with UWI's Department of Sociology and Social Work.[4] This department has undertaken complimentary work on male identity formation,[5] as well as on perceptions of family roles by children.[6] Thus UWI's work on Caribbean manhood and fatherhood has been much more about discerning the cultural and social meanings underlying the behaviours manifested in men's fathering roles, and how these roles inter-relate with women as mothers and as partners.

The early 1992 UWI research ascertained that men generally display more positive child-directed and family-directed behaviour and attitudes than popular stereotypes would suggest. Men were also able to state clearly the personal, cultural, and social obstacles which they perceive hinder their ability to be better fathers. The research pointed to the need for a *men's agenda* in relation to children and family life. It is evident, more than ten years later, that men themselves are increasingly expressing the need for such an agenda. In the recently published compilation of papers on *Children's Rights: Caribbean Realities*, Barrow provides the context for this urgency: manhood is increasingly being redefined, particularly among younger Caribbean men, through the exercising of fatherhood roles. As fathers, men are recognising the vulnerability of their father–child relationships, which are almost totally dependent on negotiation through mothers:

> *In this cultural environment of female autonomy, female household headship and extensive female-centred families and kinship networks, motherhood is the privileged half of the parenting duo and women have the power, for whatever reason, to undermine father–child bonds. In a word, it is difficult to be a father without a positive relationship with the mother, and fragile, unstable conjugality frequently disrupts fatherhood.[7]*

In another chapter of *Children's Rights*, Chevannes adds to this picture the 'jacket', in which a child's paternity is attributed to an unsuspecting partner who is not the biological father.[8] Many men who discover they have been given a 'jacket' accept these children as their own, particularly if others don't suspect the truth.

This phenomenon underlines the woman's power to name the father of her child, and thus 'establish' the child's bloodline. A man may accept a jacket because it enhances his image in relation to others, or because a bond with the mother and child has formed which is of value to him. As long as the relationship with the child's mother remains firm, biological paternity is likely to remain relatively immaterial. But if the parents' relationship deteriorates or is severed, contested paternity can become a weapon for either parent, and the father–child bond is usually the victim.

This power of women in relation to their partners is not unlimited. It can be said to be a woman's defence against the power men exercise in a patriarchal society, including physical power, as evidenced by high levels of domestic violence. Branche places the image of the Caribbean matrifocal family (mother-dominated, posited on male absence or marginality) within the wider social context of 'male privileging', which is socially reproduced within the family first, and then reinforced by many institutions thereafter. Branche states:

The study of the matrifocal family was always also a study of marginal men,
but marginal men whose marginality could only fully be understood in
relation to their privilege, in relation to patriarchal dominance. Matrifocality,
therefore, is a myth if it is taken to mean that this emphasis in Caribbean
family studies could be the basis for launching a feminist agenda.[9]

The privileging of boys begins with differential child-rearing strategies and parental expectations.[10] Boys are freer of chores and home responsibilities, and are expected to learn many of life's lessons from older boys and men 'on the street'. Girls, on the other hand, learn structured responsibility within the more closely supervised home 'yard'.[11] The concept of male privilege has added relevance to discussions of gender equity; in the analysis[12] and subsequent discourse it has become clear that privilege can in fact lead to some disadvantages for men. It has aided our understanding of male under-performance at school and high male drop-out rates, and has added a dimension to the dynamics of the man–woman domestic relationship. When men start examining the negative as well as positive effects of structured male privilege within their own lives, and the resultant vulnerabilities in their relationships with their children and partner(s), they advance their own fatherwork. Reflective men are recognising the constraints on their own development that narrow social definitions of manhood and fatherhood provide; but there are as yet few social forces that support this reflection or include broader nurturing and caretaking tasks within concepts of manly fatherhood, particularly if financial provision is absent or limited.

Two UWI symposia in the late 1990s, one on constructing Caribbean masculinity, and the other on the family and the quality of gender relations, enlivened the already rich debates and research on gender issues generated by the earlier research, particularly the work of the Gender and Development Units of the three main UWI campuses. There is therefore a solid academic foundation for improving the historical and cultural understanding of men's positions within the common patterns of gender relations and family life in the Caribbean. But greater understanding does not necessarily lead to prescriptive clarity for men's and women's daily lives. The research activities to date have pointed to the need for men to address their needs and challenges as fathers in contexts of economic hardship, non-residential unions, having children with more than one partner, and vexed relationships with women. Most fatherhood programme approaches, including many cited below, begin from women's perspectives and assumptions about what men *should* be doing, rather than from men's own initiatives to define themselves as fathers, to establish how they want to interact with their children, and to tackle challenging issues of gender inequity and new role paradigms.

Some of the perspectives emerging from men's opportunities to talk about their own needs naturally create tensions with those who have urged gender-equity perspectives – when for instance the message from a church-based group is that men must 'reclaim' their role as heads of their families, or when men decide to organise to fight 'the maternal bias of the legal system' in custody battles for their children, after marriage or conjugal relationships break down. This should not be surprising, particularly in the Caribbean, where inter-gender distrust is deeply socially embedded, and women's achievements in challenging gender bias in most sectors have been extensive.

There *is* therefore a need for men's agendas in relation to children and family to be encouraged and developed as a *foundation for respectful debates and negotiations* that can reduce tensions, foster deeper understanding and healthier relationships, and which take children's needs seriously into account. Despite the fact that parenting groups and fatherhood programmes for men are relatively recent in this region, there is tentative evidence that such an approach can in fact help to advance gender-equity concerns:

- Many men who have begun to seriously examine social roles and issues of gender have broadened their own understanding of women's positions, and of their own participation (whether deliberately or unconsciously) in systems of inequity within the society. This has sometimes led to men's greater domestic role sharing within the family, and a more open recognition of their domestic contributions as not just 'women's work'.

- Many women have had opportunities to listen to men's perspectives, including men's pain on issues of family, and to re-examine the broad-brush stereotypes of Caribbean men as uncaring and irresponsible in relation to their children. Women have also been challenged to look at their own socialisation, and the ways in which they may be perpetuating patterns of behaviour that keep men marginalised from full participation with their children.

- Men themselves often express the wish to share new perspectives gained from a men-only discussion or workshop with their female partners. The comfort women generally take for granted in discussions of child-rearing and relationships does not automatically pass to men included in these discussions; men's own socialisation has not prepared them for this. But when encouraged, in settings in which they feel 'safe' from the negativism they have come to expect, many men are welcoming the opportunity to talk about their questions, issues, pain, and pleasures in relation to their families.

Intervention experience in the Caribbean

While Caribbean research has been helping to focus debates on some of the dilemmas facing fathers and their families, practitioners at the community level have proceeded to respond to calls for fatherhood initiatives, often unaware of the research, or impatient to move forward despite the lack of tested effective models. Social workers and educators both in and outside of government, media professionals, church groups, and other community-based workers and volunteers have been fuelled by an urgency to *do something* to increase the positive and significant participation of fathers in the lives of their children. Whether motivated by a deficit perspective, religious injunctions, economic, socio-cultural, or personal development considerations, or by role-model assumptions, there is general consensus that:

- Fathers need greater attention and support; this is demanded by both men and women. Children's needs in relation to their fathers are being increasingly recognised; research is assisting our understanding of these needs.

- Global trends affect the Caribbean no less than elsewhere: more women are working outside the home, and men are under more pressure to help with childcare and domestic responsibilities. For unemployed or under-employed men, this often conflicts with the cultural assertion that manhood is defined by financial provision for the family, not by doing 'woman's work'. Many women concur, and do not encourage men to take on childcaring roles.

- 'Backlash' positions from men who feel threatened by women's growing financial and psychological independence, particularly if men feel socially or economically vulnerable themselves, move us further from achieving gender equity, feed levels of domestic violence, and negatively influence children's lives. These positions need to be challenged openly.

- Traditional ideas of men's roles and behaviours are beginning to be challenged by a growing awareness of the needs and aspirations of men in relation to their wives and children (as women's needs and aspirations beyond the home brought similar challenges), and the growing dysfunctional nature of these narrow roles for men and for women in today's world.

A limited review of Caribbean interventions undertaken by the author for the Bernard van Leer Foundation in 2002 follows; a few have been subsequently added which have come to attention more recently. This introduces the range of players that has become involved in fatherhood initiatives, and the range of programme initiatives. The outline is not exhaustive, but seeks to represent the known 'front line' examples of such interventions to date in the region.

Programme initiatives for and by fathers

Work with vulnerable, 'at risk' men

Belize and Dominica have organised parenting courses for men who are in prison. Belize's National Organisation for the Prevention of Child Abuse and Neglect (NOPCAN) selected men with short prison sentences, due to be released within two years of the programme. The men were offered a series of workshops on parenting issues to examine aspects of their relationships with their children, and to work to improve and strengthen those relationships during their incarceration and in preparation for their release. Dominica's Social Centre, with the National Council on Parenting, also provided men with a short course on parenting, and in addition visited the spouses and mothers of these men to ascertain their willingness to work with the men on family issues on release. Both programmes found the men responsive to the sessions and more positive about their relationships with their children; both programmes are seeking funds to follow up and assess the impact on the men and their families since release. An interesting spin-off in Dominica was the request of the warders for a similar course for themselves.

Jamaica's Family Planning Association provides workshops for probationers, pre- and post-prison, who have been found guilty of domestic or sexual abuse; the victims of the sexual abuse are often the men's young daughters. The courts assign men to this programme as a condition of their probation or parole, thus making this one of the few programmes that works with offenders as clients, rather than just as perpetrators of family-based crimes.

Trinidad and Tobago is the home of the only known organisation of men in the Caribbean who, like the White Ribbon Campaign in other countries, stand up collectively against domestic violence. Men Against Violence Against Women (MAVAW) is an organisation primarily for men who are trying to change their history of abuse against their girlfriends or spouses, and they work closely with the Gender and Development Unit of the Trinidad campus of UWI in providing workshops and public forums on domestic violence and gender equity.

Men-only public forums on issues of fatherhood and manhood

Churches and umbrella church organisations in several countries have mounted conferences and workshops that call on men to 'shoulder their God-given roles and responsibilities'. Few, however, have developed on-going programmes to help fathers accomplish this. One exception is a group of church-based young men in Jamaica (the Gappists[13]), founded by university students, who initiated a summer camp and leadership training for boys. They also worked to articulate a theoretical framework for understanding the roles of Christian men within the family and society. This framework acknowledges the importance of the UWI research in describing the changing context for men, and it attempts to reconcile social demands for changing roles with the need to challenge or re-interpret some of the traditional cultural and religious assumptions that confine manhood and fatherhood to narrowly prescribed roles within and outside the family.

Barbados is home to MESA, the Men's Educational Support Association, which hosts monthly public seminars for men only. Its subcommittees deal with issues of law, health, counselling, education, and fundraising. The chairman produces a weekly 'Men's Forum' in a local newspaper.

Conferences and workshops on fatherhood issues

Several regional conferences have been devoted exclusively to issues of men in their family roles, or have provided sessions within a larger agenda to deal specifically with fatherhood issues. A 2003 UNESCO and UWI regional conference on mainstreaming gender equity in the Caribbean included three presentations on issues affecting men in their family roles. Two regional Early Childhood Development conferences have held workshops on fatherhood issues for delegates (in Jamaica in 2000, and Guyana in 2002), and a 2001 regional parenting and public-education workshop placed fatherhood as one of the central issues.

In 2001, Belize held a National Conference for men only, focusing on men's own parenting and on their children's development. The men also explored the cultural meanings of masculinity, fatherhood, and gender roles within the diverse ethnic groups of Belize, as well as issues in their relationships with their wives and partners such as trust, sexuality, and financial support. One outcome of this conference was a series of sub-regional focus groups with young and older men on cultural issues of gender socialisation within different ethnic-group populations, and plans for school-based discussions with children on gender issues, using the conference participants as facilitators.

In Jamaica, an annual 'Model Father' essay contest run by Fathers Incorporated, a twelve-year-old support group for fathers, added an all-day 'retreat' for some of the nominated model fathers in 2003. The group discussed their fathering experience in depth, including whether their children were planned or not, how pregnancy and children affected their relationships with their partners, what they valued most in their relationships with their children, and what factors within society encouraged and discouraged them in being positive fathers. The outputs of this workshop will be organised by the group into a booklet for new fathers, for publication in 2004.

Parenting-education activities which target fathers

The government of St. Kitts-Nevis has organised thirteen-week courses for men in seven different communities on issues of parenting; the men help select the topics of greatest interest to them. Response has been positive, attendance high, and the media have helped with recruitment publicity as well as covering 'graduations'. Women are now beginning to say, 'What about us? We need to be included'. The men have now requested a fourteenth session to include their partners, in order to share the results of the sessions and to try to improve communication. The importance of this initiative, as well as its difficulties, were experienced in the first attempt at a session for partners. The participants found sharing their feelings with their partners difficult, the session was at times confrontational, and the outcome disappointing. The programme has recently recognised the need for a thorough evaluation of the training at this point, to better understand how to use this opportunity to work more effectively towards improved partner relationships and parent–child interactions.

Trinidad and Tobago has reported PTA meetings for men only, within a government outreach programme on gender relations. Response to this initiative was very positive; one school reported that 129 men attended one session; another that they had more men in attendance for one session than the total attendance of men and women at any previous PTA meeting. Barbados' PAREDOS, a parenting-education NGO, gives increasing attention to seminars and workshops on a range of parenting and gender-socialisation topics for men, and finds them very responsive.

There are few known sustained attempts to build father-support groups. Fathers Incorporated in Jamaica is the oldest known such group. Fathers Inc. has remained small but dynamic, and undertakes a range of public service and public-education tasks to bring positive fathering models to wider attention. In late 2003, the group launched a pilot project to assist communities to start and sustain father-support groups over a period of a year, linked to the resources and leadership of the 'parent' group.

Father–child programmes

Few programmes are known that are specifically aimed at strengthening the father–child relationship. Primary schools have held special 'Dads and Sons' days in several countries (St. Lucia and Jamaica are examples), responding to the widespread desire to bring fathers more actively into their children's school life. There was also concern about the high drop-out rates for boys and their increasing under-performance relative to girls in key school exams. 'Dads and Sons' days consist of education and recreational programmes during the school day, and girls do not attend that day. In the Bahamas, at least one pre-school annually turns the school over to the boys and their fathers (or male surrogates) with careful guidelines, and activities include baking in competitive groups, playing pre-school games, and arts and crafts. The fathers have been very enthusiastic about this approach to introducing them to the 'rigours' of pre-school life (for teachers and children) as well as to a rewarding day with their sons.

In Jamaica, Youth.now (a project which focuses primarily on the needs of adolescents and young men) has recently launched a pilot programme of community-based activities for fathers and their sons in an inner-city community. The programme aims to bring fathers, many of them non-residential, into more satisfying relationships with their sons.

Pre-parenting interventions with children and adolescents

Several countries have developmental performing-arts programmes for young people. Ashe (Jamaica) has taken its music and drama performances onto the streets, into schools, and around the Caribbean, with themes dealing with responsible sexuality, child abuse and incest, and most recently positive parenting, engaging young audiences in discussion afterwards on the issues raised in the performance. Gender equity is a consistent theme of this group. A long-standing Adolescent Development Programme of SERVOL in Trinidad and Tobago ensures that all the students who have dropped out of school and attend their trades-training programme also take life-skills courses, which include pre-parenting topics and hours of practical experience in on-site day-care programmes. Evaluations over several years suggest that direct results of these aspects of the programme include delayed pregnancy and a greater appreciation of the demands of child-rearing.

Reproductive health programmes

Reproductive health has been a common entry point for efforts to engage men more effectively in family planning and protection from sexually transmitted diseases. Rising rates of HIV/AIDS transmission have multiplied the numbers of programmes which are trying to address the pandemic's impact. Trinidad and Tobago and Jamaica report some success in establishing separate clinics (or clinic days) for men and for adolescents. Reproductive health information and treatment are the primary areas of interest, but this approach has also encouraged men to seek information about other male health issues and risk-taking behaviour. Some hospitals in the region are becoming more father-friendly, particularly in pre-natal care and birth procedures, but in general, family-health services are reported as giving little thought to access and participation of fathers as equal partners in child-rearing and child health.

Gender-equity approaches

Every country in the region has a Women's Bureau, or Gender Affairs desk. Few, however, serve both genders as actively as the Ministry of Community Development and Gender Affairs in Trinidad and Tobago, which has a male support co-ordinator. This post and budget were created to address three issues: the under-performance of boys and young men at all levels of schooling; issues of increasing general and domestic violence; and the need to advance community-level discourse on gender equity within the wider society. The Unit works closely with the Gender and Development Unit at the St. Augustine campus of the UWI to plan workshops and interventions around the country on these issues.

A CIDA fund for gender equity based in Jamaica has encouraged proposals for programmes that include approaches to reduce violence against women, and address more directly the root causes of these behaviours. It is too early to know if any of these programmes are effective in engaging men, or men and women together, on these issues.

Public-education approaches

The media, while often reflecting stereotyped images of men and women throughout the Caribbean, have also been purveyors of new images of fatherhood, and have reflected and fostered public debates on issues of positive fathering. A long-running weekly television programme in Jamaica called 'Man Talk' debated cultural definitions of manhood and fatherhood in an informal bar-type setting. In Tobago, a radio talk-show host regularly devotes his 'Mike at Nite' programmes to phone-in debates on male issues, sometimes requesting only men callers. He has found that men have welcomed this anonymous space for opening up personal issues from their own perspectives, and they sometimes using it to vent perceived injustices by the courts (in maintenance and custody issues) and by their partners (when denied access to their children). The question of how such a radio programme can link people to other, more structured, outlets for problem-solving remains open. The level of distrust and anger between men and women in family matters, which is reflected throughout the Caribbean in public debates on sensitive family and relationship issues, indicates that such a linkage is necessary.

Fathers Incorporated (Jamaica) has public education as one of its major activities, through, for example, peer-counsellor training for its members, Fathers' Day concerts and celebrations, radio and face-to-face debates, and sponsorship of two African anthropologists who spoke around the country on patterns of African fatherhood. For seven years, Fathers Inc. has mounted a 'Model Father' essay contest, with the winning candidate receiving several prizes at a public ceremony honouring responsible fatherhood. The contest and winner always have considerable media coverage during the Fathers' Day period. The essays themselves have been a rich source of reflections on what children value in their fathers. It was revealing that in one year's analysis of 53 of the essays, no one spoke specifically of financial provision by fathers as being important; the writers were more expressive of psychological and emotional support provided by their fathers.

Summary comments on programme interventions

What is clear from reviewing these varied examples is that there is as yet no overall regional strategy for advancing a men's agenda in the area of fatherwork, much less in the area of gender equity. There is little communication among programmes; most don't know about each other. There is as yet no sense of a Caribbean 'movement' or even recognition of common interests and efforts, except at regional meetings and conferences in which fatherhood issues are central, or between elements of programmes. Fatherwork remains primarily a *concept tool* for analysis and reflection about existing programmes, rather than a consciously adopted approach in practical work.

What is also seriously lacking to date is evidence of any systematic effort to evaluate the impact of any of these approaches. St. Kitts-Nevis has recently expressed the desire to thoroughly evaluate their three years of fathers-only courses, for impact on the men and their families; it is hoped they will soon do that. But beyond post-session evaluations by participants, which are usually positive about participation and content, and the anecdotal evidence of benefits from a given intervention claimed by programme organisers or by fathers and their families, the author could discover little in the way of evaluative material that could confidently guide others planning interventions with scarce resources and little time to waste on unproductive efforts. Better-informed interventions are needed, and a broader regional approach to fatherhood issues could be more effectively built on such research.

Lessons from the interventions

Having said this, however, there are some preliminary lessons to benefit planners from these programme initiatives.

> **Approaches from a deficit perspective can be effective only when men themselves identify the deficits as their own, and want to do something about them.** Men in prison, men on probation, or other such 'captive' audiences may respond positively *if* they acknowledge the ways in which

their behaviours have negatively affected their children or partner relationships. Otherwise, both captive and voluntary audiences of men will resist approaches which they perceive begin with negative judgements and aim to 'fix' them, usually for the benefit of others.

Developmental approaches, in which desired outcomes are stated in terms of men's own expressed desires for improved relationships with children and partners, greater personal satisfaction, and increased investment in their family, are psychologically and emotionally, as well as financially, more likely to be attractive to men as fathers or potential fathers. This is particularly likely when the programme is consultative in terms of choice of topic, venue, and timing, is participatory in nature, and is facilitated in a non-judgmental way.

There is a clear need to create spaces with men alone, for them to become comfortable and non-defensive in talking about subjects that would place them 'under fire' in many mixed groups. Men have not generally been socialised to talk about their family relationships in the ways that women have. However, in many of the cases cited above, men have welcomed opportunities to learn more about child development, about the importance of fathers to children, and about their own behaviours and feelings in relation to their children, without having to defend themselves.

Inherent in the lesson above, however, is **the danger of polarising men's positions versus women's on family issues**, increasing rather than decreasing levels of tension and misunderstanding. Women have often felt excluded from these approaches, perhaps forgetting that the women's movement itself progressed out of many such separate and strengthening debates that were also often about anger, the need for redress, tensions about power relationships, *as well as* about self-examination, personal change, and challenges to grow in different directions. It is significant that the UNESCO conference on gender mainstreaming recognised that after considerable progress for women's equality throughout the Caribbean, true gender equity will not ultimately be achieved without the engagement of men at all levels of the debate and the search for solutions, taking men's and women's agendas into account.[14] Perhaps this stage of men-only engagement needs to be continually interpreted not as an end in itself, but on a continuum towards a healthier dialogue with women on all the issues that constrain male–female relationships and family health.

The needs of children, and for a father's contribution in their lives, seems to be a positive entry point for engaging men in broader issues of gender equity. The welfare of men's children cannot be discussed realistically without engaging in a discussion of the relationship(s) they have or had with the children's mother(s). Aspirations for sons and daughters cannot be discussed without engaging in debates about how boys and girls should be socialised. The UWI research outlined the many ways in which children hold meanings for men that can be explored in developmental ways, because most fathers (like most mothers) do aspire to be better parents.

A children's rights perspective can help to promote gender equity. Children are entitled to a relationship with both parents, *except when the relationship has proven harmful.* Both parents are entitled to a relationship with their children, *even when not living with them.* However, mothers have been the traditional gatekeepers of men's relationships with their children, as the bitter testimony of many men seeking custody or visiting rights to their children shows. Even without legal contest, many Caribbean women discourage or sever the relationship between their children's father(s) and the children when the partner relationship breaks down, and particularly when the man's financial contribution is seen as insufficient. Fatherwork, by keeping central the developmental needs and feelings of children, can help to avoid polarising gender positions, and can aid gender relations in the process.

Recommendations for future Caribbean fatherwork

This brief review of research and programme experience in the Caribbean suggests that the greatest responsiveness from men is elicited through approaches that are not heavily prescriptive; are sequenced sessions, not one-shot encounters; are highly participatory; and that take the specific needs and interests of men into account. Men-only sessions can provide an environment more conducive to self-examination. These approaches need to be shared and replicated with guidance and support from those with confident experience.

- **Ways need to be tested for the more effective transfer of the benefits men derive from men-only discussions to discussions with their spouses and partners** about their relationships with them and with their children. The levels of distrust, hurt, and anger between men and women over family matters is one of the most common threads throughout the work reported, and calls for carefully implemented programmes that assist in the acquisition of communication and negotiation skills that can build mutual respect.

- The materials and modes of delivery used in interventions have not been rigorously evaluated for effectiveness or impact on either the fathers or their families. **Carefully designed impact studies for the Caribbean are needed,** and should be selected for their potential to inform the region's planning and implementation efforts. Impact studies require considerable time and money, and need to be planned long before programmes are underway. These conditions have been hard to meet within the resource constraints of the Caribbean. However, practitioners deserve to know if their well-meaning efforts are having the desired results, and how they can alter programmes to make better use of limited financial and human resources.

- **There has been insufficient Caribbean research on the significance of fathers from a child's perspective.** Branche and Ramkissoon have both called for the addition of more psychological studies to our sociological and historical research.[15] Ramkissoon's recent work confirmed that physically absent fathers were not necessarily psychologically or emotionally absent from their children's lives, but in fact often played strong roles. Barrow also reminds us that we have not begun to examine the value of stepfathers and social fathers within our Caribbean context; these men often play very significant roles, especially when biological fathers are not present.[16] Research in this area would spark more programme attention to father–child relationships.

- **There is a great need for more regional networking on fatherhood issues,** to share approaches, materials that work, and lessons learned. Most organisations are developing programmes for fathers in virtual isolation, with extremely limited resources, few materials, and without the support of a guiding framework from collective regional experience.

- Finally, **a developmental, rather than a deficit approach, offers a more auspicious framework for programme efforts examining fatherhood roles with men from many diverse backgrounds and in diverse family arrangements.** A *fatherwork agenda*, developed with and by men, should be the point of departure for developing support for the expressed desire of Caribbean men to learn and grow as men, as partners, as fathers, and as contributors to their communities.

Acknowledgement

This paper summarises a longer case study undertaken for the Bernard van Leer Foundation, The Hague, and is submitted with their permission. Fathers' participation with children was the focus of this review of programmes within the Caribbean region, and not the promotion of gender equity *per se*. While the author draws attention to some actual and potential outcomes which address more equitable relationships and load-share between men and women, there was no deliberate examination of the extent to which issues of gender equity have been successfully addressed by the focus on fatherhood. Further work is required to uncover initiatives that have focussed more directly on the ways in which men and women, as well as children, have benefited from these programmes, and from others with gender equity as a clear objective.

Notes

1 D. Dollahite, A. Hawkins, and S. Brotherson (1997) 'A conceptual ethic of fathering as generative work' in A. Hawkins and D. Dollahite (eds.), *Generative Fathering: Beyond Deficit Perspectives*, Newbury Park, C.A.: Sage.

2 'Partner' is the common Caribbean term used to denote wife, common-law spouse, or the steady girlfriend who may also be a 'baby-mother'(the mother of a man's children). Marriage rates in the region remain nearly 20 per cent, so the majority of children are born and remain in non-legal unions.

3 J. Brown (1989) 'Survey of Services to Young Children: a 12 Country Report', report to UNICEF, CCDC, and UWI, Mona, Jamaica.

4 J. Brown and B. Chevannes (1998) *Why Man Stay So?*, Kingston, Jamaica: UWI and UNICEF.

5 C. Branche (1998) 'Boys in Conflict: Community, Gender, Identity and Sex', paper presented at a workshop on 'Family and the Quality of Gender Relations', UWI, March 1997, Mona, Jamaica; B. Chevannes (1999) 'What You Sow is What You Reap: Problems in the Construction of Male Misidentity in Jamaica', Grace Kennedy Foundation Lecture, Kingston, Jamaica; and B. Chevannes (1996) 'Surviving Against the Current: the Real Position of Caribbean Men', paper presented at a conference on 'Caribbean Males: an Endangered Species', UWI, Mona, Jamaica.

6 W. Bailey, C. Branche, McGarrity, and S. Stuart (1998) *Family and the Quality of Gender Relations in the Caribbean,* Institute of Social and Economic Research, Mona, Jamaica: UWI; and M. Ramkissoon (2001) 'The Psychology of Fathering in the Caribbean: An Investigation of the Physical and Psychological Presence of the Jamaican Father', M.A. thesis, UWI, Mona, Jamaica.

7 C. Barrow (2002) 'Child rights and Caribbean family life: contesting the rhetoric of male marginality, female-headed households and extended family breakdown' in C. Barrow (ed.) (2002) *Children's Rights: Caribbean Realities*, Kingston, Jamaica: Ian Randle Publishers, pp. 208–9.

8 B. Chevannes (2002) 'Fatherhood in the African-Caribbean landscape: an exploration in meaning and context' in C. Barrow (2002) *op. cit.*

9 C. Branche (2002) 'Ambivalence, sexuality and violence in the construction of Caribbean masculinity: dangers for boys in Jamaica', in C. Barrow *op. cit.*, p. 89.

10 J. Brown and B. Chevannes (1998) *op. cit.*

11 B. Chevannes (2001) *Learning to be a Man*, Kingston, Jamaica: UWI Press.

12 See M. Figueroa (1996) 'Male Privileging and Male Academic Underperformance in Jamaica', paper presented at a workshop on 'Construction of Caribbean Masculinity: Towards a Research Agenda, Centre for Gender and Development Studies, St. Augustine, UWI.

13 From The Bible, Ezekiel 22: 30.

14   'Mainstreaming Gender for Development' regional consultation sponsored by UNESCO, University of the West Indies (Mona Campus), 30–31 January 2003.

15   C. Branche (1998) *op. cit.*, and M. Ramkissoon (2001) *op. cit.*

16   A social father is a man who performs fathering functions for a child or children as a member of the extended family or neighbourhood, but is not the biological father. See C. Barrow (2002) *op. cit.*

Addressing men's role in family violence:
the experience of the 'Sakhli' Women's Advice Centre, Georgia

Rusudan Pkhakadze and Nana Khoshtaria

Introduction

The 'Sakhli' Women's Advice Centre has been working since 1997 on the problem of family violence in Georgia, supported by Oxfam GB. The centre provides psychological and social counselling and legal advice to victims, works to inform public opinion and raise public awareness, and lobbies for the development of an appropriate legal framework.

As one of the post-Soviet states, Georgia is in the process of transition from a totalitarian regime to a democracy. The country is therefore undergoing significant economic, political, and social changes, which are having an impact on all aspects of public life. This chapter describes this shifting context, and in particular highlights the links between economic hardship, unemployment, and men's violence within families. It then outlines Sakhli's growing experience in tackling these issues, and concludes by setting out some ideas for the development of this work in future.

Changing gender relations in Georgia

In Georgia, transition has been accompanied by economic and political crisis. Former Soviet industries have collapsed; unemployment and inflation have soared; civil wars and ethnic conflicts have erupted across the region; and corruption has flourished. Even basic services such as energy and gas supplies have seriously deteriorated, damaging housing conditions and people's health. As a result, poverty and insecurity have become serious problems for the majority of Georgia's population. According to the Economic Development and Poverty Reduction Programme of Georgia, from 2001, 52 per cent of the population has been living below the official subsistence minimum.[1]

Gender-disaggregated data are not available with respect to poverty. However, the evidence suggests that certain population groups in which women are the majority (such as older people, internally displaced people, people with disabilities), as well as single mothers, have been increasingly marginalised.

Gender and poverty among internally displaced people

The problems facing internally displaced people are especially acute. In 2002, 55 per cent of Georgia's 264,217 internally displaced people were women.[2] They live in so-called 'organised settlement centres' in abysmal conditions, which affect their health and well-being and that of their families. Women suffer most from this situation, as they undertake most domestic labour and have to cope with the problems caused by inadequate housing (in caring for their children, for example). Many women also find paid work outside the formal labour market, and often become the main family breadwinners. In such circumstances, shifts in gender relations may occur, resulting either in a gradual renegotiation of family roles, an increase in women's authority, or in cases of domestic violence. Such changes may take place even if the women try to avoid challenging men's traditional control over family decision making.

Although in theory men and women have equal rights before the law under the Georgian Constitution (Article 14), in reality women remain subjugated to men in many spheres of life. For instance, in the legislative and executive branches of government, the rates of women's representation are very low. Only six per cent of MPs are women, and between only two and three per cent of those holding decision-making posts in the civil service. There are also few women active in political parties.

Longstanding patriarchal attitudes and behaviour patterns are firmly entrenched in Georgia, and the society remains a male-dominated one. The traditional image of a woman's role and responsibilities is that she should keep the family together, look after the children, and maintain the home. A man, meanwhile, is considered to be the head of the family, and he does not view a woman as an equal partner in family decision making.

As in other former Soviet states that gained independence following the official fall of the Soviet Union in 1991, a nationalist political discourse in Georgia has identified reproduction and housekeeping to be women's primary responsibility, and has sought to remove women from the public domain. In Georgia, as elsewhere, women have always been subject to traditional gender roles and expectations: the experience of the majority of women – that of carrying the double burden of working and caring – pre-dates the demise of the USSR, discrediting the myth that gender equality existed in Soviet times.

Shifts in gender roles are now increasingly evident. In the process of transition to a market-based economy, women appear to be not only responsible for housekeeping and childcare, but are also breadwinners. The traditional family model of male provider and female homemaker, which was standard during the Soviet era, is changing. In the middle and lower classes of society (the majority of the population), women find employment more easily than men (although such work is largely unregulated and often exploitative), whereas men are increasingly confronted with the problems of unemployment, poverty, and lack of opportunity.

In the last decade, the government and the wider public have become more aware that gender-related issues – such as inequality, discrimination, and domestic abuse – are causing serious concern and require urgent action in response. Through the activism of the women's movement and the influence of the international community, problems that were previously considered less important or non-existent have been put on the State's agenda. Women's NGOs, in particular, have been very active in running seminars, conferences, and training events, in undertaking research, and in producing publications on a wide variety of topics.

The main thrust of this growing recognition of the importance of focusing on gender has been on improving the circumstances and status of women. Raising men's awareness of (and involvement in) achieving gender equality has not been given any consideration. There is currently no understanding in Georgia of the importance of studying masculinities, or of the need to generate public debate on this issue. Major obstacles persist, including stereotypical views of gender roles and widespread indifference – not only among men, but also among women.

The nature of family violence

In 2002, Sakhli conducted a survey in Tbilisi to study public attitudes towards domestic violence. Half of the 400 participants were men and half were women.[3] The results obtained from respondents were very revealing. They showed that:

- The majority did not consider violence to be a broad social problem, but a private issue that occurs in the domestic domain and should be settled within the family (62 per cent of men, 52 per cent of women).
- Domestic violence, protection against violence, and the development of relevant legislation are more important for women then for men (50 per cent of men, 79 per cent of women).
- Economic hardship and unemployment were named as the major cause of family problems, of conflicts and domestic violence, of undermining family functioning, and of the creation tension between family members (48 per cent of men, 46 per cent of women).
- The majority of respondents, male (46 per cent) as well as female (63 per cent), consider men to be the main perpetrators of family violence.

Unfortunately, it is difficult to define precisely the extent of family violence and to identify whether it has worsened in recent years, as official statistics do not exist. But the findings of our research, together with our practical project experience, suggest that the increasingly difficult economic and political climate in Georgia is having an impact on gender relations – and that family violence may be increasing as a result.

Comparative analysis of the views of male and female respondents in the 2002 Sakhli survey showed that their attitudes to the opposite sex are mutually critical. Overall, the research revealed a tendency among men and women to interpret the behaviour of the other sex as being aggressive, and to shift responsibility for conflict onto other members of the family. Such antagonism makes attempts at conflict resolution and the prevention of domestic violence extremely hard to achieve.

An especially important finding from the research is that the majority of both women and men believe that men are the main perpetrators of family violence. This recognition leads us to argue that violent behaviour is generally perceived as an integral part of male behaviour, and as a normal feature of 'being a man'. Violence within the family is increasingly common, and is often socially condoned, or accepted as a sign of 'normal' masculinity. It is not therefore a bearer of a negative meaning for men.

Paradoxically, however, the dominant view within Georgian society is that in theory physical violence towards woman is unacceptable – indeed the results of our survey show that 84 per cent of respondents, both men and women, consider it to be inadmissible. Yet what is being referred to here is, in fact, violence outside the family. Unfortunately, there is a disparity between the widespread condemnation of violence against women in public, and an acceptance of gender-based violence in private. To combat domestic violence, it is therefore crucial to challenge such contradictory attitudes within society and to break down the boundaries of 'public' and 'private' that maintain discriminatory practices towards women.

Developing Sakhli's response

In order to increase the impact of Sakhli's work on the problems women face, we concluded that it is necessary to work with men, and to increase their awareness of, and sensitivity to, gender issues. This recognition was strongly supported by evidence from our advice and rehabilitation work that engaging with both partners of a couple was more effective in resolving family problems than working with just one (usually the woman).

Engaging men through such work helps to make them aware of the issues their spouses face, and to look at their own behaviour from the viewpoint of their wives. Once this shift in perspective happens, and men are willing to co-operate, positive changes occur. If rehabilitation is undertaken only with female victims of domestic violence, the position of the women usually improves to some extent. But family problems will not be resolved completely if male partners continue to behave in the same way.

We believe that involving men in the settlement of family conflicts and the prevention and elimination of family violence is an important aspect of work to reduce domestic violence. But in practice this is not always possible. It is often only women who are prepared to seek psychological help to address their problems. In contrast, men are usually reticent to seek expert assistance from outside in what they regard as internal 'family matters'.

Although Sakhli has not as yet established programmes specifically targeted at men, men are nevertheless increasingly involved with the organisation's work. In addition to participating in the research outlined above, men form eight to ten per cent of those obtaining advice at the centre. Men have also taken part in a range of activities to raise public awareness, including round-table debates, TV programmes, and training events. Below, we set out some examples of the activities Sakhli undertakes with men, including individual counselling and wider social action.

Counselling

In Sakhli's practice, we are mainly approached by women who suffer from domestic violence and who are materially dependent on their husbands. So far, it has been very difficult to reach out to the husbands of these women, as they are resistant, and do not acknowledge the role that counselling can play in family disputes. As indicated above, we think that at the root of their resistance is the traditional perception that whatever happens in the family is nobody else's business. However, we firmly believe that the problem of domestic violence will not be eliminated unless men are involved in initiatives to tackle domestic violence, and unless the public acknowledges domestic violence as being socially unacceptable and criminal behaviour.

Although men are only a small proportion – around one in ten – of the centre's beneficiaries, this can still be considered a relatively high figure, taking into consideration existing stereotypes and traditions. Men who come to Sakhli for support are mainly seeking help with psychological problems, depression, alcoholism, difficulties in personal relationships, unemployment, and legal issues. Several case studies are presented below, illustrating domestic violence and the results of men's involvement in rehabilitation and advice work.

Case study 1

A 46-year-old man visited the centre. He faced problems in his relationship with his wife. After ten years living together, their marriage was about to collapse. The major cause of the problems was infidelity and psychological abuse by the man. The counsellor talked to the couple separately and together in an attempt to clarify the issues and to explore the couple's common interests and problems. As a result, the couple came to understand each other's position, and expressed their willingness to make efforts to overcome the family crisis. The problem was settled, and the couple was able to maintain the marriage.

In this case, the man's initiative to ask for psychological help to resolve the family problem, and his readiness to make significant changes to maintain the family, were particularly interesting. By talking to a psychologist, he was able to identify solutions to his problems. This is not a typical case, however, and the man concerned only took the initiative in a crisis situation.

Case study 2

A 28-year-old young man visited the centre. He had been involved in an informal relationship with a woman for five years. He claimed to love her very much, and did not want to end the relationship with her, but he could not accept the fact that she had had a relationship with another man. The man seeking help felt very aggressive towards his girlfriend but, at the same time, he felt great affection for her. Being torn in two directions was undermining his emotional and psychological health. After several visits to the centre, his aggression diminished, and he came to look at his situation from a different perspective. Eventually, he managed to make a decision and, crucially, acted upon it by ending the relationship. The couple separated peacefully, and the man was able to rebuild his life.

In this case, the man considered himself to be a victim. In reality, his problem was that he wanted his partner to conform to his stereotypes and to service his needs, and he wanted the relationship to conform to his own standards. The relationship was terminated, as the young man could not accept his girlfriend's viewpoint and position. He realised that his own attitude was not wholly justified.

Case study 3

A 32-year-old woman visited the centre. She had been married for nine years and had two children (eight and six years old). If she disagreed with her husband, she was subjected to psychological, physical, and sexual violence. As a result of getting psychological assistance, significant improvements occurred – in particular her self-confidence and her trust in the psychologist increased. These improvements in the woman's self-esteem were evident within the family. Her husband noticed the change, and decided to come to the centre to try to re-establish control over the 'disobedient' wife. He attempted to get the counsellor to help him strengthen his authority over his wife, but as he was not ready to analyse his own motivations and make changes, he remained hostile to his wife and to the counsellor. Consequently, settlement of the family problem was only temporary.

As in the previous case, this case illustrates that even when improvements in the wife's situation occur, it is still difficult to settle a family problem if the husband does not see the need to change his attitudes and behaviour.

Psychological intervention gives clients the opportunity to learn more about themselves and their partners, and to see the potential for improvements in awareness and personal growth. They can get information on domestic violence and help to identify their problems; they can learn to control their own behaviour and to overcome loneliness and marginalisation. However, the problem in Georgian society remains that men do not usually seek such assistance, and their female partners cannot make them agree to receive counselling.

Wider action to prevent domestic violence

The extent and nature of domestic violence in Georgian society suggest that, in addition to individual counselling, wider preventive measures are necessary to break down men's denial and resistance. Sakhli has therefore initiated a number of activities towards this end, which are briefly described below.

Public-awareness campaign

Domestic violence was the topic for discussion at a series of four round-table debates that were held in Tbilisi in 2002, within the framework of a public-awareness raising campaign. The participants of these debates, about 80 in total, were representatives of the social services, law enforcement bodies, educators, and the mass media. The organisers paid special attention to involving men in these discussions. A TV debate was also broadcast, during which women and men discussed the causes and consequences of domestic violence.

During these events, men and women talked about the social and economic roots of violence. The participants tended to believe that rapid shifts in the division of gender roles were one of the major reasons for the violence. If men can no longer play the role of the major breadwinner in the family, they fear that they may cede control of family issues to their wives, a belief which in turn aggravates family conflict. (Alongside this perspective, it is also important to note that traditional male dominance in the family can be a cause of family violence too, and that domestic violence is not a recent problem).

The main conclusions from the discussions were that:

- men who are highly aware of gender and related issues represent a huge resource for initiating and developing work with men, and can strongly influence other men;

- activities on domestic violence and on gender issues initiated and arranged by men are more acceptable to other men;
- such work needs to be sustained if it is to reach the target audience and trigger their interest.

Sensitising the police

In Tbilisi in 2002, Sakhli piloted a project within the police service to raise staff's awareness of domestic violence. In addition to providing information about the problem, we encouraged participants (95 per cent of whom were men) to express their opinions and attitudes freely during discussions, rather than give lectures. In this way, the project succeeded in developing an atmosphere of collaboration and trust among the participants.

The police training was interesting, because it was the first ever initiative in Tbilisi with representatives of law enforcement agencies on the issue of domestic violence; in other words, with individuals widely viewed by the public as perpetrators of violence within a structure where corruption is rife. But through dialogue with the participants, it emerged that they also considered themselves to be victims of institutional violence. Of particular importance to them were the problems they face in their work in general, and in relation to domestic violence. They highlighted, for example, that they experience negative attitudes from society, which act as an obstacle in their work. They also feel unsupported by the State and the law. They feel their powers and rights are limited, they are inadequately remunerated for their work (very often they receive no remuneration at all), and their working hours are long and anti-social.

As with the general public, male police officers regard domestic violence as a private, family matter, though a number of participants recognised its wider, social aspects. But the absence of appropriate legislation on domestic violence, and of adequate methods and resources make it difficult for law-enforcement agencies to respond.

As a result of the project, it became clear that, on one hand, police-service thinking about domestic abuse and strategies to combat this problem need to be developed. On the other, intensive work needs to be undertaken to increase the public's trust in law enforcement.

Recommendations

In addition to continuing intervention at the individual level both with the victims and perpetrators of violence, there is a need to develop sensitive strategies for increasing men's gender-awareness and support for gender equality, and for challenging the widespread acceptance of domestic violence as a 'normal' aspect of life. Beyond the specific activities promoted by Sakhli, further action is required by government and other key stakeholders to explore the links between economic hardship and domestic violence, and to respond to the dominance of aggressive forms of masculinity within Georgian society.

Taking into consideration the traditions and cultural norms present in Georgian society today, a comprehensive approach might involve:

- a commitment to non-violence by individuals, communities, and government at all levels;

- a government-sponsored media campaign to increase public awareness through TV programmes and debates;

- focus-group discussions involving men and women to explore problems faced by men in Georgian society;

- legal reforms to remove the acceptance of violence;

- the development of services for the rehabilitation of victims of domestic violence and perpetrators; and

- improved information and research into the nature of masculinity, and into men's attitudes towards gender equality and gender-based violence.

Our main conclusion from working on the problem of domestic violence is that the involvement of both women and men is of prime importance if effective anti-domestic violence strategies are to be developed.

Notes

1   'Economic Development and Poverty Reduction Program of Georgia', Tbilisi, June 2003, p. 11.

2   Source: 'IDP's Reference Book', Migrant Association, Georgia Ministry of Refugees and Accommodation (2002) Tbilisi: Pirveli Stamba, p. 395.

3   The full distribution of respondents was as follows:
> by age group: 23–35 (49.8 per cent); 35–50 (39 per cent); older than 50 (21.3 per cent);
> by the amount of individual income per month: about $20 (17.3 per cent); $20–50 (19.3 per cent); $50–100 (16 per cent); $200 (32.8 per cent); without individual income (14.8 per cent).
>
> The great majority (90 per cent) of respondents were Georgian. The share of other nationalities (Russians and Armenians) constituted 10 per cent of respondents.

'Liberation for everyone, not just men'
A case study of the Men's Association Against Violence (AMKV) in Timor Leste[1]

Mario De Araujo

Two days after Asosiaun Mane Kontra Violensia (Men's Association Against Violence – AMKV) was established, we held a press conference. TV reporters covered the event, and news of the press conference was broadcast on Timor Leste TV. The next day, we received congratulations from women's organisations – but from men we received insults. One said, 'You in the AMKV are all a bunch of queers,' another said, 'What a strange world this is where instead of supporting each other, men are defending women's rights.'

This, unfortunately, is the mindset of many men in Timor Leste. In our new era of independence, which follows 24 years of violent struggle against Indonesia accompanied by unrelenting human-rights violations, the rights of East Timorese women remain largely neglected. The continuing severity of gender inequality raises the fundamental question: has independence in Timor Leste resulted in liberation for men only?

Gender inequality issues in Timor Leste may have their solution in the future, but their roots are embedded in the past. Timor Leste is a strongly patriarchal society. Men have complete control and dominate all aspects of social, economic, and political life. Men are the unchallenged decision makers in affairs relating to tradition, law, and custom. This unchecked power results in men having the freedom to do whatever they want. At its most extreme, this power extends to having control over the life and death of a woman.

Domestic violence in Timor Leste is very common. A study conducted in 2003 reported that 43 per cent of women had experienced at least one incident of violence by their partner in the last year.[2] Police figures suggest that between 40 and 50 per cent of all incidents reported involve domestic violence.[3] As in many other countries around the world, this type of behaviour by men towards women is tolerated, as there is a widespread view that culture or tradition allows a husband to 'educate' his wife and children by whatever means necessary.[4]

This chapter begins by describing how violence became rooted so strongly in Timor Leste, and how the Men's Association Against Violence was established to counter it. It then describes the aims of the organisation, its links with women's groups, and its activities, both in the field and nationally. Although AMKV's

140

work is still developing, the chapter concludes with some reflections on what has been learned from the work so far.

Establishing the Men's Association Against Violence

The Indonesian occupation created a culture of violence in Timor Leste. The use of violence and force was promoted as an acceptable way of resolving individual or group problems and disputes. Violence against women, including the rape and torture of women and girls, was used as a deliberate tactic by the Indonesian military and police to achieve political and psychological advantage over the population. While cases have been recorded of violence against women perpetrated by the East Timor Resistance fighters and the Japanese army in World War II, the number of cases was small, and the tactic was used less systematically than during the Indonesian occupation.

This history of disrespect for the rights of women in periods of conflict, and also in their homes in times of peace, has resigned women to believe that they have no rights and no control over their own lives. If this situation is allowed to continue, the gender inequality facing Timorese women and girls will continue to grow, and our new nation will never achieve true independence.

The legacy of violence against the Timorese people, including the unacceptably high level of gender-based discrimination and violence (mainly perpetrated by men against women and children) provided the motivation for the establishment of the Men's Association Against Violence in June 2002.

AMKV was founded by 20 concerned men from various parts of the country, the majority of whom had participated in an international exchange on gender-based violence held in March and April 2002. The exchange, organised by a national NGO (La'o Hamutuk) and Oxfam Community Aid Abroad, brought Timorese men into contact with Puntos dos Encuentros, a men's group from Nicaragua that is working against violence in a post-conflict, *machismo* culture. During the exchange, Puntos dos Encuentos conducted training with 38 male participants on gender, violence, and masculinity. This workshop encouraged the participants to confront and reflect on their behaviour towards the women in their families and as a society.

The workshop had two main outcomes. First, it provided an opportunity for men to discuss violence and discrimination against women, a subject that many of the participants had reflected on but never discussed openly with other men. As one said, 'I have seen the suffering of my mother and I have seen that women's life is harder, but I have never talked to other men about it'. Second, a proportion of the participants were sufficiently inspired by the work of Puntos dos Encuentros to want to work together to address the problem in Timor Leste. 'I suppose I wanted to tell and show other men that you could change,' said another participant. 'I also wanted to change. I don't want to hurt the women in my life or see them hurt by others … now in Timor we have the space, peace, and opportunity do this.'

The vision of AMKV is to build a democratic, independent, and just society, free from violence and discrimination. It aims to raise the awareness of men and women about gender-based violence, and to eradicate such violence from all levels of society. AMKV seeks to achieve this by running community-based education and discussion forums, undertaking advocacy, and building an effective network bringing together community groups, national non-government organisations, and the government.

From the outset, AMKV was committed to supporting the substantial work already being done on gender and gender-based violence by women's groups in Timor Leste. The response of women activists to our organisation and programme has been very positive, and we recognise that the very existence of AMKV is an endorsement of the work of women's organisations in the past to raise awareness of gender inequality. 'Having men involved in gender is a relief,' one women activist remarked, 'If in all our districts men did what you are doing, then East Timor would be a peaceful society. We wholeheartedly support this initiative and you must go into the remote areas to share your experiences with the men there.'

AMKV works in close co-operation with women's groups and government departments that are promoting gender equality. We share funding and resources, enter into collaborative programming, and belong to the National Movement Against Violence. As AMKV is still a small volunteer group, the extent of our activities and amount of funding we have required until now is relatively small compared with the larger women's groups. The close working relationship we have with other groups working on domestic violence (including women's groups) has created opportunities for collaboration on awareness campaigns, and has also prevented competition over resources.

AMKV's activities

Initially, AMKV set up a national volunteer structure involving men from all over the country. The volunteers would facilitate communication and co-ordinate activities in their districts. In addition to formally establishing the Association, we planned the first stages of a five-year campaign against gender-based violence, to be carried out in collaboration with women's groups across the country.

Internally, we recognised that key to our success would be the capacity of AMKV members to make positive changes in their own lives. We established a monthly reflection meeting for our members. In this meeting we discuss cases of discrimination and violence against women, but we also analyse our own behaviour towards women. We encourage our members to get feedback from their wives and families, and in general our families are very supportive of our work with AMKV. Not all members have found this process easy, and if it becomes clear that a particular man has no commitment to controlling his own violence, then we would ask him to leave. However, in most cases the other members are able to provide the positive reinforcement needed to sustain the changes.

AMKV's main activity is to conduct weekend discussion forums in communities and high schools, always involving participants of both sexes. Before the forums started, we were apprehensive as to how people would receive us and whether we would be able to influence their beliefs or behaviour – especially for male participants. We were acutely aware that men are usually the perpetrators of violence, so would they feel threatened? Would they be willing to change? We reflected on our own behaviour: we used to be like that and then slowly, with guidance from other men's groups and each other, we changed. The answer was simple: if we can change, then so can others.

Using a popular education approach, we focus on domestic violence and problems related to the tradition and customs that influence our perceptions of gender. We use common situations that would be familiar to the participants, and we talk about our own personal experiences of change. We always promote examples of practical and realistic behaviour-change, so that on leaving the forums participants have the knowledge to make immediate change in their own lives. There are often heated debates during the discussions, but there is also a lot of humour and goodwill as participants reflect on the origins of their traditions, beliefs, and behaviour around gender differences.

In a discussion in a village on the topic of housework, one man remarked, 'Some of the things you've talked about, I have done ever since I got married. For instance, when my wife gave birth, I washed and cooked and even bathed her. That's nothing out of the ordinary for me – because we have to understand the circumstances our wives are in.' When a man like this comes forward – and inevitably they do in each discussion – we use his story to disprove the theory that tradition dictates our actions, and encourage participants to see that they have the power to control their own behaviour. We take the analysis further by asking the man who has stood up whether he would be willing to support his girl children to be educated and his wife to have a voice in village decision making. Most importantly we ask him, 'Are you willing to eliminate the use of violence in your household and your village?'. Our experiences with these activities are varied, but generally communities are enthusiastic, even though participants are asked to reflect critically upon and to challenge themselves and their society.

AMKV is also involved in gender advocacy. We have lobbied the Gender Advisory Unit within the Department of Education to remove gender bias from school materials from primary to tertiary levels. We have also been involved in drafting the legislation on domestic violence, and we monitor gender-based violence in the criminal courts.

These activities have generated some criticism and ridicule from men in different sectors. Ridicule is directed at our sexuality and it is common for people to think that we are gay. Criticism comes from colleagues and friends who believe that we should be using our energy and influence to tackle other more pressing developmental issues such as poverty reduction, sustainable livelihoods, and economic empowerment. On the other hand, we increasingly receive positive feedback from key national figures such as the President, members of parliament, the police, and departmental ministers. At the community level, there are men who are responsive and willing to be involved. However, at all levels of Timorese society, there is still a high level of disinterest and apathy around issues of gender and gender-based violence.

Lessons from our experience

From the activities undertaken by AMKV, we have learned that it is important to explore everyday issues in discussion, and at the same time, to give examples of positive experiences and change from other regions of the country. We realised early on that talking about textbook analysis or gender theory did not interest participants, and often resulted in conflict between the men and women present. High levels of illiteracy also impact on our approach to the discussions. Feedback from participants reveals that they prefer to learn and explore issues through drama, and by analysing everyday situations that occur in their village or lives. We attempt to engage their emotions during the session, for example we ask them, 'If your daughter was rejected for a job because she was female how would you feel? Is it fair? If it is not fair, why does it happen? Who makes the rules?' 'Men'.

AMKV uses a strong human-rights approach in talking about gender-based violence. AMKV has been established at a time when people in Timor Leste, exhausted by years of constant violence and conflict, have a strong commitment to protecting human rights. The Constitution, of which East Timorese are very proud, enshrines the rights of all people, and of women in particular. We use this passion and commitment to human rights to promote good citizenship.

We point out that domestic violence is a violation of human rights, and that under the Constitution of Timor Leste it is considered a crime, and can result in imprisonment.

We use this process to talk about all forms of violence in communities. We explore with participants the reasons that people solve their problems with violence. We explain that violence is a learned response that has been passed from generation to generation. In role-plays, we ask people to act out a violent argument. Invariably, participants comment that, to an outsider observer, the aggressor humiliates himself when he allows himself to get out of control. Most people don't realise that they are humiliating themselves when they are violent. Even more surprising is that many participants don't know what alternatives there are to using violence. By exploring their options with them, we hope that in a small way we have given people some confidence and tools to make changes.

A central component of our programme is the ongoing commitment of the volunteer network. It is important that the volunteers have made positive changes to achieve gender equity in their own lives, and that their personal behaviour reflects this before they go out to discuss gender in the communities. We use peer-monitoring and we mentor each other on this issue, recognising that hypocrisy would destroy our programme and the credibility of AMKV with communities and with other organisations.

In reflecting on our programme, we have come to the conclusion that sharing experiences with groups through discussions is not sufficient to bring about sustainable change, and that this programme alone will not necessarily engage people living in severe poverty.[5] There is a need to combine action on gender with other entry points in communities, such as income-generation pro-grammes and other economic and social support initiatives that address men's and women's real needs in practical ways. Our next challenge is to explore how we can do this, while retaining an informal volunteer structure. It is also our hope that in the coming year we can convince our wives to be part of the network, in so doing strengthening people's confidence that change is really possible.

AMKV recognises that we have a long way to go both as an organisation and as men working in the field of gender. We too are susceptible to the cultural norms of the society we live in, and it is a constant battle to be questioning long-held beliefs and customs against strong opposition. Even with the guidance and support of a Timor Leste women's movement, it will be a long and difficult journey to be accepted by both men and women alike. However the history of resistance in Timor is strong, and in a new era of nationhood we are optimistic, and determined that liberation will be for everyone, not just for men!

Acknowledgements

The author wishes to thank colleagues in Oxfam CAA, Australia: Keryn Clark, Inga Mepham, Antonius Maria Indrianto, Sebastiana da Costa Pereira, and Zubaedah. He would also like to thank his wife Teresa Costa and his family, who always support his attempts for greater gender equality in his home and country.

AMKV is grateful for funding received from Oxfam CAA, Australia and UNIFEM.

Notes

1   Timor Leste, officially named the República Democrática de Timor-Leste, is also known as East Timor.

2   International Rescue Committee (IRC) (2003) 'Prevalence of Gender Based Violence in Timor Leste', author: Vijaya Joshi. The research sample size was 365 women.

3   Timor Leste Domestic Violence Legislation Policy Paper, December 2002.

4   In a study by Oxfam in Covalima district of Timor Leste, it was found that it was common for men and women to see violence as a legitimate form of education: 'Underlying Causes of Gender Inequality in Cocalima District', 2003.

5   Timor Leste has the lowest HDI ranking in East Asia, and is one of the poorest nations in the world.

How do we know if men have changed?
Promoting and measuring attitude change with young men: lessons from Program H in Latin America

Gary Barker with Marcos Nascimento, Márcio Segundo, and Julie Pulerwitz

Introduction

'Program H' is an initiative developed in Latin America to promote more gender-equitable attitudes among young men. It works in both group educational settings and at the community level to change community norms about what it means to be a man. The initiative is called Program H because of the Spanish word for man – *hombres,* and the Portuguese *homens.* In addition to educational sessions and community campaigns, the initiative also includes an innovative evaluation model for identifying and attempting to assess changes in attitude resulting from project activities.

Program H tries first and foremost to tap into the 'alternative' voices that exist in low-income communities, that is, young and adult men who have been questioning traditional views of what it means to be a man. These voices of resistance to the dominant versions of masculinity helped us to develop a set of objectives (what we expect or hope from young men after their participation in the initiative) and to develop an evaluation methodology. The entire process has been developed with young men from several low-income communities in Brazil and in Mexico, who helped us to define project objectives, test and develop the materials, and offer ongoing advice on how to reach other young men with messages about gender equality.

Learning to be men

It is useful to present some of the assumptions and background research that led to the Program H initiative. Although there are tremendous variations across cultures, we know that views about what it means to be a man and a woman are rooted in children's earliest experiences. In nearly all societies, a key aspect of gender socialisation and a source of gender inequality is that mothers and other women or girls are mainly responsible for caring for babies and children. This means that boys and girls generally come to see caring as a 'female' task.

By the age of two or three, children imitate the behaviour of same-sex family members. Mothers, fathers, and other family members usually encourage boys to imitate other boys and men, while discouraging them from imitating girls and women. Boys who observe their fathers and other men being violent towards women or treating women as inferior may believe that this is 'normal' male behaviour. Similarly, in observing their families, boys may believe that doing domestic work and taking care of others is women's work.

Studies from around the world confirm that from an early age, girls are generally kept closer to their mothers and to home, while boys are encouraged to spend most of their time outside the home. In their adolescent years, boys in many cultural settings spend more time outside the home in male or mostly-male peer groups.

These early childhood and adolescent experiences may have a lifelong impact in terms of how men treat women. This means that promoting change among young men has a potentially powerful impact on their lives, in the present and in the future, and on the lives of their partners.

But socialisation is a complex process. Cultural norms about what it means to be a man or a woman are filtered through the family, the peer group, the community, and the individual. Boys and girls are not passive learners, or 'sponges' of cultural norms. Instead, they filter experiences and construct their own meaning from them. Indeed, boys and men – and women and girls – have the ability to question traditional gender norms, and many do.

Even in settings where traditional notions of gender may be predominant, we see alternative views. In a survey carried out with 749 men in low-income areas of Rio de Janeiro, Brazil, up to two-thirds of young men believed that violence against women was acceptable when a woman was unfaithful, and a quarter of all men aged 15–60 had used physical violence at least once against an intimate female partner.[1] However, while many men in this study had used physical violence against a partner, and many men supported such violence, a large number did not. In focus-group discussions and individual interviews, we heard many justifications for men's use of violence against women or for men not participating in the care of their children. But we also heard other voices – of young and adult men who question the traditional views around them. For example, we met João, a young father aged 19, whose words and actions displayed a dedication to his daughter, and who said this:

'... there's this guy who's a friend of mine, and he had a girlfriend, and she got pregnant, and he abandoned her when she was pregnant, and he never liked to work, he doesn't do anything, just takes from his mother. So, his girlfriend had the baby and he doesn't work at all. He doesn't give anything to the baby,

nothing for the girl, doesn't want to work. My point of view is different.
I think about working because I want to have a family, a really good family.
I want to be there when they need me, accepting my responsibilities. Even if
I were to separate from the mother of my daughter and have another wife,
I'm not gonna forget about my daughter. She'll always be first ... But lots of
young guys, they don't think about working, just think about stealing, using
drugs, smoking. Here that's normal. But ... not me – I stay away from that,
drugs and smoking and stuff. They can think I'm square, so I'll be square then.'
(Barker 2000a)

Indeed, in many settings, boys and men are able to question traditional views about manhood and show different attitudes, including treating women as equals in the home and in the workplace. It is these voices of resistance, or more 'gender-equitable' men, as we have called them, who have offered us tremendous insights on how to promote change and who have inspired Program H.

What, then, do we know about promoting change in terms of gender norms among men? As a starting point, we know that new social ideals of manhood have emerged in various parts of the world, spurred in large part by women's increasing participation in the labour force and by the women's rights movement, and also by some men questioning their relatively limited roles in the lives of their families. We also know that changes in gender norms and individual attitudes are often gradual, with old and new paradigms existing simultaneously. In addition, several studies from Latin America confirm a continuing gap between men's discourse about gender roles and their actual behaviour.[2] In other words, men sometimes pretend to change in terms of gender equality, but their actions suggest otherwise.

In reviewing the literature, there seem to be various common factors contributing to changes in men's attitudes and behaviour related to gender and gender roles. One study in Chile found that men who showed more gender-equitable patterns of behaviour reported having fathers or mothers who carried out non-traditional gender roles or tasks. For some men, knowledge mattered; having experience of seeing men caring for children or carrying out other domestic tasks was a useful step towards carrying out these tasks themselves.[3] Another study from Chile found that men sometimes changed in terms of gender roles and norms when they started new relationships, or in other special circumstances, such as the birth of a first child.[4]

Life histories researched by Program H with young men in a low-income setting in Brazil found that there were similar factors associated with young men who showed more support for gender equality:

- being part of an alternative male peer group that supported more gender-equitable attitudes;

- having personally reflected on or experienced pain or negative consequences as a result of traditional aspects of manhood (for example, having a father who used violence against the mother, or a father who abandoned the family); and

- having a family member or meaningful male role model (or female role model) who showed alternative gender roles.

The following quote from Gustavo, aged 18, from a low-income neighbourhood in Rio de Janeiro, hints at the personal reflection that we saw in many of the young men who showed alternative views of masculinity:

> '... a lot of guys will have a have a girlfriend, then they'll go and cheat on her. So then later when they want to find a girlfriend, it'll be difficult. Because then the girls will think, "Does this guy want to be with me, and then he'll go with someone else?" So then girls don't want to go out with him. So then the guy will start to think, and he'll go slowly. He'll start going out with just one girl.' (Barker 2000a)

The Program H intervention

About Program H

These examples of resistance and reflection, combined with our research and direct experience of working with men in various parts of the Americas region, led to the formation of 'Program H – Engaging Young Men in the Promotion of Health and Gender Equity'. Program H is theoretically based, and has been empirically shown to positively influence attitudes related to gender equality, including greater sensitivity to issues of gender-based violence, increased intention to use condoms, improved partner-negotiation skills, increased attention to health needs, and a greater desire to be more involved as fathers (for those young men who are already fathers). The initiative was developed in 1999, by four Latin American NGOs with significant experience of working with young men: Instituto Promundo (co-ordinator of the initiative, based in Rio de Janeiro, Brazil), ECOS (in São Paulo, Brazil), Instituto PAPAI (Recife, Brazil), and Salud y Género (Mexico).

Program H focuses on helping young men question traditional norms related to masculinity. It consists of four components:

- a field-tested curriculum that includes a series of manuals and an educational video for promoting attitude and behaviour change among men;

- a lifestyle social-marketing campaign for promoting changes in community or social norms related to what it means to be a man;

- an action-research methodology for reducing barriers to young men's use of health services; and

- a culturally relevant, validated evaluation model (the GEM Scale: Gender-equitable Men Scale) for measuring changes in attitudes and social norms around masculinity.

These components were developed using our baseline research, mentioned above, which identified important implications for the programme: firstly, the need to offer young men opportunities to interact with gender-equitable role models in their own community setting; and secondly, the need to promote more gender-equitable attitudes in small-group contexts and in the wider community. Our research also confirmed the need to intervene at the level of individual attitude and behaviour change, and at the level of social or community norms, including among parents, service providers, and others who influence individual attitudes and behaviours. In sum, given that gender norms are promoted at the community level, we work with community leaders and through youth culture to promote positive change. And we work with individual young men to enhance their ability to question some of the negative views about what it means to be a man.

The Program H manual series

The activities in the manual series are designed to be carried out in a same-sex group setting, and generally with men as facilitators, who also serve as gender-equitable role models for the young men. First and foremost, the activities in the manuals and the group educational process focus on creating a safe space to allow young men to question traditional views about masculinity.

The activities described in the manuals reinforce each other, and make appropriate links between the specific activities and themes. The activities consist of role-plays, brainstorming exercises, discussion sessions, and individual reflections about how boys and men are socialised, positive and negative aspects of this socialisation, and the benefits of changing certain behaviours. The themes used in the manuals were selected based on a review of the literature on the health and development of boys and an international survey of programmes working with young men, in collaboration with the World Health Organisation.[5]

The themes of the manuals are

1 sexual and reproductive health;

2 violence and violence prevention (including prevention of gender-based violence);

3   reasons and emotions, which focuses on mental-health issues and young men, particularly communication skills, dialogue, emotional intelligence, and substance abuse;

4   fatherhood and caring, which encourages young men to reconsider their roles in care-giving in the family, including caring for children;

5   HIV/AIDS, including both prevention and caring.

The manuals are printed in Portuguese, Spanish, and English, and are currently widely used in Latin America by NGOs and by government ministries of health.

Educational video

The manuals are accompanied by a no-words cartoon video, called 'Once Upon a Boy', which presents the story of a young man from early childhood, through adolescence, to early adulthood. Scenes include the young man witnessing violence in his home; interactions with his male peer group; social pressures to behave in certain ways in order to be seen as a 'real man'; the young man's first unprotected sexual experience; having a sexually transmitted infection (STI); and facing an unplanned pregnancy. The video was developed in workshops with young men in diverse settings in Latin America and the Caribbean.

Being a cartoon, the video quickly engages young men, and easily transfers across cultures. And because it has no words, facilitators work with young men to create dialogue and to project their personal stories into the video. The video uses a pencil as a metaphor for gender socialisation, erasing certain kinds of behaviour or thoughts. After viewing the video, young men discuss how they were socialised or raised to act as men, and ways in which they can question some negative aspects of that socialisation. The video has been nominated for numerous awards in Brazil, and is currently used as part of the Brazilian National AIDS Program.

The manuals and the video were field-tested with 271 young men aged between 15 and 24, in six countries in Latin America and the Caribbean (Brazil, Peru, Mexico, Bolivia, Colombia, and Jamaica). Qualitative results of field-testing found that participation in the activities led to increased empathy, reduced conflict among participants, and positive reflection among them about how they treated their female partners. One young man who participated in the field-test process in Peru said, 'After the activities, we came to see the ways we are *machista* ... you know, treat women unfairly.' Another young man said, 'I realised how I sometimes became violent, because that's the way I was treated. I saw the connection.'

In addition to Latin America, where more than 20 countries use the materials, training in the use of the Program H manuals has been carried out in Asia and the USA. In Brazil and Mexico, Program H materials are being used in collaboration with the public-health sector to make the approach part of national adolescent health-promotion activities. With support from a number of international organisations, including Oxfam GB and the Ford Foundation, the Program H Brazilian partners – Promundo, Instituto PAPAI, and ECOS – have recently formed a network of NGOs in the north and northeast of Brazil to implement Program H activities with diverse populations, including men of African descent, men in the Amazon region, and men in low-income areas in shantytowns around Brasilia.

Lifestyle social-marketing campaign component

In addition to the Program H curriculum, Promundo, JohnSnowBrazil (an international consulting firm), and SSL International (makers of Durex condoms) have developed a 'lifestyle social marketing' process for promoting a more gender-equitable lifestyle among men in a given cultural setting. This involves working with men themselves to identify their preferred sources of information, identifying young men's cultural outlets in the community, and developing media messages – in the form of radio spots, billboards, posters, postcards, and dances – to make it 'cool' to be a more 'gender-equitable' man. JohnSnowBrasil and Promundo have worked with SSL International to incorporate these ideas into campaigns which are currently ongoing in Rio de Janeiro and Brasilia, with expansion planned for other major cities in Brazil, Mexico, and in parts of Asia. The campaign encourages young men to reflect on how they act as men, and enjoins them to respect their partners, not to use violence against women, and to practice safer sex. We have engaged several major rap artists in Brazil to endorse the campaign – which they have called a 'campaign against *machismo*' – and have presented it during various concerts in Brasilia and Rio de Janeiro. In 2003, the project was nominated for an award for innovations in HIV/AIDS prevention by the Global Business Council on HIV/AIDS.

The campaign taps into youth culture – music, theatre, and a knowledge of where young people hang out – to promote more gender-equitable versions of manhood. Just as many private-sector advertising campaigns seek to promote a lifestyle associated with their product, the lifestyle social-marketing campaign uses mass media and youth culture to promote a gender-equitable lifestyle among young men. In Brazil, the campaign has been called '*Hora* H', or 'In the Heat of the Moment'. The phrase was developed by young men themselves, who frequently heard their peers say, 'Everybody knows you shouldn't hit your girlfriend, but in the heat of the moment you lose control', or, 'Everybody knows that you should use a condom, but in the heat of the moment ... '. Campaign slogans use language from the community, and images are of young men from the same communities, acting in ways that support gender equality.

Developing the GEM scale: measuring change

Program H believes it is important to evaluate the work from the start. In part, this is to measure impact – do these programme components actually lead to change? But it is also important to have a greater understanding of how change takes place, and to bear in mind clear objectives for the change we want to produce. Too often, we start our work with men and women with unclear or unrealistic objectives.

Identifying outcomes

The first step in the development of Program H and its evaluation component, was to define the kind of attitudes and behaviours we wanted to promote. We asked ourselves, what did we really want to accomplish? What kind of change was possible and desirable in the settings in which we work? From our baseline research, we identified four characteristics of more 'gender-equitable' young men – attitudes that we observed among some young men in the communities in which we work. We concluded that if some young men in these settings had achieved these alternative and positive views, their attitudes could serve as our benchmark.

Specifically, the Program H activities seek to encourage young men to act in the following ways:

1   to seek relationships with women based on equality and intimacy, rather than sexual conquest. This includes believing that men and women have equal rights, and that women have as much sexual desire and 'right' to sexual agency as do men;

2   to seek to be involved fathers, for those who are fathers, or to support substantial involvement; meaning that they believe that they should take both financial and at least some caring responsibility for their children;

3   to assume some responsibility for reproductive health and disease-prevention issues. This includes taking the initiative to discuss reproductive-health concerns with their partner, using condoms, or assisting their partner in acquiring or using a contraceptive method;

4   to oppose violence against women. This may include young men who were physically violent toward a female partner in the past, but who currently believe that violence against women is not acceptable behaviour.[6]

These objectives are based on interviews with and observation of young men who acted in these ways. As such, our evaluation model is grounded in the real-life behaviour and attitudes of young men, and not in an idealised or theoretical idea of what more gender-equitable behaviour and attitudes should be. To be sure, we have prioritised certain outcomes over others, but these benchmarks are based on young men's actual gender-equitable attitudes and behaviours, and not on a list of desired behaviours which may have little to do with young men's lives.

The desired outcomes are also based on our ongoing discussion and interaction with a group of young men who serve as peer promoters and advisers to us. They have also emerged from listening to adult and young women in the communities, who affirmed that these were the attitudes they wanted from men. And they are based in part on international human rights and women's rights declarations and conventions, including, for example, the Programme of Action of the International Conference on Population and Development, held in Cairo in 1994.

The GEM scale

We used these four desired outcomes to develop indicators in the form of a scale of questions about attitude. It is important to emphasise that the scale, or group of attitude questions, is only one part of our evaluation. We also carry out interviews and discussions with group facilitators, with young men who participate in the groups, with young women who are the girlfriends of the young men, and with public-health staff and other professionals working with young people.

The scale of questions is particularly useful, however, because it can be used with a large number of young men in a relatively short amount of time. It is not perfect, of course, and it fails to capture much of the rich detail that focus groups and in-depth individual interviews can. However, when time and resources are scarce, the attitude questions can be a relatively fast way to get a general sense of whether the young men who participate in these activities are changing in positive ways. And, by being able to apply the questions to a large number of young men, the data is useful for influencing policy makers, who are often interested in achieving large-scale impact.

Briefly, the GEM Scale – or Gender-equitable Men Scale – consists of about 35 attitude questions related to gender roles in the home, including childcare; gender roles in sexual relationships; shared responsibility for reproductive health and disease-prevention; intimate-partner violence; and homosexuality and close relationships with other men. Attitude questions or statements included affirmations of traditional gender norms, such as: 'Men are always ready to have sex', 'A woman's most important role is to take care of her home and cook for her family', and 'There are times when a woman deserves to be beaten'. They also included affirmations of more gender-equitable views, such as, 'A man and a woman should decide together what type of contraceptive to use', and 'It is important that a father is present in the lives of his children, even if he is no longer with the mother'. These attitude questions were based on the four objectives, as well as a review of the literature on gender norms and socialisation among young men.

The attitude questions were tested in a community-based survey, and data from this sample were used to test the usefulness of the items and to create the final scale. For each item, three answer choices were provided: I agree; I partially agree; and I do not agree. The baseline study was carried out in three communities in Rio de Janeiro, two of which were low-income areas and one of which was a middle-income neighbourhood.

The research team, consisting entirely of male interviewers, used a questionnaire with a total of 749 men aged between 15 and 60, with young men aged between 15 and 24 being over-sampled to allow for greater analysis. The questionnaire was administered via a household survey to a random sample of men in each of the three neighbourhoods. The survey also included questions relating to a number of variables that were theoretically linked to gender-equitable norms, including socio-demographic status, relationship history, history of physical violence, and current safer-sex behaviours. These questions are not part of the GEM Scale, but are used to analyse statistical associations, and in some cases as outcome indicators themselves (such as self-reported condom use, self-reported use of violence against partners, and self-reported use of health services in the last three months). Some of these questions (for example, on self-reported use of violence against a partner) were adapted from several existing international questionnaires (from the WHO, among others), which allows us to compare our data to studies on young men in other settings. Focus groups also allowed us to test the concepts and to identify new questions. The refusal rate was less than two percent.

This baseline research confirmed the coherence of the attitude questions, that is, that young men answered in fairly internally consistent ways. For example, a young man who said he tolerated or even supported violence against women was also likely to show traditional or male-dominant views on other questions, such as believing that taking care of children is exclusively a woman's responsibility. In addition, the ways in which young men answered the questions were correlated to the ways in which they said they acted: a young man who showed *machista* attitudes about gender was likely to say he acted that way in his daily life.[7]

In summary, our baseline research confirmed that the GEM Scale is a useful tool for assessing where men are on these issues, and to assess their current attitudes about gender roles, and it is also useful for measuring whether men have changed their attitudes over time, or after a given project. We found that young men's attitudes were highly correlated with one of our key outcomes: self-reported use of violence against women.

The significant associations found between the GEM Scale and important health outcomes such as partner violence and contraceptive use supports the contention that the scale is valid. Other implications of these analyses are also of note: the research confirms that young men's attitudes about relationships with women and about gender norms matter. They are not merely parroting the values they perceive around them, but in many cases internalise or adhere to these norms and act on them, often with negative consequences for their partners and for themselves. These associations indicate that support for gender-equitable norms and behaviour is an important aspect of reproductive and sexual-health decision making, and that gender-related norms should be explicitly addressed when designing and implementing effective prevention programmes for HIV and STIs, unplanned pregnancy, and violence.

Impact evaluation

In 2002, with the GEM Scale validated or tested, PROMUNDO and the Horizons Program started a two-year impact-evaluation study to measure the impact of the manuals and video in a population of 750 young men aged between 15 and 24 in Rio de Janeiro, Brazil. The study included three groups of young men in different (but fairly homogeneous) low-income communities. With each group of young men, the activities were carried out with various levels of intensity (14 hours of activities in one group, 28 hours in another, and group activities combined with an intensive lifestyle social-marketing campaign in a third). In one of the communities, the intervention was delayed, with the evaluation questionnaire being used twice before any intervention was carried out. This allowed us to increase the possibility that any attitude or behaviour change measured was the result of the intervention, rather than due to other factors.

Analysis of the results from one of the communities, from about 160 question-naires, found positive change on a majority of GEM Scale questions, and increased condom use. While final results from the study will not be available until 2004, these initial results already confirm that Program H interventions have a positive impact on attitudes related to gender, and that the GEM Scale is a relevant and valid model for measuring this change. Qualitative methods, including interviews with young men, with those who know them, and with their female partners, are being used to triangulate or compare to the quantitative results.

Some young men, in in-depth interviews after their participation in the activities, told us that the workshops had helped them question their views about masculinity. One young man said:

> '... *I learned to talk more with my girlfriend. Now I worry more about her (worry about what she likes sexually). Our sex life is better ... it's important to know what the other persons wants, listen to them. Before [the workshops], I just worried about myself.'*

This same young man's girlfriend, in a separate interview, confirmed that he had in fact started to talk to her more, to listen to when and how she wanted to have sexual relations, and to see that having sex was not the only important part of their relationship. Another young man also said that he began to respect his girlfriend more, saying:

> '*Used to be when I went out with a girl, if we didn't have sex within two weeks of going out, I would leave her. But now [after the workshops], I think differently. I want to construct something [a relationship with her].'*

In addition to evaluating the impact on attitude and behaviour change, we are carrying out an analysis of the cost-effectiveness of Program H. A very preliminary analysis of the costs associated with the intervention suggests that a typical Program H project in an urban area with a population between 500,000 and one million inhabitants indirectly reaches approximately 20,000 young men (target population ages 15–24) with messages related to sexual and reproductive-health promotion, HIV/AIDS-prevention, and gender equity; directly reaches 2000 young men involved in project activities; and reaches 15,000 men with condoms (with more than 100,000 condoms sold). The project also indirectly benefits approximately 10,000 young women who are the partners of the young men. Total annual, unduplicated, project beneficiaries are approximately 30,000 young people. Annual operational costs (excluding start-up costs) to implement project activities and achieve attitude and behaviour change in an urban setting of between 500,000 and one million inhabitants range from US$150,000 to US$200,000.[8] More precise cost-effectiveness figures will be available in 2004, but these numbers offer a rough idea of the scope and cost of the interventions. We believe it is important to have these costs – and benefits – analysed, to demonstrate that changes in young men's attitudes and behaviour are achievable, and positive for both men and women.

Conclusions and recommendations

Given the short timescale of many interventions with young men, it is often unrealistic to expect changes in behaviour, and difficult to measure such change. The GEM Scale thus provides a potentially more sensitive evaluation instrument for measuring the attitude changes that suggest a movement or change in the direction of gender equality on the part of young men. The work of Program H suggests that attitude and behaviour change are possible to achieve, but require work at the individual, community, and policy levels.

While the examples reported here are from Latin America, initial testing of the GEM Scale and the use of the Program H components is starting in other parts of the world. Testing of the GEM Scale items and the development of culturally appropriate tools is starting in Mumbai, India, with the Horizons Program, working in collaboration with a network of youth-serving organisations. Local researchers report that the areas of gender norms and masculinity that are currently being addressed in the Brazil study appear relevant for the Indian context. Other issues which were not addressed in Brazil – such as concerns about sexual performance – were raised as being particularly relevant in India, and will be added to the intervention topics and included in the evaluation of the intervention. Initial project development in India found that youth groups in low-income settings in Mumbai often galvanise around a leader, and their behaviours are to a great extent determined by shared norms and beliefs. The study group plans to recruit young men from a selection of these groups.[9]

Clearly, no scale or intervention can include all the variables related to promoting gender equality among young men. Nonetheless, the steps and components of Program H and the GEM Scale are rooted in the norms and attitudes related to gender that exist in a given cultural setting. In addition, they focus on change at the individual and social levels, with a clear vision of the kinds of more gender-equitable norms that men and women in the same communities say they want.

In terms of final recommendations, our experience suggests the following:

- Programmes working with men to promote gender equality should rely on the voices of men and women at the community level to develop realistic indicators or outcome-measures. The alternative voices of men who show greater equality should inform programme development. These young men should also be engaged at all levels of programme development.

- Evaluation must include both individual men, who can be encouraged to question and reflect about traditional views, and the community, where norms are promoted.

- Attitude questions applied through a questionnaire, as well as qualitative research, should be combined, so that we understand how change takes place and can more closely listen to the voices and realities of the women and men involved.

Finally, it has been a concern of the Program H partners from the beginning that we did not want our programmes to become yet another 'jewel box' – small-scale programmes reaching a handful of men, with little potential for replication. We have sought to identify practices and methodologies that can be replicated elsewhere at a reasonable cost – and that can, together with other partners, contribute to our collective goal of gender equality.

Acknowledgements

Gary Barker, Márcio Segundo, and Marcos Nascimento all work with Instituto Promundo in Brazil. Julie Pulerwitz is with the Horizons Program, Washington DC, USA. The lead author wishes to acknowledge key individuals in the Program H partner organisations: Jorge Lyra and Benedito Medrado, Instituto PAPAI; Benno de Keijzer and Gerardo Ayala, Salud y Género; and Jose Roberto Simonneti and Sylvia Cavasin, ECOS. Program H has been supported by a diverse range of funders, and has a number of collaborators, including the International Planned Parenthood Federation/WHR, the Summit Foundation, the Moriah Fund, WHO/PAHO, SSL International (Durex condoms), the Interagency Working Group on Gender/USAID, Horizons/Population Council, the Ford Foundation, Oxfam GB (supporting Instituto PAPAI to implement Program H in northeast Brazil), and UNFPA. The GEM Scale research was funded through the Horizons Program (USAID), the MacArthur Foundation, and SSL International. Additional thanks to Miguel Fontes and Cecilia Studart of JohnSnowBrasil, Peter Roach of SSL International (Durex), and Christine Ricardo of Instituto Promundo.

Notes

1   Instituto Promondo and Instituto NOOS (2003) 'Men, Gender-based Violence and Sexual and Reproductive Health: A Study with Men in Rio de Janeiro, Brazil', Rio de Janeiro: Instituto Promondo/ Instituto NOOS.

2   See D. Alméras (1997) 'Compartir las Responsabilidades Familiares: Una tarea para el desarrollo', Santiago, Chile: CEPAL (Comisión Económica para América Latina y el Cariba, Septima Conferencia Regional sobre la Integración de la Mujer en el Desarrolo Económico y Social de América Latina y el Caribe, 19–21 November, 1997), background document for participants; A. Kornblit, A. Mendes Diz, and M. Petracci (1998) 'Being a Man, Being a Father: A Study on the Social Representations of Fatherhood', presented at the 'Men, Family Formation and Reproduction' seminar organised by the International Union for the Scientific Study of Population (IUSSP) and the Centro de Estudios de la Poblacion (CENEP), Buenos Aires, 13–15, May, 1998; and B. Medrado (1998) 'Homens na arena do cuidado infantil: imagens veiculadas pela mídia', in M. Arilha, S. Ridenti, and B. Medrado (eds.) *Homens e Masculinidades: Outras Palavras*, São Paulo: Ed. 34/ ECOS, 15–30.

3   D. Alméras (1997) *op. cit.*

4   J.Olavarria (2000) 'La Reproducción: *Los Padres Populares en la Crianza y las Actividades Domesticas,* Santiago, Chile: FLACSO.

5   G. Barker (2000b) *What About Boys? A Review and Analysis of International Literature on the Health and Developmental Needs of Adolescent Boys,* (Geneva, World Health Organisation).

6   G. Barker (2000a) 'Gender equitable boys in a gender inequitable world: reflections from qualitative research and programme development in Rio de Janeiro', *Sexual and Relationship Therapy,* 15 (3), 263–82.

7   J. Pulerwitz and G. Barker (2004) 'Measuring Equitable Gender Norms for HIV/STI and Violence Prevention with Young Men: Development of the GEM Scale', unpublished mimeo.

8   These costs can, of course, vary tremendously by country, depending on relative costs, but these figures give a general sense of the costs.

9   Personal correspondence, Ravi Verma and Julie Pulerwitz, December 2003.

Strategies and approaches to enhance the role of men and boys in working for gender equality: a case study from Yemen

Magda Mohammed Elsanousi

Introduction

In 2000, Oxfam GB initiated a programme to address violence against women in Yemen, in partnership with thirteen civil society organisations and the Women's National Committee.[1] This chapter first reviews the factors that have contributed to and sustained gender inequality in Yemen. Drawing on empirical fieldwork, it then identifies strategies and approaches to the involvement of men and boys in initiatives to end violence against women by fostering partnership between women's organisations and influential men in Yemeni society. The paper concludes with recommendations for development practitioners establishing similar programmes elsewhere, particularly in conservative societies in which gender equality remains a sensitive issue.

Gender equality: the Yemen context

Socialising women to be powerless

Yemen is one of the least developed countries in the world.[2] Although levels of poverty vary between social groups depending on factors such as class, race, age, disability, and gender, the Poverty Reduction Strategy (PRS) for Yemen has shown that the overall percentage of those living in poverty increased from 19 per cent in 1992 to 33 per cent in 1998. More recent indicators show that 42 per cent of the population is incapable of obtaining all their food and non-food requirements (shelter, clothing, transport, etc.).[3]

The position of Yemeni girls and women in general is shaped by social and cultural factors that tend to marginalise them and to restrict their participation in social, economic, and political affairs.[4] For example, boys have greater access than girls to education, and men are over-represented in decision-making positions. Men dominate the paid labour force and have high mobility, while women's participation is restricted; the latter tend to work unpaid, on family farms in rural areas. Due to a range of factors including religious beliefs and a preference for male children (who will support their parents in old age), fertility rates are high, and families are often large.

Women are socialised to be obedient, powerless, and voiceless, and men's abilities are valued more highly than those of women. Women are raised to fulfil the role of 'good wives and mothers'. Although women rear children, care for the sick and elderly, and maintain the household (through cleaning, cooking, and fetching water, for example), their labour remains largely invisible. Unequal gender relations are reinforced in households (by mothers, fathers, and older women and men), and influence individual and community behaviour and social institutions and structures. For instance, the school curriculum encourages the development of gender stereotypes for girls and boys. Women are rarely engaged in sports or community activities (apart from the activities in which only women participate). Men are visible and dominant both in public and in private life. The space for women is more in the private sphere, in which they have less power than men, and little recognition for their reproductive roles.

Following the unification of Yemen in 1990, a process of democratisation began. This provided some space for civil society and women's organisations to build their constituencies and agendas for the promotion of women's rights. Women in Yemen have been unable to build a strong women's movement, however, and as a result they have not had sufficient strength to challenge the embedded patriarchal power in Yemeni society.[5] Overall, the gender-power gap is unchanged, and women remain followers rather than leaders or equal partners in the process. Women as voters have been manipulated during elections by various male-dominated political parties. During the parliamentary elections in April 2003, political parties excluded women from standing for election; as a result, there is only one woman in parliament out of a total of 302 representatives.

It is important to note, however, that gender inequality is strongly associated with poverty and other kinds of inequality. Economically independent women in urban areas feel less threatened by their men, because they are able to make choices. Educated middle-class women now derive part of their identity from their affiliations to political parties; many support their party's agenda and mobilise poor women during elections on behalf of the party. But for poor and marginalised women and rural women, with less education and skills and who are economically dependent on their male counterparts, democracy makes little difference. They 'silently' accept men's domination because they have no alternative. The greater challenge for them is to address issues of their poverty and survival.

Socialising men to be in control

The socialisation process in the household supports patriarchal institutions in society, and prescribes the gender roles and responsibilities that consolidate gender inequality from birth throughout the life cycle. Unequal power relations extend into the wider community, and are reflected in the policies and practices of government institutions.

Boys and men are socialised within a narrow concept of 'masculinity'. They are supposed to be strong, dominating, earners and breadwinners, guardians of their female counterparts (mothers, sisters, wives, daughters, and female relatives). Reflecting this image, the national costume for men includes a knife worn at the front, emphasising the importance of courage and the ability to fight.

In 2002, Oxfam GB held a workshop with partner organisations in Yemen to explore men's identity and socialisation. The participants were a group of male directors of NGOs drawn from the middle class, intellectual, and élite strata of society, and a group of middle class, educated, and activist women. Between them, they illustrated how Yemeni women and men are socialised.

- Boys are treated as superior to girls in the family.
- Women in the family serve men; the best quality food is provided for men.
- Boys' education is given precedence over girls' education.
- Men are discouraged from performing domestic work (cooking, cleaning, etc.).
- Money is spent on boys' education and entertainment.
- Males are allowed complete freedom of movement in public life, and boys can come home late without it being questioned.
- Men are meant to be strong, but not emotional; they should not weep or cry. An often-heard statement in Arab families when a young boy cries is, 'Don't cry. Are you a girl?'
- Men are guardians of their sisters – and even of their mothers.
- Men are brought up to be decision makers and to hold power over women.
- The educational curriculum reinforces the pattern of men's and women's socialisation (for example, girls clean and cook, boys play outside).
- Men are socialised to be violent (with toys such as guns and sticks, and aggressive games).
- Misinterpretations of Islam enforce men's domination.
- Recreational activities, including sport, are restricted to men.
- Girls' schools don't provide sporting activities.
- Social clubs are available only to men.
- Activities take place during *Qat* sessions that exclude women – for cultural reasons, women are not allowed to sit with men during *Qat* chewing sessions.[6]

Participants then went on to describe aspects of men's identity that hinder gender equality.

- Men dominate in the family, the wider society, and the State.
- Men dominate politics and decision making.
- Men are guardians of women.
- The culture of masculinity dominates at different levels (for example, a 'real man' should be a fighter, and violent).
- Men have limited understanding and vision in relation to gender issues.

Finally, the participants identified aspects of men's identity that support the vision of a society free of violence.

- Men are responsible and care about their families.
- Men have strong and loving feelings as parents.
- Men protect women in the family (for example, fathers and brothers protect their daughters and sisters when treated badly by their husbands).
- Men accept women's work in the formal labour market in public.
- Society dishonours men who mistreat or insult their wives and daughters in public. It is a great shame for a man to batter his wife.

It is essential, however, to emphasise that Yemeni men generally resist two concepts: 'gender' (which they consider to be a Western concept), and 'equality' (which they regard as 'impossible', basing their arguments on Islamic codes). Although men of different classes and positions enjoy different degrees of power, they are united as a group by the power they hold over women – a power that remains largely invisible to them. 'Gender equality' is a threatening concept for men, who are upset at the idea that they may lose their entitlements. Men believe that their privilege and power are natural, normal, and just. A man might lose his power in society, but maintain control over the women in his household.

Factors that reinforce unequal gender power relations

Patriarchy in Yemen operates in a systematic and organised manner. The space provided to women is related to the demand for women's labour and other inputs that help to maintain the functions of society and the State, and expands and contracts according to men's needs. Similar constraints apply to women's space in relation to democratic participation. The challenge that active women's groups and organisations face is to change the way patriarchy operates within households, communities, and the State. In other words, they must change men's attitudes towards women as 'suppliers', so that men realise that women also have demands, and that men have a responsibility to support these. This necessitates working intensively with men at different levels to encourage them to work for gender equality.

During the last two decades, gender relations and women's status have been affected by two major factors: the reunification of North and South Yemen, and the global spread of fundamentalist movements. These factors have reinforced existing gender relations, and bolstered traditional gender roles and responsibilities.

The unification of North and South Yemen

Following the unification of North and South Yemen to form the Republic of Yemen in 1990, women from the south argue that they have lost several of their legal rights. The minimum age at which women can get married has been left open in law, and guardianship has been enforced for female marriage, depriving women of rights and choices over their decisions. Women are now poorly represented in decision-making positions and inadequately represented in certain professional fields: for example, the number of women judges dropped drastically by nearly 80 per cent following unification. And whereas very few Yemeni women used to wear the *Hijab* (black veil) before unification, now they do so for fear that men will harass them if they don't wear it.

The spread of fundamentalist movements

Sharia' law (Islamic law) is the main source for the Yemeni constitution and laws, in particular, for family law.[7] The spread of radical Islamic movements, which has affected Yemen, has resulted in the presence of institutions which often misinterpret Islam to endorse gender inequality. Early marriage, polygamy, and divorce are often legitimised by misinterpreting religious discourse to enforce women's subordination. For example, a man may divorce his wife without notification or even giving a reason, but a woman often has to present witnesses to claim a divorce; this process may take years, as male-dominated courts and male judges often support men, and delay women's cases in court.[8]

The classification of Yemen's society is based on tribalism, and race and gender relations should be seen within that framework. In rural areas, for example, where women are burdened with a triple role (productive, reproductive, and management in the community) the gender-power gap is significant; women are left with less bargaining power.

Promoting partnership between women and men to combat violence against women in Yemen: the conceptual framework

Oxfam GB's programme to end violence against women (EVAW) in Yemen

In 2000, Oxfam GB in Yemen started a programme to 'End Violence Against Women', based on a definition derived from the 1993 UN Declaration on the Elimination of Violence Against Women.[9] National studies have revealed that violence against women is a widespread phenomenon, manifested in wife battering, forced early marriage, and honour crimes. It is also linked to – and helps to sustain – the exclusion of girls from education, the denial of women's inheritance rights, and the limiting of women's opportunity to claim divorce or alimony. All of these factors contribute to women's material and non-material poverty (deprivation, exclusion, threats, fear, voicelessness, and so on). The programme was developed in partnership with civil society organisations and the Women's National Committee, and its components included awareness raising and educational campaigns, advocacy and lobbying, research, and legal and psychological support for women survivors of violence.

During 2000, partner organisations included men and boys extensively in joint work-based awareness-raising sessions with women and girls. This approach was exciting and unique in the context of the Arab world, where the conventional approach of the women's movement with regard to gender-equality work has been to focus on women only.[10]

When women's organisations were asked why they were inviting men to forums to discuss gender equality, some argued that work is the only public space where women and men interact. In Yemen, women and men do not associate outside the workplace, so ascertaining men's attitudes and perceptions of gender equality could only be done through these forums. Other women's organisations responded that changing men's attitudes had been recognised by women as being crucial for women's development, especially given the absence of a strong women's movement to articulate their demands.

However, the initiatives to integrate men and boys into the programme were limited in the extent to which they were able to develop lobbying and advocacy activities to encourage positive action by men in support of gender equality and ending violence against women.

Collaborating with Oxfam's 'Gender Equality and Men' project

In May 2002, building on the initial experience of partner organisations in working with men and boys to promote gender equality, Oxfam in Yemen collaborated with Oxfam GB's Gender Equality and Men (GEM) project (see the Introduction to this volume for further details about GEM). A workshop was held with partner organisations to explore the potential for women and men to work together to end violence against women. The collaboration sought to formalise the efforts of partner organisations to work within a comprehensive framework which would not only aim to raise men's and boys' awareness of gender issues, but also to work with them as key actors to influence gender power relations and to reduce gender inequality. Participants in the workshop were encouraged to include men in their analysis and actions on gender equality, and to use the outcomes of the workshop to assist further integration of the GEM approach into the programme to End Violence Against Women in Yemen.[11]

The workshop explored a conceptual framework for developing partnerships between men and women. The core components were:

* **establishing shared goals,** such as an end to gender-based violence, improved livelihoods, better governance, or poverty-reduction, and understanding that both men and women have a role to play in achieving these goals;

* **fostering co-operation,** based on the understanding that working together is more effective than working in isolation. The division of labour, however, will reflect differing levels of power and voice;

* **understanding complementary roles:** a division of labour will consist of different tasks that will fall along traditional power and gender lines. Men and women will articulate agency, willingness, and efficiency to perform separate tasks differently;

* **showing commitment:** the motivations for men and women may be different, but a commitment to the process is crucial for partnerships;

* **gaining trust:** the benefits of partnership will be shared equally; each partner will uphold their end of the bargain so that unequal power relations will not be re-established.

The framework also suggests that partnerships may become stuck at some stage; but in the end, it is usually possible to negotiate to a point of trust, where equality can be realised. Female partners emphasised the importance of building the collaboration between men and women working to end violence against women, and that requires the development of trust between the male and female individuals and organisations involved. At an Oxfam meeting with partners in Taiz in March 2002, women participants had doubted whether the men who wanted to work with them in EVAW genuinely believed in and were committed to challenging unequal power relations. In short, could men working to challenge gender inequality shed the conventional framework of masculinity within the patriarchal society they lived in?

Strategies and approaches

Working with men as allies

Oxfam encouraged partner organisations to put pressure on key policy makers and community leaders to tackle gender inequality and violence against women, using the entry point of awareness raising among men. Here we review practical initiatives to build partnerships involving men as allies, relate these to the conceptual framework above, and explore the different approaches to the implementation of each strategy.

To enhance partner organisation's lobbying, alliance building, and advocacy, Oxfam encouraged partners to form advocacy groups of potential key male actors in their area of work and in their respective provinces.[12] Below we examine this approach through a case study of the experience of three women-led partner organisations: the Yemeni Women's Union in Taiz and Hadhramaut and the Women's National Committee.

Establishing common goals

The Yemeni Women's Union is a large pioneering NGO with branches all over the country. The Union's mandate is to promote women's status (through income-generating activities, literacy classes, etc.) using a 'women in development' approach. It was working exclusively with women before the EVAW programme was established.

Beyond Oxfam's expectations, both branches of the Union targeted men in key positions who have a role to play in challenging violence against women in a very strategic way. In Taiz, the Yemeni Women's Union (YWU) formed its advocacy group from 15 men and three women (the head of the branch, the co-ordinator of Oxfam's EVAW programme and a secretary). When the project started in August 2002, the Union held eight meetings with the advocacy group, and formed its mandate jointly with the members, who devoted their time voluntarily to supporting the Union's goal of ending violence against women. The Union stated that the main aim of the advocacy group was *'promoting the rights of men and women in society, monitoring and documenting cases that violate women's rights (and in particular domestic violence and harassment in work), and raising the awareness of women and men on issues related to violence against women'.*

The men in the group include policemen, judges, lawyers, and academics, and are described by the leadership as respected in the community. They have a lot of influence, and are committed to supporting women's equality and human rights in general.[13]

In the YWU branch in Hadhramaut, a similar structure was established for the advocacy group, but there was a gender balance in representation (ten men and nine women). The male members include the chairperson of the Legal Affairs Office, the director of the Security Office, the director of the Lawyers' Union, the vice-chair of the Criminal Department in the Ministry of Justice, the director of the Social Affairs Office, and three people working in the media.

To gain the support of key male actors, the starting point for the YWU branches was to develop dialogue, to show that women have problems that cannot be resolved without men's support. The message that women's issues concern men too generated great interest among the men. The process helped to develop a common goal, which targeted and brought together both women and men. This was expressed in an interview with two female members of the YWU in Taiz:

> *'We cannot work to end violence against women by focusing only on women and ignoring men. Men in the advocacy group have been of great help in raising the awareness of other men, in particular police officers. Key men in society who joined us have helped to strengthen the role of both women and men in combating violence, and have reactivated grassroots linkages with poor women. Men in the group know by now what types of violence women experience, which encourages broader society to acknowledge that violence against women exists'.*
>
> (Interview with Ms. Soad and Ms. Ishraq, Yemeni Women's Union, Taiz, September 2003)

Fostering co-operation

Because of the socialisation process and the lower status of women in society, the impact of action by women in Yemen to raise awareness of gender issues among men remains minimal. In relation to sensitive issues such as violence against women, HIV/AIDS, or gender equality in general, men should take a leading role in educating other men. Most of the female trainers who have run awareness-raising sessions on violence against women, especially in rural and traditional areas, have been harangued by men and accused of promoting family destruction. During a field visit to the YWU in Taiz, we met with a male member of the advocacy group, and explored how he collaborates with the Union in combating violence against women. Mr. Hussein Alademeei, a human-rights activist said:

'I am collaborating with the YWU to raise the awareness of men and police and security on the rights of women and men in detention. Because Yemen is a conservative and religious society my starting point has been to use Islamic codes, then to move to national law, and thereafter make links with international Human Rights Conventions. I don't use the term "gender", which is not accepted in Yemen. It is about absolute equality between women and men, which is not possible in Yemen. We may need to "Yemenise" the gender concept.'

This reflects the understanding women have of their limitations in addressing gender issues without men's support in Yemeni society, which necessitated their co-operation with men.

Understanding complementary roles

Given the position of women in Yemen and their limited access to and control over decision making, the YWU has found that men can play a significant role in complementing their efforts. For instance, female lawyers in the Union's branches have been providing legal support to female survivors of violence, but when these cases are considered by the courts, women are discriminated against by officials. The complementary role of key male actors from the advocacy group is illustrated in the excerpt below from an interview with two female members of the Hadhramaut branch:

'The presence of men from key positions in Hadhramaut in the advocacy group has really provided us as members of the Union (which used to be only open to women), with great moral support. Having men who came to support us was so meaningful for us. When we talk now, we feel that men understand us. Their presence has changed the way society used to think. Women's issues are not any more women's issues; it is now women's and men's issues. In Hadhramaut, men occupy key positions in government ... and institutions such as the courts and police service, where women are not represented. They have access to power and decision makers; therefore they act as mediators between decision makers and ourselves. They facilitated and helped in many cases of women prisoners and women who are discriminated against in court through the dialogue and actions they have pursued with other men. The presence of men in the advocacy group gave the group strength, because it fosters a new image in our society, one where men are with us in combating violence against women'.

(Interview with Alyaa and Hanan, Hadhramaut, September 2003)

Showing commitment

It is important to emphasise that the socialisation of men, and gender roles more generally, are strongly rooted in Yemeni society. It requires considerable courage for men to work for gender equality. Promoting full gender equality may not be the main motive behind men's support for women's issues; but commitment to work in this direction is a prerequisite that may eventually shift men's attitudes towards full commitment to gender equality.

Dr. Mohammed is a lecturer in the faculty of law in Taiz University, and also a member of the advocacy group. When asked about his motive for joining the group, he said:

> 'At the beginning the YWU asked me to provide training for police on the rights of accused persons. That request was appealing for me, because I have seen that accused women and men are treated badly, aggressively, and sometimes violently. I wanted to change that practice to ensure that the accused are treated according to law. Just for police officers to come to the Union and receive the training is a success in itself. I then joined the group, because I thought it is amazing that a women's organisation took that initiative. This has further motivated me to encourage new graduates from the School of Law to take action. I have a group of new graduate lawyers – women and men – who provide legal support to poor women free of charge.'
> (Dr. Mohammed, Taiz, 2003)

Another group member argued that:

> 'Women are half of the society. The woman is the mother, the sister. Women are our daughters, wives, and colleagues at work. I believe in women's legal and social rights and recognise the violations of these rights. I highly encourage any man who cares for his mother, sister, wife and daughter to join the advocacy group to advocate for women's rights and to enable the society to understand that women have rights that should be respected. I have been advocating for that among male colleagues in the workplace'.
> (Interview with Mr. Abdelrahman Saeed, Hadhramaut, September 2003)

From the above, it is quite evident that men hold strong feelings of humanity and justice that support their commitment to gender equality. In the Yemeni context, men value the extended family, and men's obligations towards female family members are substantial. This provides a strong platform for convincing them that what is at issue are 'gains for the family', rather than 'gains for women'.

Gaining trust

In working to gain trust, women's organisations have initiated dialogues with key policy actors. The Women's National Committee (WNC), for example, has established contacts with the Ministry of Endowment, the highest religious institute in Yemen, whose work relates to Sharia Law. Members of the WNC have argued that the Ministry is open to considering women's issues and to understanding violence against women, even though key actors in the Ministry have stated that gender equality contradicts the principles of Islam. Ministry officials have asked the WNC to identify the messages they would like to be sent through mosques with regard to violence and women's rights; the Ministry is taking these forward so that they can be included in Friday prayers. Persuading officials of the Ministry of Endowment to support work to end violence against women reflects the awareness of the WNC of the importance of linking with religious leaders – and of looking at the whole discourse on violence against women in the context of what is achievable in the Yemeni context.

The WNC has succeeded in mobilising male policy makers and improving their understanding of women's issues; the men's attitudes have slowly shifted, and they have been encouraged to begin to challenge the harmful practices that affect women. For example, under the law, women are entitled to be issued with travel documents on request; however, the male-dominated Ministry of the Interior requires that any travel documents for women must be issued via a male guardian – a practice that has no legal basis. The WNC raised the issue with the Deputy Minister of the Interior, who immediately sent a circular to all officials to enforce the rights of women to request travel documents independently – if officials do not apply the law properly, they will be reprimanded.

Conclusion and recommendations

Based on examples of practice, this chapter has focused on building partnerships at organisational level between women and men, to promote gender equality and to work to end violence against women. It has looked at the work of partner organisations with men and boys on gender-based violence prior to the introduction of Oxfam GB's GEM (Gender Equality and Men) approach in 2000, and the significant changes in partners' work with men and boys following its implementation in 2002. The main findings indicate that although gender inequality is embedded in patriarchal institutions and reproduced through family socialisation processes in Yemeni society, there is great potential to work with men as allies for gender equality.

In line with GEM's partnership methodology, enlightened male academics, human-rights specialists, and government officials demonstrated co-operation and the commitment to promote gender equality, and took real action. In doing so, they used approaches that are acceptable within the constraints that are present in this society, and promoted dialogue based on justice and human dignity. Trust has been built between men's and women's organisations, recognising the power of access and influence that particular men hold over others. However, operating within the current limits of men's identity in Yemeni society means that male allies for gender equality must keep a relatively low profile, and avoid being provocative and outspoken.

The chapter highlights some effective approaches to involving men in strategies to mainstream gender equality. It suggests the following guiding principles for development workers in similar contexts:

- Practitioners need to be aware that successfully integrating boys and men in development programmes depends on recognising both the negative and the positive roles they can play. The GEM approach is based on minimising the negative and building on the positive attitudes of men and boys towards gender equality.

- In most developing countries, including Yemen, there are many women's groups and organisations that work to promote women's rights, but there is little focus on men; promoting partnership between women's organisations and key male actors in government and non-government organisations can result in effective alliances to support work for gender equality. As a starting point, development workers should seek to promote dialogue between women and men, so that the fears of both sides can be understood, and the most useful approaches for promoting partnership can be identified.

Drawing on these principles, development workers should take practical action to:

1 Understand the dynamics of gender inequality at macro level and among different social groups, through in-depth gender analysis and mapping of the various aspects of gender relations. External factors that affect gender relations and the potential impact of changes should be considered, so that workers can exploit opportunities and avoid risks.

2 Analyse the socialisation process and external factors in depth, breaking such analysis down by social class, race, age, religious affiliation, and so on; radical religious movements, individual laws, and household poverty are all examples of factors which reinforce gender inequality. Development workers should carry out these analyses in the first stages of programme formulation (problem identification and analysis) in their work with partners.

3   Identify the economic, social, and political spaces that women would most like to explore, based on the above analysis, and support women's struggles. Practitioners should test out approaches to working with men and boys that allow more space to be opened up for women; the specific intervention adopted in each case will depend on the level of men's resistance. For example, improving access for girls to education may face less resistance from men than does increasing women's political participation.

4   Build partnerships between women's organisations and key male policy makers through:

- establishing dialogue with women's groups and organisations to foster their understanding and acceptance that men hold power that they could use to support gender equality;

- encouraging women's organisations to use discourses that are accepted by policy makers and key male actors, and avoiding approaches that challenge men's identity too overtly, which may threaten them;

- providing training on gender equality for potentially 'gender-sensitive' men to shift the attitudes of men in the community, and influence change using appropriate and accepted dialogues in the community (for example, in the Yemen context by building on Islamic codes and concepts of morality);

- encouraging women's organisations to consider partnership with men at all levels to promote gender equality;

- exploring the positive characteristics of men that lead them to support gender equality, and understanding the risks they may face as a result of their support, and how to overcome them.

It is important to emphasise that men own the private and the public spaces in Yemen. Women own as much space as men wish to allow them. To achieve equal gender space requires integrating men and boys into development programmes to challenge and change their patriarchal attitudes.

Notes

1   The Women's National Committee is the government body with lead responsibility for promoting women's rights.

2   Yemen is ranked 133 out of 148 countries in the Human Development Report (UNDP, Human Development Report 2001).

3   Republic of Yemen, Poverty Reduction Strategy Paper (2003–2005).

4   For a more detailed description of gender relations in Yemen, see M. Colburn (2002) *Gender and Development in Yemen*, Bonn: Friedrich-Ebert-Stiftung/Oxfam GB.

5   For example, in January 2002, the Islamic parties in the parliament wanted to pass the *Bait Al Ta'a* law ('the house of obedience'), which means that wives can be dragged to their husbands' homes against their wishes. However, enlightened women activists from the Yemeni Women's Union in Aden (South/Socialist) succeeded in halting the endorsement of the law by sending strong messages to the government via the media. The cost was high: women from Aden were excluded from the Union's elections in September 2003.

6   *Qat* is a green leaf that is chewed, mainly by men, but also by women. It is classified by the WHO as a narcotic. It has contributed to the poverty crisis in Yemen, as growing *qat* has replaced growing vegetables and fruit in many areas. *Qat* therefore has a social and economic impact on households.

7   Family law in Islam has not been turned into civil law. Polygamy, husbands' absolute right to divorce, and male guardianship over women have not been challenged so far.

8   Under Yemeni law, a man has the entitlement to divorce his wife if she has a chronic health problem. Women are not entitled to divorce their husbands for this reason.

9   The declaration defines 'violence against women' as any act of gender-based violence that results in, physical, sexual, or psychological harm or suffering to women, including threats of such acts, coercion, or arbitrary deprivation of liberty, whether occurring in public or private life.

10 The author participated in two regional conferences in Lebanon and Cairo on the status of Arab women and CEDAW (Convention on the Elimination of All Forms of Discrimination Against Women), and on violence against women in 2002 and 2003 respectively. Both regional conferences were for women only.

11 The core discussion was based on how partners view a violence-free society, and was guided by five questions: what would a violence-free Yemen look like (physical violence in public and in the home)? What is it about men's identity that prevents the achievement of this vision? What is it about men's upbringing and socialisation that creates this identity? (Why are men this way?) How do women and men need to change the way they think and act to reinforce the positive? What can the participants do differently to make Yemen free of violence? What new partnerships, programmes, changes in ideas and beliefs (policy, practice, and ideas), are needed?

12 In the administrative structure of Yemen, the country is divided into provinces. Each is composed of a number of districts, and each district is divided into local councils.

13 Based on the nature of their employment, the male members of the advocacy group have been divided into six committees, including: monitoring and documentation; rights and freedom; awareness raising; security and defence (working with the police and security in raising their awareness of violence against women, with a particular focus on juvenile rights, media, and legal support for women).

What men think about gender equality:
lessons from Oxfam GB staff in Delhi and Dhaka

Sharon Rogers

> *'The greatest harm done to this movement is done by gender fundamentalists.'*
>
> *'Gender is not only a women's issue.'*
>
> *'Gender equality is not a "piece of work". We can't address it once or twice in a project and expect big results.'*
>
> *'We need to practice and say it and believe from our hearts. We start from our own lives and start from now.'*

South Asia is the only region of the world where men outnumber women. According to UNICEF, 'an estimated 79 million women are "missing" through discrimination, neglect and violence'.[1] Extreme forms of culturally specific violence, such as honour killings, acid throwing, and female infanticide, along with a very high incidence of domestic violence, sexual harassment, trafficking, and sexual exploitation, severely inhibit human and economic development in the region. They serve as an indictment of governments' failure to protect their citizens' human rights.

Within this context, Oxfam GB has come to believe that we need to build from our current programmes that target violence against women, which have focused on service provision, awareness raising, policy advocacy, and changing the practice of institutions such as the police and the judiciary. Oxfam GB understands that changing laws and institutions will continue to be ineffective in the face of mass attitudes which devalue women's lives and which justify control of our production, movement, and sexuality, and has therefore chosen to campaign for a fundamental shift in the attitudes and beliefs among men and women that perpetuate gender violence. The organisation is currently working to develop and launch popular campaigns in five countries: Bangladesh, India, Nepal, Pakistan, and Sri Lanka.

Developing a campaign primarily targeted at ordinary men and women, rather than policy makers, is new for Oxfam GB. In thinking through how to bring all our staff into the planning process, it has become clear that the campaign is a pilot for Oxfam, not only in terms of campaigning for behaviour and attitude change, but also in terms of gender mainstreaming. The audience for the campaign must include not only the general public, but also, and perhaps fundamentally, all Oxfam GB staff and partners.

Men working for Oxfam GB in the region appear to be interested in the campaign concept, and have participated actively in visioning exercises and initial discussions. Yet their interest is combined with guarded scepticism about how much they can or will be involved, and about how the campaign will target men in general. All agree that Oxfam must seek both men and women as allies and change agents, and that the campaigns must not portray men solely as perpetrators. Some discussion has also revolved around the extent to which women in South Asia perpetuate gender inequality and perpetrate gender violence. To date, however, male staff in the region have had few opportunities to discuss how gender equality and gender violence relate to their work, and even fewer to discuss the issues in relation to their personal lives.

As the regional campaign adviser, I felt that the development of this book provided an especially well-timed and constructive opening. This article highlights the voices of 25 men working in Oxfam GB's offices in Dhaka and Delhi,[2] and explores their experiences with and views and feelings about gender and gender equality, using the following questions as a guide:

- How do Oxfam men understand gender, gender relations, and gender equality?
- How have gender issues become visible to them? What generated their commitment to gender equality?
- What barriers do they face in working for gender equality? What discourages them?
- What recommendations do they have for Oxfam GB and other organisations trying to mainstream gender equality?

Male colleagues organised, facilitated, and recorded men-only discussions in both the Delhi and Dhaka offices. Staff in Dhaka set up separate conversations among men of the Bangladesh team and among the local administrative and finance staff of Oxfam GB's Regional Management Centre. Discussion notes recorded both consensus views and, to some extent, anonymous individual voices within the talks. In addition, I conducted nine follow-up interviews with staff in Dhaka and two with the smaller Delhi team. There is a range of opinion, experience, and emphasis represented among the contributors. I tried to note instances where only one person raised a particular issue, as well as where there seemed to be a significant number of men conveying the same message.

I have sought to explore the implications of the men's views for people and organisations seeking to involve more men in gender-equality work. The learning and recommendations that have emerged highlight possible sources of men's resistance or indifference to the work for change that Oxfam GB has been doing so far. The interviews have also helped me as an individual activist, and Oxfam GB as an organisation, to identify entry points for wider discussion and co-operation between men and women to achieve gender equality. Beginning this dialogue now, even in a limited number of our offices, is a first step towards mainstreaming a commitment to gender equality among our own colleagues, and making it more than women's work. Unless Oxfam actively involves men, they are unlikely to buy in to our campaign against gender violence, and the campaign is unlikely to be successful.

Understanding gender relations and gender equality

'Men are dominating our society ...'

Although none of the discussion questions specifically asked for an analysis of gender and the state of gender relations in Bangladesh or India, Oxfam staff in Dhaka and, to a lesser extent, in Delhi, offered several views. A significant number of comments reflected the contributors' recognition of male dominance in society and women's subordinate status. As one man said during a group discussion:

> 'Men are dominating our society, so what males like, what males want, what males desire, or what males want to see, is happening ... At this moment, women are getting few rights, [and it is difficult for them] just to have [a] ... movement [for equality]. Men are not fully ready to reduce their control over resources, decision-making processes, or even over female counterparts.'

In the same discussion, another man highlighted the undervaluing of women's traditionally gendered roles as wives, mothers, and teachers, and the way in which Islamic customary law in Bangladesh denies women equal inheritance: 'Women's contributions are not recognised, and they don't get an equal share of resources.' Discussion drew out the participants' understandings of gender as socially constructed, with formal education, culture, religion, and families all mentioned as contributing to creating and reinforcing gender norms. 'God created the earth, male and female, with balancing, but as humans, we have created imbalance for our own benefit.'

Gender inequality: a personal or structural issue?

Recognising male dominance, women's subordinate status, and the social construction of gender does not necessarily translate into a clear analysis of the causes of gender-power imbalances. Some men within Oxfam feel that there is a tension between believing in gender equality as a principle, and feeling that an undue burden is placed on men to answer for women's subordination; a tension that is highlighted by the quotations below. The discussions also highlighted men's uncertainty about how individual men and women can contribute to or undermine gender equality.

One man stressed the systemic causes of gender discrimination:

> *'Some people have a firm conviction that men are responsible for gender discrimination as a community, but I disagree. It's social structures and religious barriers, for example, which prevent women from leaving the house. We need to address the social, political, and economic systems at once. ...*
> *The family is not exempt from the external environment, so it's better to look at the structural level of things and how that influences the family [if we want to change gender relations there].'*

Although gender inequality is structural, the emphasis on structure obscures the disproportionate power that men continue to have, both as individuals and as a group, to control and benefit from the structures that perpetuate inequality. It also creates an opportunity for some men to deny or ignore their power to affect gender relations at a personal level. Institutions like the family are created and maintained by people; they don't exist on their own.

At the other end of the spectrum, some contributors focused on individuals' roles to the exclusion of other factors. For example, one man commented, *'It's not a question of discrimination ... it's a reciprocal relationship.'* Such an approach can reduce gender inequality to a question of negotiation between individuals, presuming that individuals have equal power and opportunities, and act on a level playing field, in isolation from other influences. Another contributor stressed that he sees men and women as equal, and strives in his day-to-day life, both at work and within his family, to treat people in a gender-blind manner: *'For me, gender is not an issue.'* Neither viewpoint seems to acknowledge the disproportionate risks and burdens women face in operating within male-dominated systems and institutions, which can be as big an obstacle as overt discrimination. Efforts to involve more men in initiatives for gender equality must include discussions of gender analysis and the various levels at which we can work for gender equality, from the individual to the institutional.

Who maintains gender inequality?

Many participants stressed that a key element of this analysis should be to explicitly recognise both men's and women's roles in perpetuating gender inequality, rather than to focus exclusively on men:

> *'I think gender is an issue for all humanity, but I also think how much women are responsible for creating imbalances. Women are responsible for making me*

male or female in terms of attitude, behaviour, and practices, because they are the masters of the socialisation process.'

'[Oxfam programme documents on gender equality] often refer to India's gender inequality stemming from its patriarchal culture, but gender inequality can happen in a matriarchy too.'

These men feel frustrated by their perception that many gender-equality activists say 'gender' and mean: women equal 'victims', equal 'powerless', equal 'weak', equal 'good'; and men equal 'perpetrators', equal 'powerful', equal 'dominating', equal 'bad'. By stressing women's roles and power in socialisation, the men indirectly challenge such an essentialised hierarchy as inaccurate and unfair, and make a case for a more nuanced analysis of men's and women's gender attitudes and practices.

Rather than assign blame for the maintenance of gender imbalances, gender-equality activists might more usefully stress the positive roles that both men and women can play in creating space for children to develop without undue gender stereotyping. It is also important to discuss the differential costs and benefits for men and women in adhering to and passing on dominant gender norms, and the obstacles they face in challenging them. For example, men socialised to exhibit 'masculine' qualities of competitiveness and independence are likely to be considered successful, while women and girls who exhibit these qualities are likely to be punished in myriad ways, including with violence. Qualitative research commissioned by Oxfam GB into attitudes to gender and domestic violence in India found that a significant number of women survivors of violence feel that, although they want their daughters' lives to be different, the abuse they suffer prevents them from modelling most of the behaviours and values they would like their daughters to espouse. To hold women, especially mothers, primarily responsible for socialisation, without acknowledging and confronting men's roles – not only in direct socialisation, but also in compelling women to conform to men's values – would be as inaccurate as to hold men solely responsible for perpetuating patriarchy.

Responsibility for gender-based violence

Discussion of gender-based violence raised similar issues. Several men commented that women, as well as men, commit violence against women:

'We need to re-analyse domestic violence and to recognise that women also commit it. Oftentimes, while a victim may be a woman, the perpetrator is also ...'

'Women are not immune from committing acts of violence; for example, some women beat their maids.'

These men, like the men quoted in the section above, seem to be challenging a definition of oppression that places men's domination of women as its centre, and labels men as the only perpetrators of violence and abuse. Their own experiences tell them that the actions of individual men and women are shaped by intersecting identities and power dynamics, of which gender is only one. In South Asia, where extended families are strong and joint households are prevalent, older women may abuse their daughters-in-law or push other family members to do so, as a way of maintaining their limited power within the family hierarchy. In other cases, as with women's violence against their domestic servants, while women are at the bottom of the gender hierarchy, they may act in dominating and oppressive ways, using their power and position within the hierarchies of class, religion, age, and so on.

There were also a few comments about women's 'violent' or 'oppressive' behaviour towards men, especially their husbands and co-workers. Since violence against women and its implicit threat is at the foundation of gender-power imbalances, it is critical that we include discussion and analysis of it in all our gender-equality work. All conflict is not oppression or abuse, which necessarily involves the use of systemic or institutional power as a means of control. When women engage in conflict with men in their families, they rarely have the same social, cultural, religious, and legal sanction for their behaviour that men do when they abuse women. Emphasising individual women's 'oppressive' behaviour toward men not only fails to recognise the lack of institutional power behind most of the women's actions, it can also minimise the overwhelming incidence of domestic violence perpetrated by men against women across all classes and cultures.

Making gender visible and generating commitment to gender equality

The majority of the men in the discussions described experiences within their families, universities, and the NGO sector as sources of their gender awareness, and several credited the women's movement. One person credited television and popular culture, which continue to play an increasing role in shaping opinions and raising issues. Overall, perhaps the strongest factor moving men to internalise commitment to gender equality has been seeing the effects of gender discrimination on women they know.

Parents and children

Many of the men view their parents and families as the most important source of messages about gender. For example, one man related that, when he looked for a wife, in contrast to most of his friends, he looked for a woman who had a job and wanted to work, because he grew up with both his parents working and learned from them to see women as equals. Another contributor had seen his parents' relationship change as a result of the growth of his own awareness of gender equality, which has provided an important source of positive reinforcement in a society where family condemnation would be a significant barrier:

> 'My father's family is ... more traditional. As a son, it's expected that I contribute money to my parents, even though they don't really need it. I used to give them one envelope, but then I realised that my mother wasn't spending any of it. Now, I give them two envelopes: one for my father and one for my mother ... Both my parents have accepted this change without a problem.'

Others stressed the ways that both fathers and mothers can perpetuate gender inequality, either by example or by direct intervention. One contributor said:

> 'We learn from how our fathers act toward our mothers. In Bangladesh, most of the time, we see our mothers practically jailed at home, so even if we know it's wrong, some of us think it's something we can do and get away with.'

Another recalled his mother and male peer group pressuring him to conform to the dominant norm of masculinity, despite his initial inclination to be different.

> 'When I was little, I liked fancy clothes, but my mother told me, no, they are only for a little girl. When I was older, I played with boys and girls both and had lots of girl friends, but then my male friends told me not to play with girls and that there are certain games particularly for boys, like football ... and there are other games for girls.'

All of these men's experiences point to the importance of creating opportunities for mothers and fathers to learn and talk about alternative models of relating to and raising their children within a framework of gender equality. Although not all parents will become role models for perfectly equitable gender relations, simply being open to their children's diverse expressions of gender can support both boys and girls to grow up without rigid beliefs about gender roles.

For the men quoted below, becoming fathers of girls has motivated them to think about gender and gender inequality and has profoundly affected the way they see the world and gender relations.

> 'For me, now that I have a daughter, who is my only child, I see everything through her eyes. For example, when I see an eight-year-old girl teased, I now think, "I want a different future for my daughter. My daughter will one day go to someone else's house. How will she be treated there? How can I prepare her?"'

'*I have seen a shift in thinking among my friends. For example, some are buying property for both their sons and their daughters, because the law does not allow equal inheritance, and boys legally get twice the inheritance of their sisters.*'

'*I have only one child, my daughter, and we have ... given [her] the kind of freedom that, in typical Indian households, would only be given to a boy ... Despite ... criticism [from our neighbours], we've withstood the pressure to control her. Now, the neighbours praise us when our daughter does things that typical girls can't do, and when she accomplishes great things ... I am really proud to see girls five to six years younger than she is looking to her as a model ... Their parents talk to us and ask advice. They are very apprehensive about the social implications of their daughters behaving differently, but my wife and I can reassure them. We can relate to their fears and concerns, but because we have dealt with them, we can also be helpful and provide support. My greatest joy is that my wife used to be under tremendous pressure, ... and people held her more responsible [for my daughter's behaviour than they did me], but now she feels justified and rewarded. I supported her, ... but it was hard for her.*'

By seeing women and girls through their daughters' eyes, these men have begun to think about aspects of gender inequality, such as sexual harassment, inheritance law, and mobility, which might not have concerned them before. They have also been moved to find ways to defy restrictive laws, practices, and social pressure, creating strategic models for their children and peer groups to follow, which in turn allow their children to become role models as well.

The women's movement and NGOs

The success of the women's movement in putting gender equality and women's issues on human rights and development agendas has also been an important factor in making gender and gender discrimination visible to men. This is particularly true in the NGO sector and in Oxfam GB, which the contributors see as a leader in opening space for men to think about gender. For example, one man noted that only after he began working for development NGOs did he begin to understand '*the types of discrimination. ... I don't like [the fact] that women are often in violent situations.*' Many men believe that the formal commitment to gender equality of Oxfam and other NGOs has resulted in men who are '*sensitive [and] highly conscious*'. They stressed that a gender-balanced staff and Oxfam's efforts to seek qualified women for all posts, even those in which it is not traditional for women to work, are signs that the organisation takes gender equality seriously. For example, '*As soon as you arrive at Oxfam [in Dhaka], you realise that something is different and that Oxfam supports gender equality, because it employs a woman as a gatekeeper, which is very unusual.*'

In Bangladesh, women's social advancement and increased participation in public life has given the message that 'women can do it', and *'has inspired [the contributors] to think positively about gender equality'.*

Informal social and professional contact with women

At the same time, a critical mass of women in schools and workplaces has created opportunities for friendship and camaraderie between men and women, which are especially important in societies like India and Bangladesh, where they are often segregated. As one father commented:

'My son is experiencing co-education for the first time in university, and it is changing him. He has women friends, fellow students, calling the house to speak with him, and he is seeing women as equals and friends now, whereas he didn't have as much of a chance before. Separate schools for boys and girls are a barrier to achieving gender equality. When I was in university, there was only one girl in my class. In my son's class, there are 30 per cent women.'

For the contributors, having the chance to work and study with women as peers *'was an important opportunity to become more comfortable working with them. It was also an opportunity to understand their problems better and to see the differences in the ways men and women are treated.'*

Communicating positive, alternative cultural models

Although only one man talked about how popular culture has shifted his thinking about gender, I include his example because television and popular culture influence increasing numbers of people, especially young people, in South Asia and around the world. From television, he took both examples of diversity and a stronger awareness of gender inequality.

'For example, on Star Trek: Voyager, *there are creatures that are neither male nor female, neither men nor women. Diversity means, to me, that every entity should have its equal rights ... A few months after joining Oxfam, I saw a television show from West Bengal in India, during which the host read a letter from a girl who wanted to change her sex to become a man so she could explore the world and experience it more. I was really struck by this; the girl didn't feel she had the right to be human as long as she was a girl.'*

Concurring with several other participants, he recommended taking a positive approach to cultural messaging, offering alternative models of gender relations, instead of simply negating the dominant values.

'Newspaper articles about women's rights and violence against women have little effect. People turn off ... this kind of news, because it's generally negative,

and there is so much bad stuff happening in Bangladesh. We need positive examples. US movies almost always end well, and we need to take a lesson from that approach and its appeal.'

Another contributor phrased it this way:

'I don't agree that we need to or should challenge [all] of Indian culture. All value systems have both positive and negative aspects, and we interpret and practice them to suit our needs. I am a product of the same general value system as other men are, and I do things differently anyway. We need to revive or emphasise the good examples of gender equality in the culture and de-emphasise the bad, without telling people everything they do and think is wrong.'

If we want to transform gender relations, we need to provide models and an alternative vision of what we want that change to look like, and we have to be able to show how it would benefit both men and women.

Barriers to working for gender equality

Several contributors emphasised that many men believe that gender equality is about 'special' treatment and quotas for women. They feel that such mechanisms are not only unnecessary, but also that they create a backlash and the perception that men's needs are unrecognised, especially by the government and NGOs. Beyond this overall frustration that 'gender equality' often translates into 'women's advancement' to the exclusion of men, the contributors talked about three other barriers to involving more men in achieving gender equality:

- fear of condemnation;
- being seen as illegitimate or foreign voices by the women's movement and by their own communities; and
- conservative interpretations of Islam.

Fear of condemnation

Fear of criticism silences a number of the men I interviewed, preventing them from discussing gender issues or, in some cases, even from interacting with women. The following story represents some contributors' fears that their good intentions will be misunderstood or mistrusted and that they will be seen primarily as potential perpetrators when engaging with women.

'It was 31st December, and I was leaving the office late. It was dark and raining and cold, and I saw a woman walking alone toward the main road [which is quite a distance from within the office park]. For a minute, I thought of

stopping and giving her a ride, but then I just stepped on the accelerator and passed her by. I thought about this incident for days afterward, and felt very badly that I hadn't stopped. I talked about it with my wife and daughter, and my daughter said, "You should have given her a ride." I finally realised that I was afraid ... that if people saw me take her into the car, or if she had been afraid and created a fuss, I would have had no explanation. People would have questioned my motives, and I might have had problems.'

In a professional context, all of the Delhi participants felt similar fear and self-protectiveness. Although they 'feel positive' about gender-equality work, in discussing whether they feel that they are welcome to contribute to gender-equality forums, they all indicated a disturbing level of discomfort; they feel 'highly defensive,' 'vulnerable,' 'cautious,' and 'afraid to be misinterpreted'. As one man put it, '*Everybody is watching you*'.

Two of the men recounted the same, now infamous, incident within the Oxfam GB India programme, in which a male staff member sent a joke to all India colleagues about differences between men and women getting cash from ATMs, characterising women in exaggerated, stereotypical terms. Neither of the contributors commented on the joke itself; however, they both stressed that they had felt attacked by the public flurry of e-mails condemning the joke, its sender, and sexism within the organisation, even though they had not been targeted directly. They suggested that the women's overall message about the problems with gender stereotyping had been overshadowed by men's defensiveness, and one felt that he could not have commented at the time without seeming to excuse the joke. Both recommended that colleagues address issues with each other one-to-one, so that the person being asked to reconsider his or her words or actions can do so without feeling vulnerable.

While the fear of being seen as perpetrators or labelled as sexist silences some men, a few contributors feel that Oxfam GB's hierarchical structure and organisational culture are barriers that make it '*difficult ... to act on innovative ideas*', and discourage people from saying things that are difficult to hear. Since gender inequality is a form of hierarchy deeply embedded into almost all organisations, these men recognise that to challenge it is to challenge Oxfam's hierarchy, even if some managers are women.

The lesson for Oxfam GB and other organisations working to involve more men in gender-equality efforts is that we need to create an atmosphere that supports open, respectful communication among colleagues, regardless of hierarchy. We need to challenge unacceptable communication and behaviour with sensitivity, without demonising the people we are challenging. We need to frame our messages in ways that people will hear, rather than reject them because they've shut down and become defensive. If we want more men to take chances engaging in dialogue and acting on their anti-sexist beliefs and convictions, we need to communicate that we view them as partners with good intentions and that we will support their efforts.

Being seen as illegitimate or foreign voices

Class prejudice and the perception that gender-equality work is an élite or counter-cultural issue is another hurdle that some men feel they need to overcome. For example, a gender programme worker in Bangladesh, who is from a village, related his experience of struggling to overcome the mistrust of prominent national women activists, most of whom come from privileged, élite backgrounds and are unfamiliar with reality at the village level. These feminist leaders question his perspective and gender-equality credentials, making it clear that he is not part of their club, despite his having a degree, and long experience as a gender-equality activist. At the same time, ordinary people from rural areas outside Dhaka often label him as 'urban élite' because of his job, although he works hard to maintain relationships in his village.

In contrast, another contributor from a more privileged background stressed that he struggles against the perception that gender-equality work, and NGO work in general, undermine the class hierarchy and the status quo.

> 'There are also social barriers to men doing gender-equality work. For example, when I told an uncle and aunt that I wanted to settle in NGO work, my aunt said, "No, an internship is OK, but a job, no." Some people in my family and also in the society I live in see NGOs as challenging social norms, and they disapprove of them. At the same time, NGOs are leading the way on gender-equality work, so we need to reposition them as more acceptable somehow.'

In both cases, talking about gender injustice and the strategies for challenging it without using language or images that will immediately alienate people, is a key strategy used by the contributors to overcome mistrust and rejection.

Conservative interpretations of Islam

A theme in the discussion of the influence of Islam was the tension between pushing for change by challenging some of people's most fundamental beliefs and finding elements of those beliefs on which to build. All of the contributors in Bangladesh stressed Islam's role in creating and maintaining women's subordinate status. For instance, one man commented:

> 'Most men are hypocrites. When wives are earning, men think it's great, but if they can't, they [the men] use religion as an excuse to force their wives to stay at home. Fundamentalist leaders will allow girls to work cleaning in their houses, but argue against women and girls working in general.'

However, although the contributors saw the widespread, unquestioning acceptance of conservative Islamic values about women as being a major barrier to working for and achieving gender equality, they all recommended caution in seeking to challenge it.

> '*No matter how loudly you shout, if you conflict with Islam, which is deeply rooted here, you will turn off many, many people. We need to show that equal relations between men and women are not against Islam. There are both good and bad examples of gender relations in Islamic texts and interpretation. We need to find entry points to show that women can do everything within Islam. What's most important is to avoid contradicting religious dictates.*'

As one contributor put it, in discussing gender equality, '*where we begin depends on our context*'. We need to encourage men and women to question the unquestionable, while acknowledging their circumstances and histories, beginning from points of reference they will trust and with which they feel comfortable. In one way or another, the importance of starting from where people are without attacking them, and then exploring gender issues on a personal basis, became a theme running through all the discussions.

Mainstreaming gender equality: transforming the workplace

Including men in gender-equality forums

The men in Delhi stressed that, currently, gender-equality forums held by Oxfam GB are '*lopsided*' and they feel '*there is a predetermined mindset that men do not know about gender issues*'. They asked, '*Why do people only talk about women in these meetings?*'. All of the men in the discussion want to contribute to gender-mainstreaming efforts, and many of them stressed that sometimes, '*men can be more gender-sensitive than [women], so men should not be excluded from forums or initiatives for promoting gender sensitivity*'. They were quite passionate in stating, in various ways, that '*Mainstreaming gender equality should not only be the gender lead's responsibility. People who focus on gender issues need to involve both men and women*'. Although it is important in some situations to have women-only spaces, explicitly inviting men to the table and including them in our vision of potential allies is a clear first step.

Considering attitudes to gender equality during recruitment

Contributors in both Delhi and Dhaka argued that Oxfam GB should work harder to develop a more complex and crosscutting practice of gender equality, starting with recruitment. They value working with women colleagues, but stressed that gender equality is not just about numbers.

> 'We don't want to understand gender equality by increased number of women staff; rather, we want to see the practice of gender equality at all levels of Oxfam's intervention.'

Condemning tokenism, the staff group at Oxfam's Regional Management Centre in Dhaka noted that, '*Compromising skills to recruit a woman is akin to undermining the dignity of women*'. Instead of using job advertisements that state, 'Women are specially encouraged to apply', which many contributors criticised, one man suggested alternative language, such as, 'This organisation promotes gender equality', or 'We are an equal-opportunity employer'. Others recommended that Oxfam GB explore candidates' attitudes toward gender equality during recruitment. For example,

> 'We hear a lot about the ideal of gender equality, but how did Oxfam manage to get so many people who are striving for it? Luck. The only question about gender equality ... in my interview was if I would have a problem working for a woman boss ... I am working for Oxfam because it is fighting against poverty, but the connection [between gender equality and poverty] was not there.'

Another man recommended that Oxfam work harder to consider '*other aspects of diversity besides gender*', which would help to avoid fostering an analysis of power inequality limited to gender.

Strengthening induction and training

From improvements in recruitment, discussions turned to improving Oxfam GB's induction and training on gender analysis and gender mainstreaming. One contributor noted that, currently, '*lack of communication mechanisms and uneven capacity [gives people] scope to say "I don't know. Nothing can be done." Our response needs to be, "We do know something. What can we do to put our knowledge to work?"*'. For example, although several of the men mentioned having taken the initiative to read some of Oxfam GB's policies and materials on gender equality, they still feel uncertain about how to apply it in their work. Most had not participated in workshops on gender issues, but would like to.

> 'I want to learn what Oxfam thinks and has learned about gender equality, not just what we do in our gender-equality programmes. The checklists alone are not enough to change our behaviour. We need training to get us to think critically. A checklist could actually close our minds. One option is to have discussion, and make developing checklists for mainstreaming gender equality a participatory process.'

Other suggestions included requiring training in gender analysis as part of all inductions, investing more in the ongoing improvement of the understanding of Oxfam staff about gender issues, and reducing staff turnover to retain gender-aware staff who could become '*ambassadors of Oxfam and gender equality*'.

Creating space for informal dialogue

For most of the men consulted, discussions for this article were the first opportunities they had had to explore gender issues in depth. They valued the chance to speak among themselves and to share their views, and also to feel that they had been heard by a gender-focused staff member. Recognising that training alone will not be enough, all of the men strongly recommended that Oxfam GB create opportunities for informal, open dialogue on gender issues and for sharing views about family life and gender relations outside the office.

Specific suggestions for taking this forward ranged from reviving informal weekly discussions about staff learning in the Dhaka office and focusing on gender, to having men-only discussions every two months, with men and women coming together twice a year to meet and discuss gender issues and to 'audit' themselves. Another suggestion was to hold workshops focused on gender equality 'beyond our programme work,' which would send the message:

> '*Treat women as equals not only at work, but also at home, in your personal lives. Even our mothers and sisters might not get the same privileges that we get as sons, and we can address this root-level inequality.*'

One colleague volunteered to start a men's group modelled on the Bangladesh Women's Forum, an Oxfam-supported group that creates space for mid-level female staff working for Oxfam partners to discuss gender issues within their organisations.

Support and example setting from management

The final area of recommendation is about the strengthening of management practice to support and model efforts towards gender equality. Several men emphasised that mainstreaming gender equality should be taken seriously as part of the performance objectives and development plans all Oxfam GB staff. One man discussed the value of clear policies against harassment and discrimination, and stressed that, although '*administrative or managerial action will not make staff more gender sensitive, ... it can set limits*' against overtly sexist behaviour. Another contributor cautioned, '*If men act from fear of losing our jobs, ... we might act with false faces. ...[Gender equality] should not be routine [and bureaucratic], because then we don't do it with full commitment and reflection.*' Most feel that individual managers' behaviour, rather than management systems and policies, make the critical difference in people's willingness to challenge gender inequality. By modelling the kind of behaviour they want from colleagues and being forthright in discussing gender issues, managers help to create the kind of open, supportive atmosphere that the men felt was a prerequisite for them to be involved in gender-equality work. As one contributor summed up, '*Guidelines, encouragement, and creating space for discussion, thought, and practice are better tools*' than punishment and rules.

Conclusion

Working on this article has given me a chance to see some of my colleagues in a new light. Taken in their entirety, most of the interviews were moving and emotional in ways I had not expected. I think this was because many interviewees spoke about themselves and about the people that matter most to them: their families. We weren't talking about projects and how they would impact upon women, gender relations, the environment, or poverty alleviation; we were talking about home.

Oxfam GB believes in story telling: that we work with people, not with statistics or generalised categories of 'poor people'. Yet, when it comes to our efforts for gender equality, the stories we have told have been, in effect, outside of us, in communities in which we have projects, but in which we do not live and with which we may not identify closely. For many of us, even if we have seen that gender equality is 'about us', it may have seemed to be a different gender equality from the gender equality we seek in our programmes. Even if we have seen it as 'about us', we haven't recognised that many of our colleagues, including men, also see it as about them. Working on this article has removed my blinkers. If Oxfam men in Dhaka and Delhi have so much to say about gender and gender equality, then it's likely that men in the rest of our offices do too, and that Oxfam would learn even more by soliciting their opinions and engaging in dialogue with them on a regular basis.

Talking to men once, for a single article, is not enough to get them on board as active participants in gender-equality work within Oxfam GB or within our programmes. To support men to contribute by asking questions, making suggestions, and sharing experiences about gender issues, we need to follow up by acting on the learning from the discussions. One man said:

> '*Why don't we start changing things at home? In my household, I share responsibility with my wife for work. ... If I don't do this, how will my wife do all of her things? If I expect something good, then I have to work for it and share family things with my wife. If we don't believe this, then our son would see it and know it.*'

The same could be said for Oxfam GB. Start at home. Spread expectations for gender awareness and responsibility for gender-equality work; if you don't, how will the few staff responsible for it be successful? If you want to achieve mainstreaming of gender equality, then you have to work for it. If we don't believe this, then new and prospective staff, other organisations, our partners, and communities will see it and know it. We won't be as effective or credible, because we won't be building on the strength and commitment our staff could generate.

Ultimately, whether we view men as potential allies, targets of our gender-equality work, or both, we need them; achieving gender equality demands radically transformed relations between and among men and women; a shift not only in attitudes, but also in power and its exercise. This can only happen when both men and women work towards it, separately and together. Achieving mere tolerance of change, mere tolerance of women's rights, women's participation, and gender-equality programmes will not be enough, if we want change to be mainstreamed. For it to take root and spread, change will need to be both personal and structural. In practice, this does mean men giving up privilege, and thinking more about the gender implications of their words and actions; but it also means women examining their own attitudes and behaviour, and men and women supporting each other when they choose to act outside of the dominant gender norms. As one of my colleagues said, '*We need to practice and say [it] and believe from our hearts. We start from our own lives and start from now*'.

Notes

1   United Nations Children's Fund (UNICEF) Regional Office for South Asia, with the Centre for Child Rights, Delhi, 'Commercial Sexual Exploitation and Sexual Abuse of Children in South Asia', prepared for the Second World Congress Against Commercial Sexual Exploitation of Children 2002, page 10, Kathmandu: UNICEF.

2   The author is grateful to all the Oxfam GB staff members who took part in this exercise, and to Oxfam staff who facilitated discussions. Not all of the participants were comfortable with being identified by name for this article, so the participants have been quoted without attribution.

Evolving the gender agenda: the responsibilities and challenges for development organisations

James L. Lang and Sue Smith

Introduction

This article explores the progress of two development organisations in tackling the place of men working on gender equality.[1] It describes internal lobbying and capacity-building initiatives within the United Nations Development Programme (UNDP), and the UK-based NGO, Oxfam GB. These initiatives are, respectively, the Working Group on Men and Gender Equality and the Gender Equality and Men project.

The role of development organisations in promoting gender equality

Many development organisations have a mission to achieve gender equality as part of their overall development goals. These organisations, especially multi-laterals and bi-laterals, help to shape policy discussions and more gender-equitable policy frameworks for governments, while at the same time implementing programmes and projects of their own with partners and beneficiaries. They have the capacity for a wide reach and influence in settings where equitable public co-operation between women and men may be relatively uncommon. They intervene in circumstances where people are vulnerable, living in poverty and in emergency situations – and many of these organisations aim to demonstrate that greater gender equality and flexible gender roles can alleviate these situations.

Development agencies have an obligation not only to help to ensure that the development-policy agenda reflects the fact that development goals will only be reached if gender inequality is addressed, but also to nurture more equality through programming – both their own programming and that of the partners they are working with. They must start internally with their own policies, staff, and organisational culture, instilling gender equality into the thinking and behaviours of all staff (male and female). This article tells the story of two organisations attempting this modelling within their own internal processes.

Why the problem? Some constraints on men's greater involvement in gender work

Conceptual constraints

After almost two decades of programming for gender equality, there is still an understanding among most development practitioners that, in practice, 'gender means women'. They could be forgiven for making this assumption: in the same way that only black people have 'race', only women have 'gender', and men – a dominant social category whose privileges are taken for granted – remain invisible.[2] Most of the resources reserved for gender equality, and most policy attention, has focused on women, working from the premise that women are the majority in the poorest groups, suffer the greater abuse of rights, enjoy less power, and have more limited access to resources and decision making than men at all levels. So the recent focus on men's potential contribution to gender equality – an analysis of masculinities and men's gender roles, a focus on if and how men 'lose out', and on how to encourage men's contribution to gender equality – has left many practitioners deeply confused. How can gender equality mean a focus on men? How is it possible to focus on men without old power dynamics reasserting themselves? What does it mean, in both theory and practice? Staff and partners in development agencies are finding the new area of gender equality and men conceptually challenging.

Structural constraints

Gender-equality goals pose particular challenges to men working within development agencies. While their external (and often rhetorical) objectives commit many agencies to working for gender equality within a framework of human rights and human development, their internal functioning often reflects the patriarchal norms and practices that maintain gender inequality. Individual male development practitioners may commit themselves to gender equality, but they work within organisations whose entrenched cultures and structures may embody male privilege.

Organisational barriers

Organisational and human-resource policies do not consistently encourage the flexible gender roles central to good development practice. For example, there are still cases where corporate policy does not include paternity leave, a sexual harassment policy, and flexible working and childcare arrangements. 'Gender competency' is often not included as a requirement during recruitment processes, and gender-equitable skills and attitudes are not yet systematically nurtured through longer-term staff development. In many organisations, the majority of senior management positions continue to be filled by men, and action to redress gendered power imbalances within organisations can still cause tensions among women and men staff.

Even when gender-equitable policies do exist, they may not be put into practice, because of the prevailing legal and cultural climate. For example, in an organisational ethos that equates 'hard work' with 'long hours at your desk', some staff – male and female – may feel hesitant to take parental leave, or to work flexible hours, as they fear sending the message that they are not serious about their work. There is also a risk that such policies can reinforce traditional gender stereotypes if they are used exclusively by women, perpetuating the notion that women are the 'natural' carers.

Personal constraints

Related to the general issues of organisational culture and structures, there are personal and interpersonal constraints. Although many women and men see men's participation in unpaid household and caring work as a positive step towards achieving equality, there is still resistance to it on the part of some men and women. For obvious reasons, there are hesitancies on the part of some women to welcome men into the struggle for gender equality. For example, concerns exist that men will manipulate the gender discourse to their own agendas, or that resources earmarked for the advancement of women will now be diverted to a focus on men and boys. More tacit resistance may have to do with the nature of these new partnerships required by more male involvement. The realm of gender was once a sanctuary for women in a world dominated by men – and more involvement of men necessitates power sharing and compromise within this one area where women were once sole proprietors.

For some men, resistance to greater men's involvement is rooted in the fact that it entails a greater focus on *their* gender and how their own privileges are maintained. One privilege of gender inequality for men is the relative invisibility of their gender. If we do not talk about men and gender, we will not understand men's positions and privilege, and we will not be able to outline men's responsibilities in work towards gender equality. Also, some men may feel that women often are more articulate in and dominate conversations about gender. For some men, gender is perceived as 'women's space', and as a result they feel intimidated discussing gender issues with women. Unless opportunities are opened up for women at the same time as encouraging men to enter the gender discourse on their own account, progress is difficult.

Some experiences

The United Nations Working Group on Men and Gender Equality

Background

The UN Working Group on Men and Gender Equality was an informal working group that grew out of gender capacity-building workshops for staff of the United Nations Development Programme in the late 1990s. The working group included both men and women – mainly staff from UNDP, UNICEF, and other New York-based UN agencies.

The group aimed to raise awareness around men, masculinities, and gender, and to challenge staff to think about the connections between gender-equality goals and their personal and professional lives. It also encouraged an understanding of the biases and barriers hidden behind some development policies and practice, and advocated for the deeper incorporation of concepts of masculinities into gender analysis and an increase in opportunities for men to play a part in work towards gender equality.[3]

In practice, the group took action as an internal advocacy and awareness-raising initiative. At its inception in February 1999, the 12 founding members released a statement to all UNDP employees, both at the headquarters in New York and in its country offices throughout the world, reaching more than 5000 staff. The statement announced the formation of the group, outlined its prospective work, and highlighted the rationale for its existence. Some of the points raised in the statement were:

Fear: Men are often fearful when first presented with a gender mainstreaming agenda. The advancement of women may be perceived as a threat to men's personal and professional status. This may be buttressed by anxiety about ridicule or compromised masculinity if one is widely perceived as an advocate of gender equality.

Lack of experience: Men recruited by UNDP, and a majority of those already working for the organisation, do not have experience – whether academic or professional – on related gender issues. Concurrently, it is frequently women who are recruited or appointed to handle gender concerns, regardless of their expertise. Therefore, any meaningful dialogue on gender equality and the role of men and women in gender mainstreaming could be viewed as disunited from a common agenda.

Organisational culture: UNDP's organisational culture is a product of accumulated legacies that can maintain inequalities between men and women. An absence of incentive structures for staff to view gender equality

as integral must be confronted and institutional acceptance of a
'zero tolerance' policy toward sexual harassment is imperative.
('Gender Mainstreaming: A Men's Perspective', UNDP 1999)

As the group expanded, it held approximately one planning meeting a month, and established an e-mail discussion list that grew to 125 members. An alternating chair convened the planning meetings and ensured that the commitments of individual members were met. The UNDP Gender in Development Programme offered an intern for one summer, space on their website, and *ad hoc* financing for the lunchtime talks, film events, and UN panels which became the main awareness-raising activities of the group. The group co-organised and sponsored three high profile events (discussion panels and film screenings) for the annual UN Commission on the Status of Women (1999–2001), as well as for the Beijing +5 conference in 2000.

From talk to transformation

A basic question which inspired the formation of the working group was, 'If gender equality is necessary for sustainable development, why are so few men in development organisations working on gender issues?'. The preliminary, more obvious answer was a combination of the structural and the institutional – that is, some of the constraints outlined in the first section of this article. Talking about these structural constraints in the abstract was second nature to the group's participants. Many development professionals, including the membership of the working group, are economists and other social scientists, who think about and discuss social systems and processes as part of their work.

But a concrete way forward to redress the problem of the lack of men in gender work within UN organisations started with 'the personal', and required self-reflection, behavioural change, and commitment. Many of the men who formed the working group indicated that their commitment to, or interest in, gender equality arose from two related sources. The first was a commitment to human rights and equality as valid political principles on which development work must be founded. The second was their observation of the inferior treatment and consequent struggles of their mothers, partners, and sisters, and especially their hopes and aspirations that their daughters' lives would be different. Later conversations focused on the constraints and burdens of living up to dominant concepts of masculinity.

Thus, men's participation in these discussions began to demonstrate the well-known feminist insight that 'the personal is political', and that potential for transformation exists when this connection is made. For some, it was also true that they were able to understand better how gender roles, modelled within their households for their own children to observe and learn from, were part of the arena for social change, as were the gender relations within their workplaces. As one working-group member states, *'For me, this was the first time I was able to make clear connections between my personal life and relationships and the structural inequalities that lie behind poverty. Understanding how gender and power play out in my own life truly helps me do better development work.'*

The transformative process followed by some members of the group can be envisioned as moving inwards, towards the personal, through a series of concentric circles. First, the group opened the conversation by discussing gender equality and development in conceptual, theoretical, and normative terms. The second, more focused circle, was defined by conversations about experiences observed within the workplace: anecdotes in which the speaker was a more or less passive observer of patriarchal behaviours, such as inappropriate jokes, sexist attitudes, and even sexual harassment. Often, members of the group confessed to having remained silent, and thus complicit, in these situations. Finally, the conversations turned inwards, towards the individual. Why do men behave the way they do; what do men feel and value? What are the inconsistencies between these values, behaviours, and beliefs? With the identification of these inconsistencies came the suggestions for behaviour modification, as well as suggestions for areas for advocacy and action for the group.

Roles for women and men

The women in the group were gender advocates, who saw the potential advantages of more involvement of men, and were willing to experiment in working more closely with them. These women in turn became strong advocates for the group with other, more sceptical, women. Overall, the group's membership was primarily men, but involving women in key positions was vital for the existence and financing of the group. The women who played key 'behind the scenes' roles in the group, from the various UN gender units, saw it as strategic that men in the group should play more public roles, as shared messages were strengthened coming from male messengers.

It proved to be vital for men to talk with other men, and for each individual to feel comfortable in this space. For example, in initial conversations about attitudes and behaviours in the workplace, and in the subsequent discussions at the personal level around self-awareness, the group was more comfortable starting the discussion with men only. This enabled men to 'let down their guard', articulating and affirming that they did not necessarily conform to, or want to conform to, dominant models of masculinity, and did not condone sexist and patriarchal behaviours.

After these men-only discussions, and having achieved some level of self-realisation, it was easier to discuss these issues with women. The majority of men involved were from a younger generation, and the working group made some efforts to attract both older men and senior management. This may reflect the fact that younger men appear to be more open to renegotiating gender roles than older men – a hopeful sign, in terms of achieving a more widespread transformation among men in future.

Conclusions

By the end of 2000, the working group started to lose momentum, when several active men within the group left UN Headquarters in order to pursue new professional interests, or took posts in dispersed locations. With the departure of several core members, the group slowly dissolved. This was accelerated by reforms in the UN system which affected many gender programmes, such as the Gender in Development Programme at UNDP.

While a residual influence of the working group still exists, activities such as the e-mail network and active support to panels have ceased to exist. Individual members, however, have carried the initiative forward in new settings, particularly at a local level. In addition, the working group was, along with other groups and individuals, part of a movement that placed 'men as partners' firmly on the UN development agenda, as evidenced by the fact that 'Men's Roles in Gender Equality' was a sub-theme of the UN Commission of the Status of Women inter-governmental review in 2004. It is envisaged that this will provide further stimulus for new initiatives and, potentially, for new forms of working groups.

Oxfam GB's Gender Equality and Men (GEM) project

The position of men in Oxfam GB's gender-equality work

Since the establishment of its Gender and Development Unit in the early 1980s, Oxfam GB has committed resources to the achievement of gender equality, both centrally and in its international programme.[4] Over nearly two decades, Oxfam staff and partners have increasingly targeted women and promoted gender equality in supported projects; put policies in place that support gender equality at both regional and central levels; published the results of their experience; and promoted gender awareness and sensitivity among staff (primarily in Oxfam's international programme). A focus on involving men in working for gender equality did not emerge until the late 1990s, when gender work in the organisation was already well developed. The focus achieved a foothold within Oxfam GB's gender and development work, stimulated by external discussions among development academics, by the appearance for the first time of male managers at the headquarters who had active responsibility for the implementation of gender strategies, and by the desire for a more complete gender analysis which would look at men's as well as women's gender roles. Milestones in the development of the focus on working with men have been the publication of an edition of the journal *Gender and Development* on men and masculinities,[5] the organisation of a seminar series by Oxfam GB in collaboration with others on the same theme,[6] and a publication on mainstreaming men into gender and development.[7] However, relatively little attention has been given to how and where men are included in Oxfam GB's international programme work, and what attention there is, is little recorded.

Many Oxfam staff and partners have talked informally over the years of the need to engage men in gender-equality initiatives. They have been aware of the effect on men of empowering women at household and community level, and the resistance of some men to such initiatives. In one example, the project officer in a partner women's organisation begged Oxfam to 'start brainwashing our men' about the importance of empowering women. Gender advisers are occasionally made aware of debates about the role of men and women in particular geographical contexts, often highlighting the difference between rhetoric and reality within programming. However, these discussions have rarely been articulated in reflections on the impact of Oxfam GB's work.

Such a long history of programme work on gender equality has created at least the rhetoric of widespread acceptance among staff in all parts of the organisation that gender equality is an integral part of Oxfam GB's mandate, that gender equality is an issue of rights and justice, as well as more effective programming. Organisational carrots, and occasionally, sticks, are in place to encourage this acceptance; as one male senior manager put it recently, *'you can't get away with not doing gender'*. This public acceptance of the discourse within Oxfam GB suggests that if male resistance remains, it may be that it exists under the surface.

Developing the GEM project

In 2001, a more active attempt to establish a holistic gender analysis which made men's roles visible was led by the Oxfam programmes in the Middle East and Eastern Europe region and in the UK.[8] In recent years in these regions, enormous economic and social changes have resulted in poorer employment prospects, with a connection to worsening health indicators and higher mortality rates for some men – particularly those in the lower social classes. In part, this is due to the difficulties men experience in adjusting to the new roles these changes demand of them. This reality led to the development of a proposal to improve gender analysis to include men as well as women. The proposal also aimed to encourage better programme practice to tackle the impact of poverty on women and men separately, and to influence gender relations positively at household and community level.

A development officer engaged Oxfam GB staff in its nine international regions in an interim study of the organisation's gender work with men. A workshop was attended by staff from six international regions, at which support for the value of this focus on men was built among key programme staff. Since then, there has been active work in one or two programme locations. In Yemen, a group of male advocates working to end violence against women has received active encouragement from Oxfam; in Georgia, male partners of women affected by domestic violence have been encouraged to attend separate counselling sessions. In the UK, One Parent Families York, a partner organisation of Oxfam's UK Poverty Programme, has made changes to the services it provides to promote the inclusion of fathers sharing care of their children (see chapters by Elsanousi, Khoshtaria and Pkhakadze, and Ruxton, this volume). Project learning has shown that engaging men in working for gender equality is slow and difficult, and that using entry points to engage men in no-blame approaches, recognising their own gender needs and roles, are more likely to be successful in the longer-term. However, Oxfam GB is a long way from establishing the right conditions and a critical mass of committed men and women to embed the focus on men into its international programme.

The programme work of the GEM project was accompanied by internal advocacy to managers and staff in all divisions of Oxfam GB, and aimed to engage male staff actively in gender-equality work. Senior managers have been broadly supportive of the project, but GEM is not yet firmly lodged in the mainstream of Oxfam's gender-equality programming, and the project is not located in a particularly influential position for making changes in programming.

Internal advocacy of the GEM project

The GEM project's objective in internal advocacy was to open spaces in the organisation in which men could start to think about their personal commitment to gender equality and what that meant in practice for their day-to-day work. It was also to engage senior managers and the organisational group charged with mainstreaming gender equality, to lend weight to the debate. Finally, the GEM project aimed to make clear that gender equality is not just an issue for the international programme, but for everyone working in Oxfam GB.

The staff involved in the project held two seminars in 2002 to examine the nature of Oxfam's commitment to the transformation of gender roles, as articulated in its overall gender policy. These policy-level seminars were supplemented by well-attended events open to all staff at headquarters, with presentations highlighting men's active involvement in ending violence against women, and exploring masculinities.

The discussion and internal debate that this sparked has been, not surprisingly, controversial. Some practitioners have maintained that Oxfam's mission to alleviate poverty should not take it into the realm of personal transformation. Others believed that the commitment to transform gender roles had to focus on those who would benefit most: women. Some acknowledged that the issue of men's personal transformation needed addressing, but that this was something that men themselves needed to take on.

Oxfam's gender policy now contains clarifications on the role of men. The new policy (2003) states Oxfam GB's commitment to 'work with both women and men to address the specific ideas and beliefs that create and reinforce gender related poverty'. It goes on to elaborate that 'we will address the policies, practices, ideas, and beliefs that perpetuate gender inequality and prevent women and girls (and sometimes men and boys) from enjoying a decent livelihood, participation in public life, protection, and basic services'. This is with the proviso that 'we will ensure that any work we do with men and men's groups supports the promotion of gender equality'.

A significant organisational innovation to promote the greater involvement of men in gender mainstreaming was the creation of an internal training session in a series of introductory courses, called 'The Gender Journey'. This is open to all staff in Oxfam GB's Oxford headquarters, and uses the principle of gender balance in both the training team and participants. The course was championed by a male senior manager and resourced by the female Human Resources director. Men are actively recruited to the course – senior male managers in particular – in order to create a pool of skilled men able to act as 'gender champions' in their departments, ensuring that staff are encouraged and supported to develop their skills and commitment. The course aims to demystify gender and to create a space in which participants feel able to challenge and explore their role in Oxfam's gender-equality work. The content is supported with case studies drawn from the UK context (from Oxfam's programme and from the wider social and economic context), to enable participants to make the connections between their professional and personal commitment. It has been a successful experiment in starting to alter the reality that few men feel they know enough about the issues, even if they are broadly sympathetic. '*It shows that we can still be lads, and care about gender equality*', was a comment on these changes by one senior manager.

The 'Gender Journey' has been assisted by slow improvements in the UK external environment, and social and economic changes which have meant greater flexibility in gender roles. A statutory requirement for employers to give staff two weeks paid paternity leave has recently been passed in the UK, although full parental leave is still a long way off, and the importance of positive male role models for children is a focus of attention in some government policy. The two male Oxfam GB senior managers interviewed for this article were convinced that it was now possible and acceptable in some Oxfam departments for men to be public about their family commitments, and that attempting to achieve a work–life balance is not always seen as a sign that men are not serious about their careers. *'There's lots of blokes picking up their children from the nursery now, and saying openly in meetings, " I've got to pick up my child now – it's five o'clock"'*, said one senior staff member.

For Oxfam GB, initial success in achieving a vocal commitment from men to gender equality appears to lie in the combination of the institutional and the personal. For these two senior managers, the inspiration to action sprang from their own lives. For one, an upbringing by a lone father in an all-male family meant a clear understanding that gender roles can be interchangeable, and an ability to give more sympathetic and active support to staff seeking more flexible working arrangements. For another, his education in the crucible of the feminist movement of the 1970s meant a lifelong commitment to gender equality. *'I always try to be proactive and positive in challenging gender inequality in any shape or form, all the time.'*, he said. Their personal experience meant they could be honest about not knowing the 'right' answers, and open to helping other men who feel uncomfortable articulating their own views. *'Since I've been running the course, people stop me in the street and say things like, "I know I should know this, but what is gender mainstreaming exactly?"'* (Oxfam GB senior manager).

Without institutional support, however, this personal commitment would be difficult to translate into practice. As a result of the many years in which gender equality became an increasing priority in its international programme, gender mainstreaming became one of four corporate priorities for Oxfam GB in 2002. Support to those male managers who take seriously their job of modelling visible commitment to gender equality has come from strong personnel and programme requirements to seek staff with a commitment to gender equality; the selection of qualified and committed men to some 'gender' posts; and performance-management systems and annual reviews which in theory require gender to be made visible. While women continue to demand vocal commitment as proof of seriousness, the male managers interviewed believed that setting a practical example was more important. *'I believe it does make a difference if you do it,'* said one. *'In people's subconscious, it registers. What we do is modelling, standing up first, taking the lead.'* (Oxfam GB senior manager).

Conclusions and recommendations

Through discussion, research, and analysis, development organisations can nurture more equitable institutional cultures and practices and help to explore and highlight what gender equality looks like at different institutional levels, such as family, community, workplace, or policy. Organisational support for family-friendly working practices, for example, demonstrates that gender equitable behaviour at the household level is encouraged. And as advocates for rights and equality, development organisations can also encourage staff and partner organisations to model gender equitable behaviours at all these levels. This suggests the following recommendations:

- Greater conceptual clarity is needed about masculinities, and what is meant by men's involvement. Men increasingly understand themselves to be gendered beings, but there is confusion about what this means for the advancement of women. Efforts such as those of the UN and Oxfam GB show the importance of connecting the personal to the professional for gender transformation.

- Dominant ideas about masculinity in many societies are often in direct opposition to the behaviours, ideas, and beliefs that are more gender equitable and beneficial for women and men. Exploring this tension between development goals and masculine ideals with male (and female) staff of development organisations is a good entry point for personal and organisational reflection.

- Development organisations should lead by example in implementing organisational policies in relation to, for example, paternity and maternity leave, flexible working hours for both women and men, childcare provision (with male and female staff), and sexual harassment. Special attention should be given to policies that encourage more flexible gender roles, such as increased opportunities for childcare for men and the reduction of the double burden of paid and unpaid work for women. These will help to rebalance gendered divisions of labour and income inequality between women and men.

- To ensure fertile ground for these policies to take root, it is important that more senior managers, particularly men, become involved as active champions in the cause of gender equality. Male managers as positive, gender self-aware role models are key to changing the attitudes of those who may be unsure or ambivalent about new gender policies.

- Gender teams, units, or gender focal-point networks should be comprised of both women and men, and the gendered personal dynamics of these teams should be discussed in various arenas.

- Organisations should establish opportunities for men to talk to other men about gender issues, in addition to discussions between men and women. Both men and women need safe, comfortable, and at times separate spaces to discuss the political, personal, and organisational dimensions of gender.

- Greater gender self-awareness and shared professional goals can lead to alliance building between women and men. Exploring the concepts of gender equality and sustainable development in terms of achieving goals, and deconstructing personal gender behaviours, beliefs, and constraints encourages deeper partnerships among and between groups of men and women.

- Adequate resources (human and financial) are needed to sustain gender initiatives, including those focused on the advancement of women, as well as initiatives such as the UN working group and the GEM project.

Notes

1   This article is based in part on the authors' observations and interviews with staff of Oxfam GB, UNDP, and other UN and bi-lateral agencies. The case study on the UN working group contains additions and edits from Alan Greig, Sarah Murison, and Geoffrey Prewitt. The case study on Oxfam GB is based on the authors' experience of developing and managing the GEM project, and discussions with two senior men in Oxfam GB with responsibility for gender equality.

2   M. Kimmel (2000) *The Gendered Society*, New York and Oxford: Oxford University Press.

3   This thinking was synthesised in the subsequent UNDP publication *Men, Masculinities and Development: Broadening Our Work Towards Gender Equality*, by A. Greig, M. Kimmel, and J. Lang (UNDP 2000).

4   For more information on Oxfam GB's work on gender equality, see *Changing Perceptions*, T. Wallace and C. March (eds.) (1990), and *Gender Works: Oxfam Experience in Policy and Practice*, F. Porter, I. Smyth, and C. Sweetman (1999).

5   Available in book form as C. Sweetman (1997) *Men and Masculinity*, Oxford: Oxfam GB.

6   'Men, Masculinities, and Gender Relations in Development', a seminar series held in 2000, funded by the Economic and Social Research Council. A selection of the contributions was published in C. Sweetman (2001) *Men's Involvement in Gender and Development Policy and Practice*, Oxford: Oxfam GB, also available online at www.oxfam.org.uk/publications

7   S. Chant and M. Gutmann (2000) *Mainstreaming Men into Gender and Development*, Oxford: Oxfam GB, also available online at www.oxfam.org.uk/publications

8   Oxfam GB's programme in these regions covers the Middle East, Eastern Europe, and the Commonwealth of Independent States; and the UK Poverty Programme reaches people in poverty in England, Scotland, and Wales.

Conclusion

Sandy Ruxton

The contributions to this book confirm that masculinities and male practices are much more diverse than conventional explanations allow. Far from being fixed by genes or social structures, they are influenced in dynamic ways by factors such as race, culture, class, age, ability, religion, and sexual orientation. Such differences result in men having interests that divide them (as well as some that unite them). Many men – especially those belonging to dominant groups in particular societies – continue to hold power over and derive services from women, and are therefore resistant to moves towards gender equality. But the authors of this collection suggest that there are other men who reject stereotypical perceptions of masculinity and rigid gender divisions, and are more open to supporting gender equality.

Reflecting the views expressed in this publication, the UN Secretary General has endorsed the importance of supporting men's active participation in promoting gender equality. As he stated in a recent report:

> 'Men in many contexts, through their roles in the home, the community and at the national level, have the potential to bring about change in attitudes, roles, relationships and access to resources and decision-making which are critical for equality between women and men. In their relationships as fathers, brothers, husbands and friends, the attitudes and values of men and boys impact directly on the women and girls around them. Men should therefore be actively involved in developing and implementing legislation and policies to foster gender equality, and in providing role models to promote gender equality in the family, the workplace and in society at large.'[1]

Encouraging increasing numbers of men to act in favour of gender equality remains a significant challenge facing governments, public and private organisations, civil society, and communities. At international level, the 48th session of the UN Commission on the Status of Women in New York in March 2004 addressed the role of men and boys in achieving gender equality. It concluded, among other things, that key stakeholders (including governments, UN organisations, and civil society) should promote action at all levels in fields such as education, health services, training, media, and the workplace, to increase the contribution of men and boys to furthering gender equality.[2]

The evidence presented in this book suggests that examples of positive initiatives are emerging – often small-scale and struggling – which are encouraging men to show support for gender equality. A small number of men and men's groups are actively working to sensitise other men to gender issues, often in alliance with women and women's groups. Increasingly, development organisations such as Oxfam GB are adding their weight and voice to such efforts, as the publication of this collection testifies.

There are both risks and resistances to attempts to reshape masculinity, as we identify in the Introduction. Gender and Development (GAD) approaches involving men seem to remain at a conceptual level, rather than being integrated into practice, reflecting uncertainty among policy makers and practitioners as to the most effective ways forward. If this remains the case, it will raise serious questions about the worth of such approaches.[3] It therefore seems timely to encourage greater efforts to test out GAD's propositions. Developing work with men from a gender-relations perspective is one way to do this.

Drawing on existing theory, the Introduction provides a conceptual framework for thinking about men, masculinities, and gender relations, and shows how this is related to the subsequent chapters. Based on this framework, and the exploration undertaken by Oxfam GB's Gender Equality and Men project, this book has sought to explore the aims and methods underpinning effective interventions with men and to record emerging practice.

The aim of this Conclusion is to identify strategies for development organisations and practitioners to involve men positively in initiatives to promote gender equality, and to explore effective practice in engaging men and learning from work on specific issues. It ends with some reflections on the challenges facing development organisations.

Effective practice in engaging men

Developing positive messages and behaviour

A consistent conclusion from the book's contributions is that it is essential to engage men with positive messages that promote their awareness and understanding. Keating and Rogers describe the reality that men often approach discussions about gender in a defensive frame of mind, believing that they will be heavily criticised for the views and feelings they express. Failure to diffuse this reticence can act as a significant block to progress. As Kaufman comments, *'Language that leaves males feeling blamed for things they haven't done, or for things they were taught to do, or guilty for the sins of other men, will simply alienate most boys and men'.*

This is also relevant to the analytical models on which interventions are based. Brown cites the example of 'deficit perspectives' of fatherhood in the Caribbean, which have wrongly, in her view, emphasised men's role as family provider or protector over that of participant. Rather than holding up 'ideal' images of fatherhood, against which men are invariably judged as wanting, Brown favours a developmental approach, based on the idea that men can work at improving their engagement as fathers over time. She concludes that if this is to happen, it is vital to respond to men's own expressed desires for improved relationships and greater family participation. Conversely, men are likely to resist efforts to 'fix' them.

Although it is important to respond to men's concerns, practitioners need to ensure that interventions do not undermine improvements in the position of women and girls, or avoid addressing some men's negative or harmful behaviours. Brown herself acknowledges the importance of making sure that women or women's voices are not ignored.

A similar caution should be applied in relation to campaign and advocacy messages. De Keijzer argues that there are initiatives that *'are successful in reaching men, but lack a gender perspective that sensitises men and empowers women'*. He criticises campaign slogans from Zimbabwe and Mexico for playing to men's macho stereotypes of themselves, and argues that such messages are likely to encourage rather than undermine a backlash against women. In contrast, Kaufman cites a positive example, in describing how the White Ribbon Campaign has used a campaign poster in many countries headlined, 'These men want to put an end to violence against women', followed by lines for signatures. This approach effectively challenges men and boys to take responsibility for change, and focuses on the positive benefits to all.

This emphasis on shared benefits for men and women is critical. Messages promoting shifts in gender relations *can* engage men by highlighting the potential positive outcomes for themselves, their partners, and their children – even in situations where men may have to give up some of their privileges.

The importance of this point is reinforced by the fact that 'men' and 'women' are not homogeneous groups. As identified at the start of this chapter, there are divisions of interest among men, and some groups of men are willing, in relation to some issues, to align themselves with women or with particular groups of women.

This is confirmed by Barker in this volume, who highlights the importance of identifying existing gender equitable commitments and behaviours among men, and building on them. This approach involves not just offering positive messages to men, but also looking for existing positive behaviours in men, celebrating them, and developing communities of support for them. A key challenge here is to support emerging initiatives such as this one, which are encouraging positive behaviour among men and alliance-building between men and women.

Identifying effective messengers

A central element in developing effective practice in work with men is to identify who are the most effective communicators of messages. Several contributors highlight the advantages, in their particular context, of getting boys or men to engage other boys or men with gender issues. This is evident, for example, in the work of AMKV in Timor Leste (de Araujo) and of TAI in South Africa (le Grange). Both describe the benefits of raising the awareness of boys and men and mobilising them to help design and deliver appropriate messages (about men's violence, and about HIV/AIDS respectively), and of supporting and nurturing such groups. Kaufman reminds us that this is important not only so that men organise themselves to work for gender equality, but also because participating in such groups can shift their relations with other men in a positive direction.

Using informed and self-critical male messengers can therefore be a very useful strategy. However this it is not necessarily the same as saying that boys (or men) need 'male role models', above all else. This assumption is often made too easily, without asking who those models should be, and what qualities they will impart; for instance, having no father is likely to be less damaging for a child than having a violent father. Gender learning is an active process, not a step-by-step progression. Just because a particular boy has a male role model, does not mean that the model will be one that the boy should, or in practice will, emulate. Similarly, some organisations claim success in appealing to men and boys by the use of celebrities, especially those from the sporting world. Here again, care must be taken to avoid the risk of reproducing stereotypes and entrenching, rather than questioning, traditional masculinities.[4]

Other contributors stress the significance of female role models – in particular sisters, mothers, grandmothers, wives, and girlfriends – in encouraging men to change. From his experience over the past decade with Salud y Género in Mexico, Central America, and Peru, de Keijzer emphasises that, '*Women play a central role in the promotion of gender equality, not only through what they are slowly and painstakingly achieving for themselves, but also by their direct influence on men they are related to.*' Among a range of factors helping to make men more aware of gender issues, Rogers cites the strongest one as '*seeing the effects of gender discrimination on people they know*'.

Workshops with men, or with men and women together, provide key opportunities for 'messengers' to raise gender issues. In many cases, having men working with women as co-facilitators with an equal voice can be an effective way of modelling appropriate behaviour. It can help to reduce the risk that male facilitators will avoid tackling power issues in relation to gender, or worse, will slip into collusion with male participants. Keating argues convincingly that for male facilitators, it is important to identify and confront this 'male–male bargain' at an early stage of a workshop. It is also worth noting the challenges for female facilitators; as Joshua says, *'Gender training offers men a perfect opportunity to assert their control over women trainers'.*[5] Women trainers, therefore, are more likely to face challenges to the idea that women face inequality. Because of these challenges facing male and female facilitators in working with men, there is a need to develop training for facilitators in this field, and in particular to increase the numbers of men who are able to undertake this work.

Engaging with men's emotional and personal lives

Throughout this book, the contributors highlight the negative impact for men, women, and children of men conforming to restrictive definitions of masculinity (see de Keijzer, Kaufman, Mehta *et al.*). The dominant notions of what a boy or a man is supposed to be and how he is supposed to behave undoubtedly vary to some extent between societies. Yet, as described in this collection, the similarities in the models of masculinity adopted by boys and men are perhaps more striking than the differences. There are many examples presented of men needing to show that they are 'strong, tough, in control, independent' – and the negative effects of these gender norms.

This reality underlines the importance of attempts to encourage men to engage more actively with their emotional and personal lives. Several articles show how it is essential to create space for men to undertake such exploration. Brown, for example, argues that men welcome opportunities to learn about fathering, and about their own emotions and behaviour in relation to their children. Pkhakadze and Khoshtaria illustrate how, although men are reticent in seeking advice on family matters, counselling can assist them to gain new insights and ways to tackle the issues that face them. And the articles by Lang and Smith and by Rogers also demonstrate that men are, in situations where they feel they will not be treated judgementally, able and willing to open up about the personal issues that matter greatly to them.

The pace of change can be slow, however, and the outcomes uncertain. De Keijzer describes how male participants in sessions on violence against women are often confronted with their own fear, sadness, and tenderness, and simultaneously with the power and privilege they hold as men. While this can lead to high drop-out rates initially, many men do come back to such groups later on.

Appropriate environment and delivery

Workers from a range of sectors (including, for instance, child welfare, sexual and reproductive health, and counselling) report difficulties in engaging men in using formal services. Some clear learning about ways to tackle this issue arise from the contributions in this volume.

Especially important is the need to be sensitive to men's concerns about their identities, and how they feel they will be judged if they do access services. Bennett relates how men failed to pick up leaflets about a particular UK organisation's activities because it offered 'support'; when the wording was amended to 'information', men attended.

It can be important to do outreach work in the places men go. Mehta, Peacock, and Bernal show that men often congregate at certain venues and times – such as at sports events and religious celebrations, in workplaces, and in social locations such as bars or cafés – and these can be focal points for intervention.

There is also evidence that there is value in creating spaces where men can meet in private. In a public setting, men are less likely to talk openly and honestly, and are very unlikely to show their vulnerability; the reverse tends to be true in private spaces.[6] This perspective is endorsed in several articles, including those by le Grange and Brown.

Le Grange goes on to describe how men, especially young men, can be encouraged to promote gender equality to their peers if given a sufficient degree of involvement, responsibility, and ownership. This approach is also referred to in other contributions, including those of Barker and Mehta, Peacock, and Bernal.

The perspectives of staff in a range of health and welfare services are highly relevant too. The attitudes of workers (both male and female) can, consciously or unconsciously, lead to men being marginalised. For instance, family services may focus exclusively on the needs of mothers and children, reinforcing the centrality of childcare as 'women's work'. And workers in a range of settings may lack confidence in communicating with male clients, and be uncertain as to their needs. Tackling these issues requires efforts to make gender visible in services, by providing opportunities for staff to reflect upon the gendered nature of the work and their practice.[7]

Cultural issues play a significant role. Elsanousi's description of how boys and men learn about gender roles in Yemen suggests that very restrictive notions of masculinity apply in that context. Nevertheless, she argues that, as long as approaches are avoided that may challenge men's identity too overtly, it is possible to influence change using references to culturally accepted codes and behaviour. An example of this in practice is cited by Keating, who shows how a female trainer in Afghanistan was able to use her familiarity with Islam and Quranic scripture to advance the case for gender equality.

The evidence presented in this book indicates that men respond more positively to the language and tone of training and educational group sessions when it is grounded in their own experiences and concerns. Young men especially value humour as a way of diffusing discussions that might otherwise be experienced as threatening, as le Grange highlights. Materials aimed at young men also need to be easily accessible and presented in a way with which they can identify. Barker draws attention to a lifestyle marketing campaign in Brazil which reflects this awareness.

Overall, it is essential to devote time and resources to appropriate communication strategies. Among these, the most important appear to be: using contemporary language, design, and branding; exploiting the potential of film, TV, radio, and the Internet; and targeting information at the places where men gather.[8]

The process of change

There is agreement among contributors that the process of engaging with men and beginning to shift their attitudes and behaviour can be slow, and that, although long-standing examples do exist (such as the initiatives described by Barker, de Keijzer, and Kaufman), much programme work to actively engage men with gender equality work is still in its infancy.

There are a number of factors that appear to support or accelerate change in individual men. Sometimes change can come about as a result of a significant life event: becoming a father or grandfather; the breakdown of a relationship; illness; or the death of a loved one. Rogers identifies other influences which have in some cases shifted men's perceptions, usually over a period of time. These include realising the impact of discrimination (especially on daughters), increased informal or professional contact with women, learning about the women's movement, and messages from popular culture.

A key element is the *desire* to change. As de Keijzer notes in relation to interventions, '*Men who only attend workshops as a result of partner, institutional, or peer pressure will eventually drop out.*' He goes on to suggest that workshops can lead men to question their socialisation, and when they do this with other men, the experience can be powerful; they may develop more gender equitable perspectives and may even become role models for other men. Nevertheless, this progression is not necessarily linear: some men start to change, but then re-establish former patterns; others learn to change what they say, but find it more difficult to change what they do.

This underlines the importance of facilitators recognising the potential difficulties that may be encountered in workshops, and structuring the educational processes in such as way as to minimise them. For example, one-off activities may have some impact, but sustained initiatives over a period of time are more likely to achieve positive results. It is also essential to tackle themes in a logical sequence. Rather than confront men directly with a personal gender-change agenda, a gradual, structured approach will probably encounter less resistance, and will ultimately achieve more. This was evident from the work of NGOs such as HASIK (Philippines), ROZAN (Pakistan), and Stepping Stones (UK and international), presented at a workshop in Oxford as part of the GEM project.[9]

Opportunities to promote change can be closely linked to the context in specific societies. As Mehta, Peacock, and Bernal make clear, economic and social crises (including, for example, the HIV epidemic, large-scale unemployment and poverty, and concern about men's violence) can all give rise to shifts in gender relations, providing new opportunities for intervention, as shown in the practical examples from Timor Leste and Georgia given in this volume.

It is also essential to locate grassroots interventions in the context of broader social measures. In the case of Georgia, for instance, the authors suggest that alongside the development of counselling services, further action – including media campaigns, legal reform, the development of services, and further research – is required by government and other key stakeholders. While action in these areas may not be appropriate in all cases, these are some of the options that it may be desirable to pursue alongside intervention at local level.

Alliance building

Considerable scepticism exists about the potential for men and women to work together in pursuit of gender equality, especially among some women.[10] Many women's groups argue that the impetus for progressive change has always come from them, and that it is hard to envisage men or men's groups becoming involved without men deflecting the agenda, or worse, taking over. They draw attention, in particular, to the backward-looking approach of some vocal 'men's movements' working to undermine progress towards gender equality.

Nevertheless, there are counter examples, though less well known, of men working together for gender justice. Perhaps the most extensive of these have been the campaigns of gay men in some countries against discrimination and around HIV/AIDS activism. And in principle, those working with men have much to learn from women's groups with a longer history and a developed understanding of working for gender equality; such connections can reduce the risk that men's groups will shore up traditional masculinities, and provide a practical illustration of how men's and women's interests can coincide (for example, in addressing violence against women).

The evidence presented in several chapters in this book suggests that useful models of co-operation exist where men and women have been able to affect change positively. Kaufman cites the well-known example of the White Ribbon Campaign, which has brought men together to tackle violence against women, working closely with women's organisations (and other key stakeholders) in many countries. This experience is mirrored at national level by Mario de Araujo's description of AMKV's work in Timor Leste. He acknowledges that *'the very existence of AMKV is an endorsement of the work of women's organisations in the past to raise awareness of gender inequality'*. Similarly, de Keijzer states that, *'One of the main influences for change is the continuous struggle of women towards gender equality in all spheres of society'*.

Perhaps the most challenging context is described by Elsanousi in her chapter on Yemen, where men hold the reins of power both in public and in private. Yet the author shows how, even here, it has been possible to build partnerships between women's groups and influential men. To make such partnerships work in similar contexts, she recommends strategies to establish dialogue between men's and women's organisations, developing training on gender equality for potentially 'gender sensitive' men, and exploring the positive characteristics of men that lead them to support gender equality.

Alliance building is not just a matter of developing partnerships between groups specifically working towards gender equality between men and women. In many cases, there is potential to construct alliances between these groups and other organisations that work with men (or women) but do not usually work directly on gender issues. Mehta, Peacock, and Bernal provide a striking example of this in EngenderHealth's 'big tent' approach in South Africa, where they and PPASA have established close working relationships with organisations – including unions, community-based organisations, and the military – capable of reaching huge numbers of men. Such efforts are likely to strengthen organisational learning, create strong coalitions for advocacy and policy change, and ensure that efforts are well co-ordinated.

Monitoring programme effectiveness

Given the embryonic nature of much gender-equality work with men, there are few examples in the literature of research into the effectiveness of such programmes. Indeed, Kaufman admits that much work over the past decade has been *'intuitive and impressionistic'* and that further evaluations are necessary. This is undoubtedly the case, both in order to demonstrate whether such work has an impact (and if so, what kind), and to clarify whether devoting resources to it is valuable. Of the few evaluations that have been done,[11] the work of Barker and others to test out their 'Gender-equitable Men Scale' is a noteworthy example.

It is likely that no one methodology can be applied generally across all countries, and different contexts would necessitate different responses according to the patterns of gender roles and models of masculinity present in each. Impact evaluations also demand considerable resources, and such constraints exist in many countries. Even so, in the long-term it is likely to prove cost-effective to invest in this work at an early stage of project design and development. Learning for practitioners and policy-makers would be augmented, and they would be better able to target the limited financial and human resources they have.

Learning from work on specific issues

Below, we analyse lessons about five issues addressed by contributors: reproductive and sexual health; fatherhood; gender-based violence; livelihoods; and work with young people. Other issues could have been chosen, but these five were identified for two main reasons.[12] First, they provide key entry points for engaging with large numbers of boys and men. Second, they are areas where the pressure of social, economic, and political change (both global and local) is having a significant impact on men's lives, and where intervention may help men to respond positively in favour of gender equality.

Different sectors in the field of development have emphasised different approaches. Some, such as sexual and reproductive health, have a more long-standing tradition of involving men, and have attracted both interest and resources (partly as a result of the spread of HIV/AIDS). Others have developed work with men more recently; for instance, rising concern about gender-based violence in many societies has highlighted men's misuse of power (see le Grange, de Araujo, Pkhakadze and Khoshtaria, this volume). And others, such as fatherhood, have been treated with some caution and been given less priority – even though they arguably have great potential to engage with men's emotional lives and to reach much larger numbers of men.

This brief overview of interventions in different sectors probably reflects the understandable desire of many practitioners to focus primarily on improving the status and safety of women. Nevertheless, there may be risks associated with neglect for a sector such as fatherhood; it is possible that failure to engage positively with men around fatherhood issues has enabled the more strident 'men's rights' movements that have emerged in countries such as the USA to fill the vacuum.

In his contribution, de Keijzer raises the interesting question of whether change in a man's attitudes and behaviour in relation to one issue will promote comparable change in relation to others. He suggests, for example, that, *'This has been reported by men dealing with their violence; many start drinking less (or stop altogether) and develop richer relationships with their children'*. However, he warns that this is by no means automatic, citing the example of men who want to be more involved fathers, but do little to improve their relationships with their partners. It is difficult to derive any firm conclusions yet, from anecdotal evidence such as this. Nevertheless, this is an important area for further exploration and evaluation.

HIV/AIDS and sexual and reproductive health

Development work around sexual and reproductive health originally focused primarily on women as targets for intervention. As HIV/AIDS spread during the 1980s, gay men in developed countries became another target, but the majority of heterosexual men were largely ignored until the1990s.

Recently, more thoughtful practice initiatives have emerged to engage men in general in issues concerning HIV/AIDS and sexual and reproductive health, prompted largely by the concerns of women at grassroots level. Underlining this shift in focus, the 2000–2001 World AIDS Campaign slogan was 'Men Make a Difference'.

Such efforts are particularly relevant to South Africa, where it is estimated that around 600 people a day currently die of AIDS-related infections. The construction of male identity is still heavily influenced by the legacy of apartheid, for example through the separation and disintegration of families as a result of labour migration. However, it appears also to be closely linked to the spread of the HIV/AIDS epidemic, fuelled by and linked with other factors, such as poverty, violence, and lack of education. In particular, unemployed men have seen their masculine identities undermined by their lack of work (or work prospects); as a result many have turned to drink, have become increasingly promiscuous, and have abandoned their families. Morrell argues that *'These steps can be understood as steps of desperation, reflecting their inability to see any other way of dealing with their predicament ... Living desperate lives is unlikely to make anybody take safe-sex messages seriously.*[13] He cautions, however, that although poverty is implicated, it is not the sole cause, and that the simplistic identification of poor African men as 'high risk' is not likely to gain their co-operation in helping to reduce transmission.

Le Grange describes one attempt in KwaZulu Natal to provide young men with accurate information about sexual and reproductive health, to educate them about the risk of HIV infection, and to explore their perceptions of masculinity. The experience of this project suggests that involving young men as 'peer educators' (in this case through football clubs) can be a very effective strategy in engaging other young men around these issues. In particular, giving responsibility to the peer educators to develop approaches in their own schools and communities with minimal guidance from project staff has encouraged a participatory learning environment. Activities provide a forum where young men can talk with trust about sensitive issues that they usually do not discuss. Even though the topics are serious, opportunities are also provided to have fun – an important element in engaging young men. A sign of the project's success is that it has become 'cool' for young men to belong to the group.

Mehta, Peacock, and Bernal's description of EngenderHealth's 'Men as Partners' (MAP) Programme also suggests some useful lessons. MAP works on a broader range of sexual and reproductive-health issues (and links these to other masculinity-related concerns, such as gender-based violence) in South Africa and a range of other countries (including Bolivia, Guinea, Pakistan, and Nepal). The authors cite the importance for individual men of providing private spaces for them to obtain services in order to encourage them to seek help, and of offering safe and comfortable environments for them to build connections with other men and to explore their identities. They also highlight the need to assist staff working in clinics and other service settings to explore their own feelings about gender and sexuality and about working with men. At organisational level, they believe it is essential to build support among senior leaders in partner agencies, and to involve all key stakeholders from the start.

Gender-based violence

Gender-based violence lies at the heart of gender inequality (and racist and homophobic violence), and is rooted in the beliefs of many men about masculinity, and their anxieties about their place in the gender hierarchy.[14] Considerable practical experience has built up over the last decade or more in challenging such violence, especially in relation to the domestic sphere, where many men still believe it is their right to use physical force to control and discipline their partners.[15]

The best-known example is probably that of the White Ribbon Campaign, founded in Canada in 1991, and exported to many other countries worldwide since then. In his contribution, Kaufman highlights some of the key features of the campaign. These include a specific focus on men's violence against women, using the white ribbon as a symbol of a public promise by a man never to commit, condone, or remain silent about violence against women; a politically non-partisan approach (the 'big tent'); working closely with and supporting women's organisations; and a small decentralised organisational structure, working as a catalyst in partnership with others (such as schools, corporations, trade unions, religious institutions, sports clubs, youth groups, government, and non-government organisations).

A number of other contributions in this book highlight similar approaches to those outlined by Kaufman. Elsanousi's contribution shows how, even in the gender-segregated context of Yemen, it is possible for women's groups to develop partnerships with influential men in order to reduce men's violence. In relation to Timor Leste, de Araujo also draws attention to the significant support of the women's movement in sustaining the work of the Association of Men Against Violence. Mehta, Peacock, and Bernal endorse the 'big tent' approach, showing how EngenderHealth and PPASA have used this to effect in South Africa.

This latter example also highlights how men react in societies undergoing transition from occupation or external control to freedom. As Connell describes:

> '[*Insurrections and civil violence*] *may put young men through a vehement if informal training that emphasises aggressiveness, physical bravery, distrust of authority, and loyalty to the immediate group. At the same time, civil conflict severely disrupts regular education and many of the ties that would have given young men a secure place in families and communities. The result may be a continuing problem in the aftermath of civil conflict, with men who were once regarded as heroes now marginalised and impoverished, possibly very angry, and well-trained in violence.*'[16]

The conditions described by Connell mirror those identified by Mehta, Peacock, and Bernal, by le Grange in post-apartheid South Africa, and by de Araujo in Timor Leste. The situation in Georgia appears similar, though the background of Soviet domination with its emphasis on formal gender equality (although not implemented in practice) is different.

A number of useful lessons arise from these chapters. For instance, de Araujo emphasises the importance of developing and sustaining the awareness of their gendered attitudes and behaviour among men who are members of anti-violence groups, and shows how concrete examples can be effective in shifting entrenched attitudes in grassroots forums. He also draws attention to the significance of international exchanges between countries with comparable histories (in this case with the Puntos de Encuentro group from Nicaragua[17]) in developing the ideas and capacity of his group.

At a broader level, Mehta, Peacock, and Bernal highlight how the movement to end men's violence resonates powerfully with civil rights and other social justice movements, and how working together can prove mutually beneficial. Pkhakadze and Khoshtaria also describe wider action on prevention, moving beyond Sakhli's individual counselling with men and women. This includes activities to raise awareness of domestic violence in the masculine culture of the police force, an issue which officers have tended to regard as a private family one.

Livelihoods

There have been very few attempts to address with men gender issues that relate to the economic aspects of livelihoods, such as production, employment, marketing, and finance. These areas tend to be seen as male enclaves, where men's traditional attitudes and behaviour make it difficult to promote gender equality. Anecdotal evidence suggests that, as a result, projects (in microfinance, for example) have often targeted women; although some have had unforeseen, and sometimes negative, effects. Ensuring that women are 70–80 per cent of the borrowers from a particular scheme may sound positive, but in practice, the project may cause women to increase their workloads in order to achieve repayment, and cause anger and resentment among men, who believe their traditional livelihoods are being undermined.[18]

Kidder's contribution suggests ways in which it is possible to explore these areas with men. In her view, livelihoods strategies need to be informed by gender analysis. In particular, it is critical to identify how livelihoods projects may be less *effective* in achieving their economic objectives if gender stereotypes are not challenged: '*When we identify the economic efficiency of addressing gender equality, some men may find these arguments more acceptable, as well as motivating*'. She goes on to cite her experiences of asking men in microfinance workshops in Santo Domingo, Senegal, and Indonesia, 'Are women better repayers?' and shows how this question has helped men to identify their gendered attitudes and roles in household finance, and changes for them that would be critical for successful microfinance.

An example from the developed world is provided by Bennett, who highlights how employment-training projects in the UK often reinforce traditional ideas of 'men's work'. According to project staff, it is only possible to begin to shift men's perceptions of masculinity and male roles *after* recruitment, but Bennett warns of the danger that projects may in practice de-prioritise or neglect this opportunity to promote change, and thereby leave existing gender relations untouched.

Keating puts a different perspective on such approaches in her article. She argues that in many cases practitioners use ingenious strategies for leading participants (both male and female) to the conclusion that gender inequality is a major obstacle to household income generation and to the achievement of sustainable livelihoods. However, she believes there is a danger that they may avoid addressing the unequal balance of power between men and women.

There is no correct answer to the kinds of dilemmas that are raised here, and choosing the most appropriate strategy will depend on the context. Both Kidder and Keating agree that both equality and efficiency approaches are valid; their difference is in how and when to introduce these ideas in a workshop.

Overall, the evidence suggests that livelihoods work is a significant area in which it is possible to engage men. Given that working on livelihoods in general has been at the heart of traditional development-sector approaches, it is puzzling that attempts to work with men on masculinity issues have neglected this topic so much. It is to be hoped that development organisations will address this gap in the near future.

Fatherhood

In recent years, traditional models of fathers as 'providers' and mothers as 'carers' have increasingly been challenged in many countries. This has come about for several reasons, including changes in the labour market (for example, greater numbers of women being in paid work, the impact of migration), changes in family structure (increasing numbers of female-headed households and step-families), and a re-evaluation of the role of fathers in child development. To some extent, perspectives and practices among mothers and fathers themselves are shifting; change is haphazard, however, varying according to class, race, and age. On the one hand, Pkhakadze and Khoshtaria draw attention to Georgian women's growing 'double burden' of working and caring. On the other, based on experience in Latin America, Barker highlights the positive attitudes and behaviour of some men (particularly young men) who are prepared to question traditional practices.

An important issue for further exploration is the extent to which the advent of fatherhood can draw men to support broader aspects of gender equality, and how such shifts can be nurtured and encouraged. De Keijzer outlines how fatherhood can be an opportunity for development work to challenge men's beliefs about authority and negotiation, domestic work, discipline and violence, emotions, reproduction, and so on. And Rogers cites evidence from India and Pakistan of how individual men have changed through their experience of becoming fathers (particularly of girls): *'By seeing women and girls through their daughters' eyes, these men have begun to think about aspects of gender inequality, such as sexual harassment, inheritance law, and mobility, that might not have concerned them before. They have also been moved to find ways to defy restrictive laws, practices, and social pressure, creating strategic models for their children and peer groups to follow, which in turn allow their children to become role models as well.'*

The significant potential of working with fathers is also stressed by other writers. Chant and Gutmann, for instance, argue that development work is needed to support men as fathers.[19] Moreover, there are risks in failing to pursue this course: *'If this does not occur, development policy and practice will be obliged to continue its current focus on salvage operations which aim to enable women to bring up their children alone'.*

More positively, Flood suggests that when men share equally with women in the care of children, their marriages and relationships improve – and that both men and women benefit from men's involvement in parenting. For this to happen, changes in gender norms and relations are needed: *'Men's involvement in parenting depends on the encouragement of boys' and men's parenting and relationship skills and commitments, more diverse notions of manhood, and co-operative and egalitarian relations between men and women in families and elsewhere.'*[20]

How can work on fatherhood best be carried out? As indicated above, Brown favours 'developmental' over 'deficit' approaches, building on fathers' strengths rather than identifying their weaknesses, and providing spaces for men to discuss fatherhood with each other. She argues that these approaches: *' ... are more likely to be attractive to men as fathers or potential fathers, particularly when the programme is consultative in terms of topic choice, venue, and timing, is participatory in nature, and is facilitated in a non-judgmental way'.*

De Keijzer shows that where trust has built up in a workshop, it is important to explore participants' experiences of having been children, as a way to understand their attitudes as fathers. Although this can prove difficult for them to talk about (given that their fathers were often absent or rejected them), this approach provides an entry-point for addressing powerful emotional issues that go to the heart of men's thinking. Many men are unable to address these issues as fathers, however, and unconsciously wait until they are grandfathers to do so.

Workshops and activities on active fatherhood are, on their own, likely to play only a small part in shifting men's attitudes and behaviour. In conjunction with other policy initiatives by development organisations and others, however, such as attempts to encourage men to make use of 'family-friendly' employment practices (as advocated by Lang and Smith), they provide powerful arenas for encouraging men to change.

Young men

Young men have been mentioned in several of the sections above. They also merit specific consideration, however, not only because it is important to meet their immediate needs, but also because they are potentially the standard bearers for future change. In many – perhaps most – societies, concern is focused on the negative actions and attitudes of young men, particularly those at the sharp end of economic and social change. This is related to the generally high levels of violence, drug and alcohol abuse, crime, and accidents among young men. Underlying these behaviours is a widespread anxiety among and between young men about their roles and their futures. In line with Connell's theory of 'hegemonic masculinity' (see Introduction), such experiences can sometimes translate into aggressive attempts by young men to shore up traditional notions of masculinity by the reassertion of male power over, for example, other marginalised men, women, ethnic minority groups, and gay men.

Based on the work of Program H in Brazil and Mexico, Barker offers a more positive perspective, arguing that even in circumstances where traditional ideas of male dominance hold sway, alternative, more 'gender equitable' voices are either present, or can be stimulated, among young men. This view reflects the conclusions of other studies. Drawing on their work with boys in UK schools, Frosch, Phoenix, and Pattman, for instance, also argue that young men can be emotionally and intellectually articulate, thoughtful, and insightful; if they are to demonstrate these qualities, they depend on the availability of close and supportive relationships.[21]

Program H, implemented by four partner NGOs,[22] aims to help young men question traditional norms relating to manhood, using a range of methods and materials. Qualitative results of field-testing this programme show increased empathy and reduced conflict among participants, and positive reflection on relationships with female partners.

This work draws on the findings of a broader review by Barker, for which he consulted 77 programmes reaching boys and young men in schools, communities, workplaces, military facilities, and juvenile justice centres.[23] He summarises learning from the review as follows: '*Broadly speaking, programmatic experiences are generating a series of priorities: identifying boys' own rationale for change; engaging relatively few young men intensively in small groups over an extended period; tapping into the positive power of male peer groups to encourage gender equity; addressing homophobia; planning high-energy activities that involve multiple themes; working with boys on self-care and prevention; and creating settings where young men can talk openly about their doubts and question issues that are often seen as unquestionable (such as what it means to be a man)*.[24] Many of the lessons identified are reflected in other contributions to this volume.

Challenges for development organisations

A range of challenges face development organisations if they are to promote GAD approaches that address men in the future. One challenge surrounds the extent to which such organisations (often based in the global North) need to be responsive to the specific cultural contexts in which they are working (usually the global South). For example, a male interviewee in Elsanousi's article argues that in his work he doesn't use the term 'gender', as it envisages absolute equality between women and men, *'which is not possible in Yemen'*. He goes on to suggest that *'we may need to "Yemenize" the gender concept'*. For some people, in particular, some women and women's groups, to obscure or downgrade 'gender' and 'gender equality' in this way is likely to compromise feminist goals too much. For others (including Elsanousi), such fears are misplaced, especially if it is possible to demonstrate positive movement towards gender equality from such approaches. While the articles in this volume do not – and arguably could not - provide a definitive answer to questions of whether to compromise on such issues, when to do so, and to what extent, it is important that they are considered carefully by organisations and practitioners.

Another key challenge is how to identify and counter resistance (usually from men) to gender equality. This resistance can include the denial of discrimination against women, appointing gender leads with insufficient power to effect change, using delaying tactics, paying lip-service to notions of gender equality, and tokenism. Each of these necessitates the development of specific strategies in response. On one level, these may include gathering and presenting clear evidence of discrimination, exploring innovative ways to implement particular programmes, and developing effective monitoring and evaluation. On a deeper level, de Keijzer shows how tackling male resistance depends on an understanding of masculinities, of the *reasons which cause* men to change, of transition *processes* themselves, and of the *contexts* in which change can take place.

Other challenges are more concerned with how development organisations operate. Chant and Gutmann, for example, suggest that the patriarchal culture common in many development organisations, with men dominating the higher management levels, has tended to obstruct progress.[25] In practice, this has enabled senior male managers to maintain dominance not only over women, but also over other more junior men who might otherwise be more sympathetic to gender issues. Moreover, this culture may have sustained WID programmes, which, by focusing specifically on women and women's empowerment, can be perceived as less threatening to male power.

The contributions to this book outline various strategies which could contribute to strengthening GAD approaches, and in particular, male participation in them. In part, this involves reviewing the direction and content of organisational programmes to ensure that the key points outlined above are incorporated in practice, and that examples of positive initiatives are publicised and shared.

At a more basic level, it involves agencies reassessing their own policies, and staff and organisational cultures, from a gender-relations perspective. For example, the UN Expert Group on the 'Role of Men and Boys in Achieving Gender Equality' recommended that in the public sector policies to tackle gender segmentation should be implemented; men in leadership positions should support and publicly endorse gender equality in their workplaces; promotion policies should be designed that encourage men to share caring work; and budgets should be examined for incentives or disincentives for gender equality.[26]

These recommendations are echoed in the articles by Lang and Smith and by Rogers in this volume. Drawing on experience from the UN Working Group on Men and Gender Equality, and from Oxfam GB's GEM project (see Introduction), Lang and Smith conclude that development organisations need to model *'gender equitable behaviours at institutional policy and project level'*. This must involve greater efforts to assist staff – especially male staff – to see the connections between the personal and the professional spheres.

Rogers similarly emphasises the importance of organisations actively creating space for informal, open dialogue on gender issues and sharing about family life and gender relations beyond the office. In some cases, it may be appropriate to provide separate spaces for men and women to talk to each other, in others, combined forums may be worthwhile. In addition, induction of new staff should provide a focus for training in gender analysis and gender mainstreaming.

Lang and Smith provide one example of what organisations can do in practice; Oxfam GB's internal gender-training course, in contrast with much gender training which focuses more on women's needs, encourages men to take a proactive approach to gender in their work. Crucial to the course's success is the fact that it has been led by an effective male-female facilitator combination.

However, in general, it is important to note that there is a great lack of skilled male facilitators working in this area. This is perhaps unsurprising, given the challenges such a role presents; on the one hand, the male facilitator can be branded a 'traitor' by other men, on the other, he may be seen as 'taking over' the gender agenda by women. Given that male facilitators must be ready to address these criticisms, there may be a need for capacity building in this area.

At policy level, Lang and Smith argue that development organisations should implement working practices such as paternity and maternity leave and flexible working hours. From the employee point of view, these are intended to encourage men to increase their involvement in childcare while reducing the double burden on women of working and caring. If such policies are to have an impact, significant efforts are, however, required to ensure men use them. Failure to do so can entrench rather than undermine traditional gender roles – especially in a context where male work hours tend to be increasing (at least in developed countries). For this reason, the authors believe that senior managers, particularly those who are male, should act as role models for others by making use of such provision.

Into the future: engaging men in working for gender equality

This book represents an attempt to record progress towards the creation of strategies and practice that actively engage men in gender-equality work. Although many initiatives require further evaluation, the diverse examples described give cause for optimism, and suggest that it is not only desirable, but also possible for development organisations and practitioners to engage with men effectively.

As this concluding chapter makes clear, positive ways forward can be identified. For work with men on gender equality to be successful, however, it is not enough to be convinced of the theoretical value of such intervention. Connell has suggested a range of broad social conditions that will support progressive work with men and boys.[27] These are: the presence of a core group of men orientated towards gender equality and social justice; support and commitment from those in leadership positions (particularly men); a women's movement that is prepared to engage in alliance politics with men; the promotion of a clear statement of the reasons why men and boys should support gender equality; and programme and policy intervention compatible with at least some of the interests of men and boys.

Contributions to this book draw attention to a range of relevant practice issues which are related to these conditions, including the importance of developing positive messages and behaviour; of identifying effective messengers; engaging with men's emotional and personal lives; ensuring appropriate environment and delivery; understanding the process of change; alliance building; and monitoring programme effectiveness.

In addition, key entry points for working with men for gender equality need to be explored and exploited. This is particularly relevant in sectors where traditional masculinities are being challenged by the pace of economic, social, and political change. These sectors include reproductive and sexual health, fatherhood, gender-based violence, livelihoods, and work with young people.

Alongside such practical measures, development organisations must re-examine their own policies and cultures at all levels, and ensure that they reinforce positive efforts to engage men in gender-equality strategies in programmes and projects – while not compromising or undermining prospects and resources for the empowerment of women.

What is the likelihood of making further progress in the near future? It is unrealistic to expect men, as a group, suddenly to shift their attitudes and behaviour completely – especially because they continue to derive privileges (such as higher incomes and caring services) from the 'patriarchal dividend'. Some men and men's movements, particularly those in the dominant positions, will doubtless be impervious, or even hostile, to change.

However, the articles in this book suggest that there are others who do understand the potential of gender reform, the contribution they can make (whether in the workplace, the community, or the home), and the potential benefits to themselves, their families, and other people. As we have seen, there are increasingly available examples of programmes and projects working with men, in alliance with women and women's groups, which are rooted in a clear support for gender equality.

It is essential to develop work for gender equality as a positive project for men, engaging their enthusiasm and energy, and encouraging them to see themselves as active participants in achieving gender equality. Such progress needs to be nurtured and sustained, and is likely to take place in different sites, at different times, among different men.

This book shows that a range of stakeholders, including not only development organisations, but also governments, UN organisations, and other elements in civil society, can play their part in implementing effective strategies, and that some initial steps towards positive change are happening at grassroots level. We hope that the contributions in this volume can add their own momentum to this process.

Notes

1   Report of the UN Secretary General, 'The Role of Men and Boys in Achieving Gender Equality', 22 December 2003, E/CN.6/2004/9.

2   The conclusions of the Commission on the Status of Women, 48th session, are set out in the Appendix.

3   S. Chant and M. Gutmann (2000) *Mainstreaming Men into Gender and Development*, Oxford: Oxfam GB.

4   M. Flood (2003) 'Engaging men: strategies and dilemmas in violence prevention education among men', *Women Against Violence: A Feminist Journal*, 13.

5   M. Joshua (2001) 'Gender training with men: experiences and reflections from East Africa', in C. Sweetman (ed.) *Men's Involvement in Gender and Development Policy and Practice: Beyond Rhetoric*, Oxford: Oxfam GB.

6   T. Lloyd (1997) *Let's Get Changed Lads: Developing Work with Boys and Young Men*, London: Working With Men.

7.   S. Ruxton (2001) 'Men and child welfare services in the UK', in C. Sweetman (ed.), *op. cit.*

8   R. Poudyal (2000) 'Alternative masculinities in South Asia: an exploration through films for schools', *IDS Bulletin*, 31(2).

9   J. Lang (2002) 'Gender is Everyone's Business: Programming with Men to Achieve Gender Equality', workshop report 10–12 June, Oxford: Oxfam GB (available on www.oxfam.org.uk/what_we_do/issues/gender/gem/).

10   See for instance S. Chant and M. Guttman (2000) *op. cit.*, pp3–4.

11   See for instance P. Welsh (2001) *Men Aren't From Mars: Unlearning Machismo in Nicaragua*, London: Catholic Institute for International Relations.

12   For example, although there are articles here about societies in which upheaval has taken place in recent years (e.g. East Timor, Georgia, South Africa), there are none about societies currently experiencing a high level of societal conflict (e.g. Iraq, Palestine). This is a theme on which further research and analysis on working with men for gender equality would be useful.

13   R. Morrell (2003) 'Poverty and HIV', contribution to UN web discussion on the HIV/AIDS pandemic, 11 July 2003, http://esaconf.un.org/~gender-equality-role-men-boys/guests

14   I. Breines, R. Connell, and I. Eide (2000) *Male Roles, Masculinities and Violence: A Culture of Peace Perspective*, Paris: UNESCO Publishing; J. Hearn (1998) *The Violences of Men: How Men Talk About and How Agencies Respond to Men's Violence to Women*, London: Sage.

15   See, for example, H. Ferguson, J. Hearn, O.G. Holter, L. Jalmert, M. Kimmel, J. Lang, and R. Morrell (2004) 'Ending Gender-based Violence: A Call for Global Action to Involve Men', Swedish International Development Cooperation Agency, www.sida.se

16   R.W. Connell (2003) 'The Role of Men and Boys in Achieving Gender Equality', United Nations Division for the Advancement of Women, Expert Group Meeting, Brasilia, Brazil 21–24 October 2003.

17   T. Montoya (1998) *Nadando Contra Corriente: Buscando Pistas para Prevenir la Violencia Masculina en las Relaciones de Pareja*, Puntos de Encuentros: Managua. See also P. Welsh (2001) *op. cit.*

18   See for example quotes from Lorraine Corner (p42) in S. Chant and M. Gutmann (2000) *op. cit.*, p42.

19   S. Chant and M. Gutmann (2000) *op. cit.*

20   M. Flood (2003) *Fatherhood and Fatherlessness*, The Australia Institute, Discussion Paper No. 59.

21   S. Frosch, A. Phoenix, and R. Pattman (2002) *Young Masculinities: Understanding Boys in Contemporary Societies*, Basingstoke: Palgrave.

22   Instituto Promundo (co-ordinator), ECOS (in São Paulo, Brazil), Instituto PAPAI (Recife, Brazil), and Salud Y Género (Mexico).

23   G. Barker (2000) 'What About Boys? A Review and Analysis of International Literature on the Health and Developmental Needs of Adolescent Boys', World Health Organisation, www.who.org

24   G. Barker (2003) Introduction to 'My Father Didn't Think This Way': Nigerian Boys Contemplate Gender Equality', Q/C/Q No 14, New York: International Women's Health Coalition/Population Council.

25   S. Chant and M. Gutmann (2000) *op. cit.*

26   UN Division for the Advancement of Women (2003) 'The Role of Men and Boys in Achieving Gender Equality', *op. cit.*

27   R.W. Connell, intervention during panel on 'Men Working on Gender', UN Commission on the Status of Women, 4 March 2004, New York.

Appendix

Commission on the Status of Women
Forty-eighth session 1–12 March 2004

The Role of Men and Boys in Achieving Gender Equality

Agreed conclusions 12 March 2004, as adopted

1 The Commission on the Status of Women recalls and reiterates that the Beijing Declaration and Platform for Action[1] encouraged men to participate fully in all actions towards gender equality and urged the establishment of the principle of shared power and responsibility between women and men at home, in the community, in the workplace and in the wider national and international communities. The Commission also recalls and reiterates the outcome document adopted at the twenty-third special session of the General Assembly entitled 'Gender equality, development and peace in the twenty-first century'[2] which emphasized that men must take joint responsibility with women for the promotion of gender equality.

2 The Commission recognizes that men and boys, while some themselves face discriminatory barriers and practices, can and do make contributions to gender equality in their many capacities, including as individuals, members of families, social groups and communities, and in all spheres of society.

3 The Commission recognizes that gender inequalities still exist and are reflected in imbalances of power between women and men in all spheres of society. The Commission further recognizes that everyone benefits from gender equality and that the negative impacts of gender inequality are borne by society as a whole and emphasizes, therefore, that men and boys, through taking responsibility themselves and working jointly in partnership with women and girls, are essential to achieving the goals of gender equality, development and peace. The Commission recognizes the capacity of men and boys in bringing about change in attitudes, relationships and access to resources and decision making which are critical for the promotion of gender equality and the full enjoyment of all human rights by women.

4 The Commission acknowledges and encourages men and boys to continue to take positive initiatives to eliminate gender stereotypes and promote gender equality, including combating violence against women, through networks, peer programmes, information campaigns, and training programmes. The Commission acknowledges

the critical role of gender-sensitive education and training in achieving gender equality.

5 The Commission also recognizes that the participation of men and boys in achieving gender equality must be consistent with the empowerment of women and girls and acknowledges that efforts must be made to address the undervaluation of many types of work, abilities and roles associated with women. In this regard, it is important that resources for gender equality initiatives for men and boys do not compromise equal opportunities and resources for women and girls.

6 The Commission urges Governments and, as appropriate, the relevant funds and programmes, organizations and specialized agencies of the United Nations system, the international financial institutions, civil society, including the private sector and nongovernmental organizations, and other stakeholders, to take the following actions:

a) Encourage and support the capacity of men and boys in fostering gender equality, including acting in partnership with women and girls as agents for change and in providing positive leadership, in particular where men are still key decision makers responsible for policies, programmes and legislation, as well as holders of economic and organizational power and public resources;

b) Promote understanding of the importance of fathers, mothers, legal guardians and other caregivers, to the well being of children and the promotion of gender equality and of the need to develop policies, programmes and school curricula that encourage and maximize their positive involvement in achieving gender equality and positive results for children, families and communities;

c) Create and improve training and education programmes to enhance awareness and knowledge among men and women on their roles as parents, legal guardians and caregivers and the importance of sharing family responsibilities, and include fathers as well as mothers in programmes that teach infant child care development;

d) Develop and include in education programmes for parents, legal guardians and other caregivers information on ways and means to increase the capacity of men to raise children in a manner oriented towards gender equality;

e) Encourage men and boys to work with women and girls in the design of policies and programmes for men and boys aimed at gender equality and foster the involvement of men and boys in gender mainstreaming efforts in order to ensure improved design of all policies and programmes;

f) Encourage the design and implementation of programmes at all levels to accelerate a socio-cultural change towards gender equality, especially through the upbringing and educational process, in terms of changing harmful traditional perceptions and attitudes of male and female roles in order to achieve the full and equal participation of women and men in the society;

g) Develop and implement programmes for pre-schools, schools, community centers, youth organizations, sport clubs and centres, and other groups dealing with children and youth, including training for teachers, social workers and other professionals who deal with children to foster positive attitudes and behaviours on gender equality;

h) Promote critical reviews of school curricula, textbooks and other information education and communication materials at all levels in order to recommend ways to strengthen the promotion of gender equality that involves the engagement of boys as well as girls;

i) Develop and implement strategies to educate boys and girls and men and women about tolerance, mutual respect for all individuals and the promotion of all human rights;

j) Develop and utilize a variety of methods in public information campaigns on the role of men and boys in promoting gender equality, including through approaches specifically targeting boys and young men;

k) Engage media, advertising and other related professionals, through the development of training and other programmes, on the importance of promoting gender equality, non-stereotypical portrayal of women and girls and men and boys and on the harms caused by portraying women and girls in a demeaning or exploitative manner, as well as on the enhanced participation of women and girls in the media;

l) Take effective measures, to the extent consistent with freedom of expression, to combat the growing sexualization and use of pornography in media content, in terms of the rapid development of ICT, encourage men in the media to refrain from presenting women as inferior beings and exploiting them as sexual objects and commodities, combat ICT- and media-based violence against women including criminal misuse of ICT for sexual harassment, sexual exploitation and trafficking in women and girls, and support the development and use of ICT as a resource for the empowerment of women and girls, including those affected by violence, abuse and other forms of sexual exploitation;

m) Adopt and implement legislation and/or policies to close the gap between women's and men's pay and promote reconciliation of occupational and family responsibilities, including through reduction of occupational segregation, introduction or expansion of parental leave, flexible working arrangements, such as voluntary part-time work, teleworking, and other home-based work;

n) Encourage men, through training and education, to fully participate in the care and support of others, including older persons, persons with disabilities and sick persons, in particular children and other dependants;

o) Encourage active involvement of men and boys through education projects and peer-based programmes in eliminating gender stereotypes as well as gender inequality in particular in relation to sexually transmitted infections, including HIV/AIDS, as well as their full participation in prevention, advocacy, care, treatment, support and impact evaluation programmes;

p) Ensure men's access to and utilization of reproductive and sexual health services and programmes, including HIV/AIDS-related programmes and services, and encourage men to participate with women in programmes designed to prevent and treat all forms of HIV/AIDS transmission and other sexually transmitted infections;

q) Design and implement programmes to encourage and enable men to adopt safe and responsible sexual and reproductive behaviour, and to use effectively methods to prevent unwanted pregnancies and sexually transmitted infections, including HIV/AIDS;

r) Encourage and support men and boys to take an active part in the prevention and elimination of all forms of violence, and especially gender-based violence, including in the context of HIV/AIDS, and increase awareness of men's and boys' responsibility in ending the cycle of violence, inter alia, through the promotion of attitudinal and behavioural change, integrated education and training which prioritize the safety of women and children, prosecution and rehabilitation of perpetrators, and support for survivors, and recognizing that men and boys also experience violence;

s) Encourage an increased understanding among men how violence, including trafficking for the purposes of commercialized sexual exploitation, forced marriages and forced labour, harms women, men and children and undermines gender equality, and consider measures aimed at eliminating the demand for trafficked women and children;

t) Encourage and support both women and men in leadership positions, including political leaders, traditional leaders, business leaders, community and religious leaders, musicians, artists and athletes to provide positive role models on gender equality;

u) Encourage men in leadership positions to ensure equal access for women to education, property rights and inheritance rights and to promote equal access to information technology and business and economic opportunities, including in international trade, in order to provide women with the tools that enable them to take part fully and equally in economic and political decision-making processes at all levels;

v) Identify and fully utilize all contexts in which a large number of men can be reached, particularly in male-dominated institutions, industries and associations, to sensitize men on their roles and responsibilities in the promotion of gender equality and the full enjoyment of all human rights by women, including in relation to HIV/AIDS and violence against women;

w) Develop and use statistics to support and/or carry out research, inter alia, on the cultural, social and economic conditions, which influence the attitudes and behaviours of men and boys towards women and girls, their awareness of gender inequalities and their involvement in promoting gender equality;

x) Carry out research on men's and boys' views of gender equality and their perceptions of their roles through which further programmes and policies can be developed and identify and widely disseminate good practices. Assess the impact of efforts undertaken to engage men and boys in achieving gender equality;

y) Promote and encourage the representation of men in institutional mechanisms for the advancement of women;

z) Encourage men and boys to support women's equal participation in conflict prevention, management and conflict resolution and in post-conflict peace-building;

7 The Commission urges all entities within the UN system to take into account the recommendations contained in these agreed conclusions and to disseminate these agreed conclusions widely.

Notes

1 Report of the Fourth World Conference on Women, Beijing 4-15 September 1995 (United Nations publication, Sales No. E.96.IV.13).

2 A/RES/S-23/3, annex.

Index